Women's Work and
Chicano Families

Anthropology of Contemporary Issues

A SERIES EDITED BY

ROGER SANJEK

A full list of titles in the series appears
at the end of the book

Women's Work and Chicano Families

CANNERY WORKERS OF THE SANTA CLARA VALLEY

Patricia Zavella

Cornell University Press

Ithaca and London

First published 1987 by Cornell University Press.
Second printing 1990.
First published, Cornell Paperbacks, 1987.
Second printing 1990.

International Standard Book Number (cloth) 0-8014-1730-9
International Standard Book Number (paper) 0-8014-9410-9
Library of Congress Catalog Card Number 87-5245
Printed in the United States of America

Librarians: Library of Congress cataloging information appears on the last page of the book.

⊗ The paper used in this publication meets the minimum requirements of the American National Standard for Permanence of Paper for Printed Library Materials Z39.48–1984.

For my children,
Laura and Anthony

Contents

Contents

Tables

Preface

Scholarly attention has increasingly focused on the feminization of the labor force since World War II, especially on the great increase in paid employment among women with children—a phenomenon that has been characterized as a "subtle revolution" (Smith 1979). The impact of this development on women themselves continues to be debated. Some people argue that women gain autonomy because of their new earning power; others show that women's employment contributes to their subordination; still others hold that the gender inequality within families is reconstituted in new forms in the workplace.

Most research on women workers in the United States has overlooked Chicanas.[1] Margarita Melville (1980) has correctly noted the dearth of research on Chicanas' participation in the labor force—a lack all the more regrettable because, at least during the decade from 1960 to 1970, the proportion of married Chicanas who entered the labor force for the first time was higher than that of white women (Cooney 1975). Recently the percentage of Chicanas who are employed or looking for work has nearly equaled that of all other women. In 1980, for example, 49 percent of Hispanic women were in the labor force, compared with 52 percent of white women. But unemployment rates have consistently been higher among Chicanas (U.S.

1. Throughout this work, the terms *Chicano* and *Mexican-American* are used interchangeably. *Chicanos* can refer to males only or to both males and females; *Chicanas* are Mexican-American women.

Bureau of Census 1982). Hispanics are the fastest growing ethnic group in the United States,[2] and these statistics reflect an increasing population of Mexican-American women. At the end of World War II, Chicanos were concentrated in Southwest labor markets, which only in recent decades have expanded to provide large-scale employment for women. The growth of Chicanas' labor-force participation has brought many changes to Chicano families, changes this book will investigate.

Chicanas living in California have often found work in the fruit- and vegetable-canning industry, which has always employed many women and ethnic minority workers and has been among the most important contributors to the economy of the Santa Clara Valley, where I did my fieldwork.[3] In recent years, however, the canning industry has declined until few full-time jobs are available, and even seasonal jobs are at a premium. Working conditions are archaic. These realities affect not only a woman's feelings about her work but the organization of her family life as well. This book examines the linkages between Chicano family life and gender inequality in the labor market, specifically the inequality associated with long-term seasonal employment in the canning industry.

Recent research on Chicano families has suggested that women gain power and autonomy when they become employed, and that therefore Chicano families are more "egalitarian" when wives work. Leonarda Ybarra (1977, 1982a, 1982b), for example, has claimed that such couples are more likely to have "egalitarian" values in regard to the household division of labor and to act on those values. Glenn Hawkes and Minna Taylor (1975) and Maxine Baca Zinn (1980) support this view, having found that decision making in Chicano families is shared more fully by working wives than by full-time homemakers.

2. By the turn of the century, Hispanics, 60 percent of whom are Mexican-Americans, will become the largest minority group in the country, surpassing Blacks. Between 1970 and 1980 the Hispanic population increased by 61 percent (reaching 14.6 million), while the rest of the U.S. population increased by 11 percent and Blacks by 17 percent. The Mexican-American population showed the greatest increase in this census decade, surging by 93 percent to about 8.7 million people (U.S. Bureau of Census 1983). These figures on the Hispanic population are probably too low because of the impossibility of counting accurately the many undocumented immigrants.

3. *Canning* here refers to the food-processing industry and the manufacture of canned, preserved, and frozen food.

This research, however, fails to distinguish women who hold full-time jobs from those who work part time or seasonally, as do the cannery workers I studied. Several incidents that occurred as my fieldwork began caused me to question whether the perspective of the existing research permitted adequate understanding of the impact of women's seasonal cannery work on Chicano families.

The first Chicana cannery worker I interviewed was Gloria Gonzales, who lived in San Jose's east-side barrio. Gloria invited me into her home to sit in the living room with her husband and some neighbors, who were drinking beer. I suggested that we go someplace else or arrange to meet again some other time, but she was eager to begin at once. Despite misgivings, I started to explain my interest in women workers. Gloria's husband, Frank, interrupted to announce, "Oh, she doesn't work, she just sits around the house all day." I explained that I had been told Gloria was a cannery worker. "Oh, she is," he said. I asked Gloria how long she had been working. "Twenty-four years this season," she replied. Evidently my presence and Frank's drunkenness had brought out a recurring marital conflict.

Gloria and I began an informal conversation about her job: how she had gotten it, what she did, and how she felt about it. Frank continued to drink and joke with the neighbors. Throughout our conversation, the others interjected their own commentary, teasing and arguing with one another. Their verbal jabs made it clear that Frank and Gloria had been quarreling. In the middle of our talk, Frank announced that Gloria was going to quit so that she could stay home and take care of their youngest son, who was seven years old. Gloria explained that she had the option to "freeze" her seniority and retire early, and that she planned to do so after next season: "It's better not to work, get unemployment, and you get by." But later, when I asked for her general views on employment for married women, she indicated that she placed a high value on independence: "Women *should* work outside the home, see what they can do for themselves. It brings you satisfaction to earn your own money when you're old and your husband is gone." With a glance at Frank, she laughed and said, "When I quit, I'm going to start a housewives' union."

Gloria's sally brought an abrupt end to Frank's patience, and he became abusive. Gloria, he complained, was lazy—and to support his charge he enumerated a long list of domestic chores (including

[xiii]

making his dinner) that she had not completed. He was so dissatisfied with her negligence, he informed me, that they now slept apart. He then questioned my motivations and integrity, demanding to know what I was going to do with the interview information. He shouted, "You could be anybody, from the union—who knows? Gloria could get fired." When I tried to explain that I was doing independent research, he launched into a harangue about people who help "those Mexican people." He obviously did not identify himself as a "Mexican" (the term I had unfortunately used) and felt threatened by my questions. His anger was intense.

It was clear that our meeting could not continue. Gloria walked with me to my car, and we scheduled an interview in my home. She apologized profusely, emphasizing that Frank had been drinking all day. Then she rationalized: "He's awful, but he's better than nothing."

At the time I was concerned that I had precipitated the blowup, but I later concluded that I had become embroiled in an ongoing struggle over the working-wife issue: Frank wanted Gloria to quit; she planned to work one more season. My questions had broken through the facade of marital harmony normally presented to strangers. This incident revealed that when Chicanas enter the labor force, the possibilities of egalitarian family practices clash with traditional gender ideology. Why was Gloria's seasonal job still a matter of contention after so many years?

A short time later I interviewed Blanca Ramírez, who had been working the four-month season at the cannery for twenty years. Blanca was a sorter, at the bottom of the cannery job ladder. She wanted a promotion and was succinct in her appraisal of her chances of moving up: "Discrimination is blatant. If you're white or know the bosses, you last maybe a week on the line. If you're brown or a woman, you work for years and never get promoted." Blanca belonged to a group of workers who only a year earlier had won a race and sex discrimination suit against California Processors, Inc. (a canning industry association).[4]

Several weeks later, at a party attended primarily by Chicano

4. In 1976 the plaintiffs were awarded five million dollars, at that time the largest award made by the San Francisco District Court in an employment-discrimination case (*San Francisco Examiner and Chronicle*, 25 November 1979). A key victory was the removal of separate seniority lists for seasonal and full-time workers. The effect of dual seniority had been to restrict women to seasonal jobs.

cannery workers, I tried to explain my research to Mary Lou, a Chicana seasonal worker, and her Anglo husband, a plant superintendent at another cannery. As I spoke of my interest in women cannery workers, her husband interrupted: "They're all women, and they all can be replaced by a machine." After a tense silence, Mary Lou said winsomely, "Where could you find a machine that acts like me?" She tilted her head and fluttered her eyelashes. In an effort to erase tension by self-mocking silliness, she told us of the crazy things she did, and then she repeated her question. Everyone laughed at her clowning and the absurdity of the notion that a machine actually could replace Mary Lou. Most of the women present were seasonal cannery workers, and they could not have been pleased to hear this management representative callously refer to the possible loss of their jobs. His insensitivity was blatant, and so was the deference that everyone's laughter accorded him.

These incidents reveal some of my informants' conflicts as they handled the roles of cannery worker, wife, and mother. The neat correlation of paid employment with rising marital equality faded. In the workplace these women were segregated in seasonal jobs with limited access to full-time work and better working conditions, and they even faced the threat of being replaced by machines. At the same time, they had made long-term commitments to seasonal cannery jobs, which in turn had brought changes that required accommodation by family members and sometimes created problems at home.

The interview with Gloria Gonzales made apparent the continuity of traditional family norms despite her egalitarian ideas.[5] Her husband still expected her to perform all of the housework. The couple's open conflict over her neglect of the housewife role indicated that egalitarianism did not flourish in the Gonzales home. Furthermore, as a seasonal worker who was economically dependent on her husband, Gloria had little power and low status. Interviews with other workers made it clear that these families did not easily change their attitudes and behavior to accommodate the demands of the wives' jobs. I learned about marital problems, women's misgivings about the fact that they worked, and changes in domestic arrangements which lasted

5. In my view, both partners in an egalitarian relationship have equal power and status as well as joint responsibility for economic maintenance and household chores.

only as long as the work season. Thus family adaptation and women's seasonal cannery work seemed interrelated, and the data I collected, along with women's repeated denials that their work had any effect on their families, showed the complexity of the issue. This crucial dimension of family conflict was ignored in earlier studies of Chicano worker families. Rather than the increase in marital influence reported by these studies, I found that, to the extent that company practices keep women in "women's jobs," Chicana workers will have difficulties effecting changes at home. Like other minority women workers, Chicanas seem to be at risk, since they are concentrated in declining industries or in occupations slated for elimination because of changing technology (Kane 1973).

My approach in this book is historical and ethnographic; it aims to merge what is most valuable in existing analyses of Chicano families with a feminist perspective. In the following chapters I construct "actor-oriented" descriptions (Geertz 1973)—interpretations of informants' renditions of their experiences—but I use women's own words to convey the meanings of their actions as they manage work and family responsibilities. I know, however, that I, like any anthropologist, came away from my interviews with only partial impressions of the society I had explored, given by informants who had varied motivations for talking with me. Nevertheless, I have tried to understand these women's views of their situations, and I hope that such understanding may contribute to the betterment of the conditions that shape their lives.

My fieldwork was conducted over fifteen months during 1977–78, while I lived in the Santa Clara Valley. Most of my data come from in-depth interviews with twenty-four cannery workers and labor organizers and from their life histories. These materials are supplemented by historical research on the canning industry and participant observation in canneries and other settings frequented by cannery workers. In the course of my fieldwork, several questions emerged: Why are Chicanas concentrated in seasonal cannery jobs? How did these women become cannery workers? How do they feel about their cannery jobs? How do cannery jobs affect their families? How do Chicanas feel about being working mothers? These questions are explored in the following chapters.

As the sample in my study is small and fairly homogeneous, I make no claims that my findings can be applied to all Chicanos. I hope, however, that my perspective will contribute to the understanding of Chicana workers in other situations and that it will stimulate more detailed observations on Chicano families in the future. I also hope my work will be useful in comparative research on the millions of part-time and seasonal non-Chicana women workers.

This book owes much to the help and emotional support I received from many people. The labor activist Jaime Gallardo originally encouraged me to focus my research on cannery workers. He, his law partner, Amanda Hawes, and Richard Rodriguez all helped me in the initial stages of my research. Andy Lucero provided important insights during a particularly hectic period of fieldwork, and Martin Brown and Peter Philips, who were conducting research on the canning industry when I was doing fieldwork, generously shared their writings and data with me.

Micaela di Leonardo read the entire first draft of the manuscript, made insightful substantive and editorial suggestions, and provided friendship throughout this project. Working with Louise Lamphere on her own "Sunbelt industrialization" research project served to clarify my ideas regarding this work. Louise has been a constant source of constructive criticism and generous support. Antonia Castañeda and Maxine Baca Zinn gave me encouragement at critical moments during the long process of writing.

Renato Rosaldo and Roger Sanjek helped in the presentation of the data and in clarifying the theoretical points. The critical readings of David Wellman, Bill Friedland, John Borrego, and Jim Borchert forced me to do some analytical rethinking; Borrego was especially helpful here. Carter Wilson helped with the subtleties of translation.

The publisher of Feminist Studies (Feminist Studies, Inc., c/o Women's Studies Program, University of Maryland, College Park, Md. 20742) gave me permission to use material first published in my 1985 article " 'Abnormal Intimacy': The Varying Work Networks of Chicana Cannery Workers" (11[3]:541–547) in Chapters 4 and 5.

A postdoctoral fellowship from the Stanford Center for Chicano Research provided a year of support and an atmosphere conducive to writing. My work also received support from faculty research funds granted by the University of California, Santa Cruz (UCSC). Deborah

Johnson and the staff at the UCSC computing center entered the manuscript into the computer. Scott Brookie and Patricia Hairston graciously provided additional word-processing assistance. Sara Hare was a very resourceful research assistant.

Many thanks go to Felipe Gonzales, who made many substantive comments and helped me to clarify the perspective developed in the following pages.

I especially appreciate the insights and hospitality offered by the cannery workers whose experiences inform this book, and I regret that they must remain anonymous.

PATRICIA ZAVELLA

Santa Cruz, California

Women's Work and
Chicano Families

[1]

"Two Worlds in One": Women's Work and Family Structure

Various theories have attempted to explain the persistence of occupational segregation, the pattern whereby women or members of racial groups are concentrated in particular occupations, industries, or jobs within firms (Reskin 1984; Blaxall and Reagan 1976; Stromberg and Harkess 1978). Neoclassical economic theories attribute job segregation to imperfections in competitive labor markets and to exogenous factors such as sexism or racial prejudice by individual employers or in schools that produce workers with less "human capital." Proponents of the neoclassical view argue that if women or minorities would get enough education, skills, or training, they could eventually have equal participation in the labor market. Labor-market-segmentation theory criticizes this view, claiming that the structure of labor markets discriminates against certain groups and that employers encourage racial or gender antagonisms. Feminist scholars are also concerned with discrimination in the labor market, but they view the behavior of men—whether they are employers, workers, or union members—or specific firm practices as playing key roles in excluding women from better-paying jobs or training programs that would provided the necessary skills for promotions (Hartmann 1979; Milkman 1976, 1982; Blau 1984; Strober 1984; Kanter 1977; Roos and Reskin 1984). Other feminist theorists examine sex-role socialization or segregation in schools or training programs that orient or prepare women for certain occupations (Marini and Brinton 1984). The pervasiveness and complexity of occupational segregation suggests that many factors contribute to the perpetuation of women's inferior position in the labor market (Oppenheim Mason 1984).[1]

Recent feminist scholarship has been concerned with how women's labor-force participation and family obligations are connected in ways that distinguish women from men workers. As paid workers, women are subject to the same economic forces as men. Yet precisely because of their female status, women are concentrated in lower-waged "women's jobs"—occupations in which more than 70 percent of the workers are female (Oppenheimer 1970; Blau 1975). In addition, women bear the burden of responsibility for private household tasks beyond their labor for wages. Women, then, are simultaneously wage workers, women workers, and family members. The relationship between women's wage labor and "private" domestic labor is obscured under capitalism (Zaretsky 1976) and comprises two major processes: the family's influence on female labor-force participation and the effect of wage work on women's roles within the families. Elizabeth Pleck (1976) has suggested that women's work and family are really "two worlds in one," and recent scholarship shows the ways in which women combine work and family responsibilities have varied historically and regionally (Safilios-Rothschild 1976; Kamerman 1979; Tilly and Scott 1978; Smith 1982; Kessler-Harris 1982; Fernández-Kelly 1983; Lamphere 1987).

Previous research on Chicana workers has focused on working conditions or on how women's employment affects their families but has not addressed the two-way relationship between women's work and family (an exception is González 1983).[2] In the following pages, I show how revisionist works on Chicano families have ignored the world of work, and I illustrate a perspective that would connect

---

1. The index of occupational segregation by sex showed no change between 1900 and 1960 (Gross 1968), declined slightly during the 1960s, and declined significantly during the 1970s because women began entering traditionally male occupations in the professions and management. Yet by 1981, 60 percent of women (or men) workers would have to change jobs to achieve identical male and female distributions (Beller 1984).

2. Studies of Chicano workers show how racism and class exploitation are intertwined; yet they focus on men and ignore sexism. Although the growing literature on women and work analyzes the relationship of class and gender, it rarely investigates the situation of minority women and often ignores the importance of race.

[2]

Chicanas' work and family lives. Socialist feminist theory is a useful point of departure in analyzing the conditions of Chicana cannery workers because it directs analysis to who benefits from women's labor and the mechanisms that create job hierarchies excluding women, and it focuses on conflict in social relations.[3]

Linking Women's Domestic and Wage Labor

Socialist feminist theorists (Milkman 1976; Hartmann 1981b; Eisenstein 1979; Kuhn and Wolpe 1978) have argued that capitalist relations in the public sphere and patriarchal family relations are linked. *Capitalist patriarchy* is a system in which the control of wage labor by capital and men's control over women's labor power and sexuality in the home are connected. In the labor market, job segregation is the primary mechanism maintaining the domination of men over women, for example, in enforcing lower wages for women. Women's labor-market activities are restricted through the bearing and rearing of children and men's efforts to control home life. Therefore, we must examine the relationship of women to men in both the labor market and families. Heidi Hartmann has stated: "Patriarchy, by establishing and legitimating hierarchy among men (by allowing men of all groups to control at least some women), reinforces capitalist control, and capitalist values shape the definition of patriarchal good" (1981b:27–28).

According to this socialist feminist argument, the relationship between capitalism and patriarchy contains an inherent contradiction: capitalists and husbands have competing interests in women's labor. In different historical periods, capitalists have preferred either that women enter the labor market (during World War II) or that they return to homemaking (immediately after World War II). In all periods, husbands have been interested in personal and family service. Hartmann (1979) has suggested that the "family wage" provided a resolution to this conflict. The family wage, which working men won in nineteenth-century struggles with capital, insured that men were paid wages high enough to support a family. Labor organizations—

3. For an analysis of different types of feminist theory—conservative, liberal, traditional Marxist, radical, and socialist—see Jaggar and Rothenberg 1984.

[3]

guilds and later unions—were crucial in limiting women's participation in the labor market. Unions often excluded women from training programs and generally supported protective legislation that denied women access to difficult "male" jobs (Milkman 1976, 1982; Hartmann 1979). The rationale for the family wage was the ideology of women's "proper place"—the notion that women are moral guardians of the home and therefore should not enter the labor force (Welter 1973; Ehrenreich and English 1975; Milkman 1982). Thus the family wage secures the material basis of male domination and ensures women's economic dependence. Women's family responsibilities—housework, child care, consumption, and emotional nurturance, which benefit individual men—also reinforce women's inferior labor-market position since it is assumed that women lack commitment to paid employment.

Socialist feminism also identifies inherent contradictions within families. Families are seen to be structured by gender and age, and this socially constructed "sex-gender system" changes over time (Rubin 1975; Thorne 1982). The gender and age of family members affects the family as an economic unit. As family members pool income and share resources such as housing or job benefits, common interests and interdependence are created. Yet women and men participate in the labor market differently, and these experiences also affect families. The domestic division of labor—who does the chores and the time spent doing them—reveals the amount of men's control over women's labor.[4] The family is the locus of political struggle, for men do not voluntarily give up their domestic privileges. Societal contradictions, then, bring conflict to families, and family members must adapt.

Family ideology—the assumptions about proper men's and women's roles—most often supports the segregation of women in the labor market. In Western culture, the family is regarded symbolically in opposition to the public world of work (Collier, Rosaldo, and Yanagisako 1982). Families are seen as havens, providing nurturance for

4. Feminist scholars have debated how housework contributes to women's oppression. One position holds that women's household labor produces use value as opposed to exchange value, which places women outside of capitalist relations (Benston 1969). Others argue that women not only provide essential services for capital by reproducing the working class but also create surplus value through that work (Dalla Costa and James 1972).

[4]

struggles in the labor market. Ideally, families are governed by feelings and moral values and form relationships that endure the vicissitudes of outside circumstances. The world of work is viewed as competitive, impersonal, temporary, contingent upon performance; in it, morality must be buttressed by law and legal sanctions. According to this ideology, families should be nuclear in composition, and women and men should marry for love rather than economic reasons (Rapp 1978). Within this view, "the concept of family is a socially necessary illusion which simultaneously expresses and masks recruitment to relationships of production, reproduction, and consumption" (Rapp 1982:170). According to this ideology, traditionally, men are breadwinners, whereas women are supposed to sacrifice their careers and minister to family needs, especially those of children.[5] This opposition of family and work posits a contradiction between women's (and men's) needs as individuals and the concerns of their families. This ideology is supported by institutions—schools, churches, media, and unions—in which women are socialized to defer to men. Family ideology serves dual purposes: It masks women's multiple statuses by defining women as secondary workers—women who work to supplement family income—and it rationalizes women's subordination in the labor force since women perform "women's work." At the same time, housework is devalued as not being "work," and thus the double day of women is discounted.

Socialist feminism is a useful starting point in analyzing change and stability in Chicano families since these families are subject to the same political and economic forces as other families. Yet Chicanos differ considerably from other groups in how women and men have participated in the labor market.[6] Chicanos face racism in its various manifestations in the labor market. They accept certain American values and beliefs, yet have a culturally specific version of family ideology. The distinct history of the Chicano people has created important differences in how Chicanos and Chicanas have participated in regional labor markets. The following discussion of Chicana

5. Sara Ruddick (1982) has noted that sacrifice is integral to "maternal thinking," the reflections, emotions, and judgment developed through the discipline of mothering.

6. Several theorists (Davis 1981; Hooks 1984; Joseph 1981; Simons 1979; Westwood 1984) have argued that women of different classes and races have varied interests and experiences, and race must be incorporated into socialist feminist theory.

[5]

labor history illustrates how a socialist feminist perspective must be modified to interpret the lives of Chicana workers.

Chicana Labor History

The particular process of incorporation of the southwestern United States (originally northern Mexico) into the capitalist world economy was critical for the development of a Chicano working class (Almaguer 1981; Borrego 1983). The conquest of the "new world" by Spain in the sixteenth century brought gold and silver to the Spanish state and fueled primitive capitalist accumulation (Chapa 1981). Almaguer (1975) has shown that in the feudal society of colonial Mexico, the class structure was based on a racial hierarchy as well: Spaniards (usually male) who were born in Spain or in Mexico (the *criollos*) held the positions of power, authority, and status, while Indians, Blacks, and "mixed races" (mestizos, mulatos, zambos) labored for the white landowners.[7] As Mexico colonized what is now the American Southwest, these class and race categories were brought north and became the basis of class and racial stratification in the United States.

The U.S.-Mexico war of 1846–48 was instigated to further capitalist development in the Southwest (Barrera 1979; Borrego 1983). After this war, in which Mexico lost one-third of its territory to the United States, the Treaty of Guadalupe Hidalgo guaranteed certain rights to the Mexican citizens who lived in the annexed territory. Mexicans had the right to choose American or Mexican citizenship and to retain their property "without their being subjected to any contribution, tax or charge whatever" (Valdez and Steiner 1972:102). During the late nineteenth century, however, capitalist transformation of the region brought many changes for Chicanos. The United States was industrializing, while the Southwest was becoming a center of agriculture and mining. Chicanos were displaced from their land. They lost landholdings to Anglos either through legal means, such as their inability to pay taxes, or through fraud, such as the infamous "Santa Fe Ring" in which Anglo businessmen conspired to take over Mexican-owned land (Barrera 1979; Acuña 1981). Mexicans increasingly were proletarianized and incorporated into the burgeoning Southwest labor markets, serving as reserve labor pools. During this period,

7. The majority of Mexicans who lived in northern Mexico were mestizos—that is, of Spanish and Indian parentage.

[6]

"Mexicans experienced downward occupational mobility, job displacement and entrapment in the lowest levels of the occupational structure throughout the region" (Almaguer and Camarillo 1983:6). The class structure institutionalized racial domination. These processes plagued the Mexican-American population for decades.

In the second half of the nineteenth century, Chicanos labored in developing the infrastructure of roads and railroads connecting the Southwest to the East Coast. Significant numbers of Chicanos worked in the mining and agricultural industries, especially after the Chinese Exclusion Act of 1882. In the late nineteenth century in southern California, Chicano sheepherders and vaqueros had to migrate in search of work that would use their traditional pastoral skills; women were forced to work as domestics or in canneries and packing sheds to support their families. These Chicana wives entered the local labor market even before their husbands did (Camarillo 1979).

It was common throughout the late nineteenth century for Chicano men to be paid lower wages than Anglo men for the same work or to receive lower wages because they worked in "Mexican jobs" (Barrera 1979).[8] Urban Chicano workers were segregated into older areas of cities, which had cheaper but dilapidated housing. These workers were often forced to abandon Mexican customs and practices and to speak in English. Chicanos were also subject to exclusion from local political processes through various practices (Camarillo 1979; M. García 1981). These changes—proletarianization, occupational and residential segregation, cultural repression, and exclusion from political participation—characterized Chicano history through the early twentieth century, especially in California and Texas (Camarillo 1979; Montejano 1981).

After the Mexican Revolution began in 1910, the first wave of Mexican immigrants entered the United States, fleeing the instability in Mexico. This migration involved "class and cultural transitions from a peasant class with a feudal patriarchal culture of Mexico to the

---

8. Mario Barrera has suggested that there was a "colonial labor system" at this time, in which Chicanos were a subject to "labor repression": There was a system of dual wages, with Mexicans being paid lower wages than Anglos for equal work, or occupational stratification based on racial status; Chicanos served as reserve labor pools as well as "buffers" in times of economic dislocation, and their geographic mobility was restricted (1979:chap. 3). For other discussions of Chicano occupational segregation in the late nineteenth and early twentieth centuries, see Acuña 1981, Jiménez 1981, M. García 1981, Trujillo 1981, Montejano 1981.

working class and capitalist culture of the U.S." (González 1983:59)[9] Mexican immigration to the Southwest contrasts with other immigrant histories of the time in an important way: rather than being solitary male immigrants, Mexican workers often brought their families with them. This was in part because the Santa Fe railroad line encouraged the migration of Mexican families to provide a stabilizing force on male workers. The fact that Mexico is on the U.S. border meant that it was easier for Chicano workers to bring their families to live near their places of work.[10] "Greaser towns," as they were called by Anglos, sprang up around various mines, and barrios grew on the "other side of the tracks." In contrast to Japanese and Filipino farm workers, Chicano farm workers often worked as families, and women and children labored alongside the men in the fields. Farmworker families were forced to migrate thousands of miles in search of *"la pisca"*—the harvest.[11]

The use of wage differentials based on race and sex was common throughout the Southwest and continued into the twentieth century (Barrera 1979). Chicana workers, especially in border towns, were victimized by the payment of lower wages than Anglo women received for the same work (M. García 1981). Chicana urban workers experienced poor working conditions and miserable wages as domestics and laundresses (M. García 1981) and as workers in the food-processing industries (Ruiz 1982) and in Los Angeles factories (Taylor 1980).

With the high unemployment rate of the Great Depression, Mexican labor became regarded as superfluous. Thousands of Mexicans and their American-born children were deported or pressured to repatriate (Hoffman 1974). Before 1950, 90 percent of all Chicanos

9. The literature on Mexican immigration and migration is extensive. See Gómez-Quiñones 1981, Hernández-Alvarez 1966, Portes 1979, Ríos-Bustamante 1981, Cornelius 1983, Gamio 1930, Tienda 1983, Cárdenas 1975. Margarita Melville (1978) and Rosalinda González (1983) have examined the conditions of Mexican immigrant women, and Wayne Cornelius and his colleagues at the Center for U.S.-Mexican studies have produced scores of monographs and articles on Mexican immigration.

10. An immigration commission report of 1911 found that 58 percent of Mexican railroad workers and 60 percent of the Mexicans employed in construction admitted that they had wives with them. These figures were much higher than those for immigrant groups from Europe and Asia. See García 1980. The immigration of Asian wives was restricted until 1965.

11. In search of farm work or other jobs, Chicanos on the migrant stream eventually settled in such remote places as Chicago and Bethlehem, Pennsylvania, or in the Northwestern states (Año Nuevo de Kerr 1975; Cárdenas 1975; Slatta 1975). See also Allen 1931a, 1931b.

resided in the Southwest, and Chicano workers were characterized by seasonal labor migration. After World War II Chicanos began urbanizing, primarily because of declining demand for farm labor due to mechanization. By 1980 about 20 percent of all Chicanos resided outside of the Southwest (Tienda 1983:153).

Chicanos and Chicanas participated in strikes and attempted to unionize in various industries. One of the major struggles of Chicano workers was over racist exclusion and unwillingness to organize Mexican workers by the labor movement (Arroyo 1975). In some cases, such as the Oxnard strike of 1903, Mexicans and members of other racial groups (Japanese and Filipinos) joined in solidarity to gain union recognition (Almaguer 1984). In other instances, Chicanos or Mexican immigrants were used as strikebreakers against Anglo workers (McWilliams 1949; Barrera 1979; Rosales and Simon 1975).[12]

The Mexican Bracero Program (1942–64) brought Mexican contract laborers to the United States to work in agribusiness and some industries. Wage rates and working conditions were negotiated by the U.S. and Mexican states. Agricultural organizing was virtually impossible until this program was repealed (Galarza 1964, 1977). The United Farm Workers, which eventually won union recognition for California's farm workers, made a concerted effort to include all family members in union activities (Thomas and Friedland 1982).

Because of occupational segregation, unionizing attempts have usually been segregated by sex and race.[13] For example, the CIO-affiliated Union of Cannery, Agricultural and Allied Workers of America (UCAPAWA) separately organized women and men and different racial groups (Ruiz 1982). Immigration status has also been used to divide workers, and Chicanas and Mexican immigrant women have had to contend with bosses calling the Immigration and Naturalization Service to deport union sympathizers (Vázquez 1980; Mora 1981). Yet women have had their share of victories in labor struggles. A prolonged copper strike in New Mexico, immortalized in the classic film *Salt of the Earth*, was saved by Chicana housewives. Although the men initially refused the women's help, they later became convinced of the need for men and women to struggle together against

12. For other sources on Chicano labor organizing, see the special issue of *Aztlán* on Chicano Labor Studies (Arroyo 1975).

13. Sources on Chicanas' participation in labor organizing include Mora and Del Castillo 1980, Mirandé and Enriquez 1979, Almaguer and Camarillo 1983, García 1980, Durón 1984.

the bosses (Wilson and Rosenfelt 1978). Oral histories of the Farah clothing-maker strikers indicate that Chicanas gained a new sense of self-worth through the strike activities, which enabled them to challenge paternalism by their husbands (Coyle, Hershatter, and Honig, 1980).

There are several theoretical points to be made regarding this overview of Chicana labor history. The most important is that Chicanos have remained in the bottom strata of the working class for more than a century. For example, using data from the National Chicano Survey, Tomás Almaguer and Carlos Arce (1984) estimated that approximately 78 percent of Chicano workers have working-class occupations, compared with 55 percent of the Anglos. Wages have differed significantly between Anglos and Chicanos. In addition, Chicano men have generally received higher wages than Chicanas (Segura 1984; Ruiz 1984). Yet Chicanos have to contend with wages among men that are often less than a "family wage." Chicano men continue to receive lower wages than Anglo men: Chicanos (Spanish origin) had median earnings of $14,700 in 1981, compared with $21,240 for white men (U.S. Census, cited in Segura 1984:64). Furthermore, migrant work is a significant part of Chicano men's labor history. Although migrant Chicano workers sometimes took their families on their journeys, they also were often temporarily separated. Economic instability and migration have hammered at the cohesion of Chicano families and have exacerbated the economic dependence of family members.

Despite some unique features of their labor history, Chicana workers have been subject to the same processes as other women in the labor market. Chicana workers have also been concentrated in "women's work" (Ruiz 1984).[14] Chicanas differ from Anglo women, however, in terms of specific patterns of segregation by industry and occupation. For example, in the midseventies the most numerous occupational category for Chicana workers was operatives, followed by clerical and service workers. At this time, the most numerous occupational category for all women was clericals, followed by service and professional or technical workers (U.S. Bureau of Census 1977). Laura Arroyo (1973) has documented the contemporary concentration

14. For overviews of Chicanas in the labor force, see Segura 1984, Sánchez 1977, Mirandé and Enriquez 1979. Collections of oral histories that include Chicana workers are Elsasser, MacKenzie, and Tixier y Vigil 1980; Coles and Coles 1978; Seifer 1976; Cantarow, O'Malley, and Strom 1980.

of Chicanas in particular industries—food processing, electronics, and garments. Chicana workers largely reside in the Southwest, where these industries are important, and they are typically "tracked" into these low-paying jobs. Factors that contribute to the occupational segregation of Chicanas include discrimination by employers, low educational attainment, and the lack of skills.[15] Chicano families tend to have more children than white families, so the lack of child care also places considerable constraints on Chicanas' participation in the labor force.

By 1980 Chicanas had experienced some occupational upward mobility into the professions and technical ranks. Denise Segura (1984) has shown that educational levels of Chicanas have risen, accounting for some of the occupational mobility Chicanas experienced between 1970 and 1980. Vicki Ruíz (1984) and Rosemary Cooney (1975) have shown that Chicanas with high educational levels are more likely to be in the labor force than those with little education. Nonetheless, Chicanas were still concentrated in "women's jobs" in 1980.

Certain analyses of Chicana employment patterns (Almquist and Wehrle-Einhorn 1978; McKay 1974; Cooney 1975; Fogel 1967; Briggs, Fogel, and Schmidt 1977) have provided important information but are marred by the misconception that Chicana cultural values determine women's labor-force participation, an argument not substantiated by the evidence.[16] These conceptual problems stem from a long-standing view of Chicano culture and families.

Perspectives on Chicano Families

There has been a curious conceptual focus in research on women's roles in Chicano families. In the past, Chicano families were often viewed on the basis of a functionalist "machismo" model. According to this view, Mexican folk tradition is expressed in "familistic" values: Mexican cultural principles of male dominance and age-based authority in decision making are considered the core of Chicano families.

---

15. Tatcho Mindiola (1981) has examined the cost of being a Chicana worker in the Houston labor market and has shown how jobs in the public sector provide less discrimination for Chicanas.

16. For critiques of this view, see Ruiz 1984, Segura 1984, Zavella 1984. I suggest that a complex set of factors, including changing labor markets in which women's jobs contract or expand, determine Chicanas' labor-force participation.

[11]

Furthermore, patriarchal values are said to define a complete segregation of roles within the family, with an authoritative husband-father who ideally is the breadwinner and a submissive wife-mother who cares for the home and rears the children.[17] Mexican-American families are considered to retain these Mexican cultural norms. Values that are conducive to success in American society—achievement, independence, and deferred gratification—are supposedly absent in the Mexican-American family.

This perspective assumes that the Mexican-American family is insulated from American institutions, functioning to socialize children and inculcate them with Mexican values. According to this view, the family also serves as an emotional retreat from a hostile world. Conjugal relations among Chicanos are said not to include shared interests and recreation or satisfactory sexual relations.[18] Chicano families are also said to be familistic in that solidarity arrangements are not focused on the nuclear family. Instead, the family of origin and *compadrazgo* (fictive kin) ties are supposed to be more important to Chicanos.[19]

Change in Chicano families is often explained by acculturation— as Chicanos acquire American "egalitarian" values and norms, the family changes accordingly. Chicano women in particular are said to be subject to acculturating tendencies.[20]

17. Several related norms are said to follow: Fathers and older brothers are seen as distant and commanding obedience and respect. Mothers are portrayed as sacrificing, nurturing, and modest. Women are viewed as manipulators who covertly influence men through children and other kin. Men and women are said to live in separate worlds, with only brief moments of interaction between them.

18. See Heller 1966, Peñalosa 1968, Ramírez 1967, Madsen 1964, Rubel 1966, Tharp et al. 1968. For an excellent summary of the trends in Chicano family studies, see Ybarra 1983.

19. This characterization is similar to ideal typical working-class families: "Blue-collarites" are seen as oriented toward the extended family, traditional, patriarchal, religious, authoritarian, liking discipline, and so on (Miller and Riessman 1961). However, few social scientists have incorporated the concept of class into their analyses of Mexican-Americans. For a critique of this perspective as applied to white ethnics, see di Leonardo 1984.

20. Manuel Ramírez (1967) has found that Mexican-American college students identify more with authoritarian family values than do Anglo students. Chicanas, however, reject the values of masculine superiority and separation of the sex roles, which Ramírez has characterized as evidence of "Americanization." He has claimed that "this is to be expected because their roles are being affected more than those of men by the increasing Americanization in the values of the culture," and he has suggested that acculturation and "cognitive dissonance in the area of civil rights"— the "need to maintain the status quo"—may create conflicts for Mexican-Americans (1967:9). See also Tharp et al. 1968, Humphrey 1944, Madsen 1964, Staples 1971, Samora and Larson 1961.

A hearty critique of acculturation theory and functionalism has developed in the past decade and a half, much of it by Chicano social scientists.[21] This revisionist body of work shows that functionalism, as it has been applied to Chicano families, reifies values and norms and disregards change and variation among both Mexicans and Mexican-Americans.[22] Although there may be ideals of egalitarian or "companionate" family relationships in the United States, behavior may radically depart from values, and the patriarchal nature of American and other Western families cannot be ignored. Structurally, the traditional American family is similar to the traditional Mexican family; the assumption that the former is somehow more modern is unfounded.[23] The acculturation model misidentifies the "nontraditional" United States as gender egalitarian and condemns contemporary Chicanos to a timeless, unvarying patriarchal culture. To the extent that functionalist and acculturation studies have any virtue, it is that they describe the *ideology* of traditional Chicano families.

Chicano family ideology is made complex, however, by the cultural and demographic heterogeneity of the Mexican-American people (Moore 1970; Grebler, Moore, and Guzman 1970). The majority of Chicanos are born in the United States, but a significant portion (one-third) are foreign-born. Estimates vary, but most observers place the number of undocumented Mexicans residing in the United States at between one-quarter and two million people (Cornelius et al. 1982). Chicanos have rapidly urbanized, more than the general population, and by 1970 approximately 90 percent of all Chicanos lived in urban areas. The majority of Chicanos speak English and Spanish; yet the portions that speak only English (13 percent in 1978) or predominantly Spanish are increasing. Mexican immigrants migrate from both rural

21. Some of the earliest critiques include Romano-V. 1968, 1970; Vaca 1970; Montiel 1970, 1973; Sotomayor 1971. See also Alvírez and Bean 1976; Zinn 1975, 1979a, 1980; Miller 1975; Mirandé 1977; Ramos 1973; Ramírez and Arce 1981; Wells 1981; Ybarra 1982a, 1982b, 1983; Zavella 1976. Renato Rosaldo (1984) has pointed out that functionalism was out of fashion at its source at Harvard by the midsixties, yet ironically continued to be uncritically applied to Chicano populations. Perhaps the functionalist social scientists were experiencing "cognitive dissonance."

22. Américo Paredes (1971) has shown how the term *machismo* was not a part of Mexican folk tradition until the 1940s. Facundo Valdez (1979) has claimed that the term is foreign to New Mexico, whereas Leonarda Ybarra (1982a) has found great variation in how Chicanos define *machismo*.

23. Barrie Thorne (1982) has criticized the functionalist perspective on families in general. She has noted, however, that the feminist theoretical concern with the underlying structures of gender and age are borrowed from functionalism.

[13]

and urban locations in every region of Mexico (Portes 1979), adding to Mexican cultural diversity in the United States.

Regional variation among Chicanos in the United States can be found in Spanish accents and vocabulary (for example, the use of sixteenth-century Spanish among rural northern New Mexicans), recipes and food preferences, folklore, and manner of ethnic identification. Ernesto Galarza (1972) has suggested that there are Chicano cultural regions that correspond to major urban centers: the San Francisco Bay Area (centered in San Jose), metropolitan Los Angeles, the San Joaquin Valley (Fresno), the Salt River Valley in Arizona (Phoenix), northern New Mexico–southern Colorado (Albuquerque), South Texas (San Antonio), and the U.S.-Mexico border area (San Diego, El Paso, McAllen). Chicago, second only to Los Angeles in the number of Chicano residents, is another Chicano urban cultural center.[24] Terms of ethnic identification alone vary considerably. The official terms include *Hispanics* or *Persons of Mexican Origin*, both used by the Census Bureau. People identify themselves as *Mexican-American, Mexican, Spanish American* or *Hispano* (primarily used in the northern New Mexico–southern Colorado area), *Raza* or *Latino* (mainly in urban areas where there are large concentrations of Latin Americans), and *Chicano*. The term *Chicano* became widely used in the late 1960s and reflects a shift in consciousness similar to that of using *Black* rather than *Negro*.[25] Ethnic diversity among Chicanos suggests that one is likely to find variation in family ideology as well.

Recent empirical studies also question some of the notions proposed by the functional approach (see Cromwell and Cromwell 1978; Cromwell and Ruiz 1979). Frank Bean and his colleagues (1977) have attempted to ascertain whether Chicano families are indeed as familistic as suggested in the literature. Their survey of 325 Mexican-American couples found that Chicano husbands are less satisfied with the marriage when their wives work than when they do not work. However, Chicanos are less dissatisfied when their wives work for reasons of economic necessity than when they work voluntarily. Blue-

24. Works that document regional Chicano history and changing cultural patterns include Gonzales 1985; Onís 1976; Brown, Briggs, and Weigle 1978; Paredes 1982; Leonard and Hannon 1977; Camarillo 1979; Campa 1979; M. García 1981; Pitt 1970.

25. For discussions of the problems, context, and regional differences in Chicano ethnic identification, see Metzgar 1974; Miller 1976; Limón 1981; Peñalosa 1970; Hernández, Estrada, and Alvírez 1973; J. García 1981.

collar Chicanos are most satisfied with the affective aspects of their marriage when their wives are not employed. Because of this variation and the similarities to working-class Anglo couples, the researchers have concluded: "There is little evidence that familism is an over-ridingly important factor in Mexican-American family life. . . . Class is probably the most important factor conditioning the relationship" (Bean, Curtis, and Marcum 1977:766).

The revisionist work that examines how women's wage labor affects Mexican-American families (Hawkes and Taylor 1975; Zinn 1980; Ybarra 1982b) is discussed more fully in subsequent chapters. But we may note now that these works convey a keen sense of the flexibility and variation in Chicano families. Maxine Baca Zinn has asserted that "future research on Mexican-American families must examine the ways in which family roles are affected by both cultural expectations and specific external linkages of family members with societal institutions" (1980:59). I suggest that we examine particular inter-connections between women's work and family, and my study of long-term Chicana cannery workers provides one example of these linkages.

A socialist feminist lens, filtered by a concern with racial inequality, opens up a field of vision with which to understand the lives of Chicana workers. Our next step is to focus on one historically specific vista, to examine how a particular sector of women of color have experienced and perceived the complex articulations of race, class, and gender.[26]

Chicana Cannery Workers

I argue that the structural constraints on women's lives and the ideology of family reinforce Chicanas' subordination. Within this con-text, women construct varied meanings of work and family. The analysis begins in Chapter 2 with an overview of women's work in the canning industry. The occupational segregation by gender and race and the diminishing number of canning jobs created an older labor force. In addition, the declining canning industry, which had high portions of Chicanas, kept women in marginal economic positions.

26. For works on Black and Japanese-American women that take a similar approach, see Davis 1981, Thornton Dill 1983, Nakano Glenn 1980.

Chapter 3 uses women's life histories to describe the context in which the women I interviewed decided to seek cannery jobs. The need for their labor at home, along with few job options and child-care facilities, limited these women to "mothers' jobs." Women had to struggle with their husbands in making the decision to seek even seasonal wage work.

Chapter 4 focuses on the cannery work culture in which networks of coworkers are an important element. I distinguish between "work-based networks," which are informal groups that socialize women into work culture, and "work-related networks," which are expanded work-based networks operating outside the factories and whose members engage in social exchange. This distinction enables us to interpret the meaning that women workers derive from the work situation. I show how work-based networks are structured and how they derive from the occupational segregation on the job. Yet work-based friendships hold important positive values for women as well.

Chapter 5 focuses on the family lives of cannery women who had long-term seasonal jobs. I show that although family ideology did become more egalitarian, the actual division of labor did not. I also examine how work-related networks operate within women's private lives and suggest that coworker relationships are one way in which Chicanas bridge the worlds of work and family.[27] A brief chapter discusses restructuring of the canning industry in the six years following my fieldwork and the decline of canning in the Santa Clara Valley.

In sum, I aim to merge a socialist feminist perspective on the political-economic conditions of women's cannery work with an interpretation of Chicanas' cultural expressions. By linking the changing conditions of women's work with changes in families, we can understand the meaning women attribute to their total life situations.

The rest of this chapter discusses the issues involved when a Chicana researcher conducts a study among women of her own ethnic group. I agree with Arron Cicourel (1964) that the very conditions of social scientific research constitute an important and complex variable, greatly influencing the findings of an investigation. My status as a Chicana affected the reception I got and the data to which I had

27. Ulf Hannerz (1980) has suggested that the flexibility of networks is crucial. While agreeing with this, I also believe that anthropologists should pay close attention to conditions in which various types of networks flourish and how networks contribute to cultural meaning for the social actors. Suad Joseph (1983) has a similar perspective.

access. My discussion of the context of the interviews and the status of the researcher assumes that the feelings of the researcher and subjects are data in themselves. Moreover, my reflections are both personal and "deeply cultural" (Cesara 1982) and allow the reader a view of the potential areas of bias arising from the anthropological interview process.

The Fieldwork Process

The Santa Clara Valley is located on the southeastern shore of the San Francisco Bay.[28] The valley was once a rich agricultural area, noted for the acres of fruit orchards that thrived in the mild climate. Santa Clara County is now a major metropolitan area and financial center, with high-rise buildings in the renovated downtown area and suburbs covering the once-beautiful agrarian landscape. The major city is San Jose, whose sphere of influence covers approximately eighty-six thousand acres (City of San Jose 1974).

I chose the valley as the research site for two reasons. It has a relatively large Hispanic population, 22 percent in 1970 (U.S. Bureau of Census 1973), which was primarily of Mexican origin. Thus San Jose differed from other places such as San Francisco, which has a large Latino population from Central and South America but a small Mexican-American component. Second, the city was large, with a population of 445,000 in 1970. It is one of the fastest growing metropolitan areas in the nation, with a diverse employment structure. I could expect to find Chicanos working in a variety of occupations. My aim, at first, was to find a job with a family-service agency so as to meet a variety of people. Then with the backing of such an institution, I planned to conduct the research full time. When I moved to San Jose it quickly became clear that finding a position in an agency would be impossible. Jobs were scarce and competition with overly qualified people was intense.

A general housing shortage in the Santa Clara Valley made it nearly impossible for my family of three to find an affordable place near the east side of town where most Chicanos reside. We ended up living

28. Census data for Santa Clara County (San Jose SMSA) will be used here since others are not available, although the valley is only the eastern part of the county and extends north beyond the county line.

on the extreme west side of San Jose. The sprawling suburban area is crossed by several major freeways, which I had to take to deliver my child to the babysitter before conducting an interview; the average driving time was forty-five minutes one way, and my most vivid memory of San Jose is of being stuck in traffic on a sweltering, smoggy day. Time was often wasted as well on those inevitable occasions when informants had to reschedule interviews at the last minute.

Living on the west side made me feel isolated at times and as if I were not part of the Chicano community. As Maxine Baca Zinn (1979b) has emphasized, fieldwork is a continuous process of entering the field and of meeting and establishing relationships with inform-ants. I did not have a neighborhood home base from which to maintain such contacts. My plight was similar to that of other migrants to San Jose. Annalee Saxenian (1980, 1984) has traced the explosive growth of the electronics industry and other changes by which the "Valley of the Heart's Delight" became known as Silicon Valley.[29] Suburban sprawl, congested freeways, and neighborhood shifts along with rising housing costs are all standard fare of life in the valley.

Initially, I tried to interview people in positions of authority in the canning industry, specifically union officials and company executives. These sources proved to be generally unsatisfactory. They were sus-picious of my motives and effectively avoided my questions. For example, while talking with a cannery-company executive whose job was to investigate litigation against the corporation and relating my plan to do plant observations, he said: "They [his fellow executives] think *I'm* weird when I talk to these workers for too long, when I ask too many questions. So there's no way they would let someone like you, an outsider, in to talk with them." At one point I met with a Chicana-plant affirmative-action officer. I hoped to become employed at the cannery and to do observations from the job. I assured her that my interests were purely academic. She found my research interest-ing but worried that I would "talk too much." She told me: "The reason why some people don't want to talk to you is because they think you're a socialist, or a Communist, or from the Cannery Workers Committee, or someone from the EEOC [Equal Employment Opportunity Commission] snooping around, or from the union, or OSHA [Occupational Safety and Health Administration]. See, all

29. Silicon Valley is located in the northern and western part of Santa Clara County.

these agencies are involved; you could be from any one." In one statement she adeptly covered all of the political fears imaginable. She promised to call me during the season but never did, and I found out later that she had been fired.

On the union front, the situation was also politically sensitive. My attempt to talk with a Teamster official was met with a curt "all of this is confidential information." The Teamsters and the United Farm Workers (UFW) unions had a jurisdictional rivalry during the 1970s, which carried over into canneries.[30] At this time there was a short-lived "Teamsters for Chávez" movement and some cannery workers wore pro-Chávez buttons at the factories. Cesar Chávez, the president of the United Farm Workers, and the Teamsters came to several agreements over which union would represent agricultural and food-processing workers.[31] They agreed in 1977 that the UFW would represent farm workers, and the Teamsters would remain the exclusive union for cannery workers. This situation raised suspicions regarding my intentions. The fact that I then used the surname Chávez, was a Chicana investigating an industry that was undergoing a race- and sex-discrimination suit, and that I came from Berkeley all raised questions about my motives. My surname proved particularly sensitive. On one occasion, I attempted to interview a union official. After forty-five minutes of my getting nowhere, he apparently decided I was harmless despite the fact that I was a Chávez, and he signaled to that effect by nodding to his coworker who hovered nearby. I was quickly ushered out the door and given two grievance-process case-books, which proved to be of little value. I found that when I identified myself as Zavella, even in something as innocuous as making arrangements for plant tours, I received more cooperation. The time spent in attempting to interview officials was largely wasted, and I redirected my energy toward establishing worker contacts.

One of my original sources was an acquaintance who introduced me to his mother and aunts at a party attended almost exclusively by cannery-worker families; several of the women I met at this party agreed to participate in the study. My other sources were two activist

30. This was the California State Council of Cannery and Food Processing Unions, International Brotherhood of Teamsters, Chauffeurs, Warehousemen and Helpers.

31. For good organizational analyses of the United Farm Workers Union that mention this jurisdictional conflict, see Friedland and Thomas 1974, Thomas and Friedland 1982.

lawyers who had worked extensively with cannery workers and their causes; they gave me names and phone numbers of several persons who agreed to be interviewed. These contacts provided access to two types of informants: those who were critical of conditions in the industry and who actively sought redress and those who were relatively apolitical. Interviewing informants from two perspectives enabled me to formulate questions better and to gain insight into the intricacies of the whole situation. Without mentioning names, I raised questions with my informants based on notions others had expressed. This allowed me to see more clearly the internal divisions among workers and how this affected their constructions of meaning regarding work, family, and political roles.

The descriptive material I collected came mainly from interviews with Chicana production workers, and the cases were selected to represent the range of variation found among the informants. I also hope to show women's personalities—their humor, strength, and sarcasm. Regardless of the stereotypes of passive Mexican-American women portrayed in the literature and despite the many constraints in their lives, these women were vibrant historical actors.[32]

I also gained information through participant observation in private and public settings—parties, barbecues, union meetings, labor "shape-ups" outside the canneries, plant tours, informal meetings of cannery workers—and through my participation in labor organizing. For two seasons I tried unsuccessfully to get a job in a cannery by waiting around company gates, a quest shared by many.

The Politics of Research

Race and gender relations had a definite impact on my research. This could be seen not only in the process of conducting fieldwork in San Jose but also in the importance of my status and of various community members' perceptions of me. The insider-outsider di-

32. William Madsen's (1964) work is probably the most infamous in this regard. For example, he has stated: "Because women are regarded as weak, suggestible, and less intelligent than males, the purity of a female must be defended first by her parents and then after marriage by her husband" (1964:20).

lemma is still salient for minority researchers doing fieldwork in minority communities.[33]

During my stay in San Jose, there were two local political controversies that affected my fieldwork. The first was a controversy over research being carried out at the local medical center, located a few blocks from my apartment. The medical research institute sponsored an Anglo graduate student in anthropology who was studying cultural values and reproductive decision making among Mexican-Americans. A Chicano organization had been agitating for months trying to prevent the medical center from cutting back services that would affect poor people. They seized upon this issue and branded the student's research as racist. Their main criticism was that the research exploited persons of Mexican ancestry, even though taking the questionnaire was voluntary and it was administered to Anglos as well. The organization's spokesperson questioned: "Why should someone use the Chicano community for their own benefit of getting a degree?" The medical center was pressured to drop its support of the research.[34]

This issue was very close to home literally and by professional association. I was the same age and gender as the anthropologist, and my research was similar. I empathized with the woman and realized I had to be very careful not to offend Chicano political groups. I was also thankful that I had not been able to work through an agency that could become embroiled in political controversy. At the same time, I could understand the community members' outrage at being used as research objects by an institution that was cutting back on services to them.

There is a long history of minority-group hostility toward Anglo researchers who are perceived as furthering their careers at the expense of other people's time, trust, and privacy. This has sparked the call for minority people to boycott such research or to demand something in return, and in some communities Chicanos have done just that.[35] In response, social scientists have called for a code of ethics

33. For an overview of the insider-outsider controversy regarding who is best qualified to conduct research with minority populations, see Zinn 1979b and Aguilar 1981.

34. *San Jose Mercury News*, 29 May 1978.

35. See Gonzales 1985 for an interesting account of a similar community protest over a racial-attitude questionnaire in which an Anglo social scientist not only was fired from the University but was pressured to leave town under threat of physical harm.

that recognizes the often-exploitive nature of research in minority communities and that enjoins researchers to reciprocate in some way (Blauner and Wellman 1973; Zinn 1979b).

Near the end of the fieldwork, I was asked to join in the campaign to get a slate of workers elected to union office. Although I was concerned with the possible repercussions this would have on my research, I could hardly refuse to participate. Because of my criticism of working conditions and my sensitivity to the ethics of research, I thought this was an opportunity to reciprocate in a very tangible way. In addition, the organizers had been generous in their support of my research, and I felt an obligation to assist. Also, I knew my participation would allow me to make new contacts and intensify my relations with those informants who were involved, and I hoped to gain further insight into the industry and union organization. I never regretted the decision. My position was campaign coordinator, which essentially involved doing more intensive research—securing and interpreting election rules, developing rosters of cannery workers, mapping cannery locations and their shift schedules—running errands, and coordinating the scheduling of meetings, leafletting, and observers at the polling sites. The group's permanent membership developed the campaign strategy and organizational ideology. I made my role as anthropologist clear to everyone involved.

A second community problem was even more serious. While I lived in San Jose there was a series of rapes that occurred mainly in the downtown area, which I frequented, near the university. Women were raped at knifepoint in broad daylight, and a nun was raped in her convent bedroom. There was such community protest that the mayor appointed a special task force and enlarged the undercover police patrols in the area. Several suspects were arrested, one who resided in an apartment two buildings from where I lived. The rapist was finally caught when he attempted to break into the convent a second time.

All of this occurred at a time when *Redbook* magazine named San Jose the second-best city in the country in which women could live and work. San Jose won this distinction based on its rating in eight areas: number of jobs for women, number of women elected to public office, medical care, concern for children, income, legislation, character of the population, and, ironically, personal safety.[36] However, both my female informants and I were extremely fearful, and I tried as much as possible to do fieldwork during the day. But since my informants worked day shifts, this was largely impossible, and I was forced to go out at night. Both the research controversy and the danger of night work affected my role as ethnographer, which, I hope, eventually led to richer research.

The interviews were informal and usually took place in the informants' homes. Most people were very hospitable, offering me a beverage, showing me their homes, offering gifts of food or produce from their gardens, pulling out family pictures, or introducing family members as they passed by. Since I did not pay them, I relied on the rapport that we established and their generosity. I was very much aware of their kindness in spending their valued leisure time with me, and I reciprocated as best I could by bringing small gifts and giving advice and information when they requested it. Occasionally, a spouse, child, or friend was present but usually not for long. The women were visibly more at ease when we were alone, and we rescheduled the interview if a husband unexpectedly showed up.

The interviews were open ended and based on an interview guide developed early in the research. I did not actually administer a questionnaire but asked general questions and allowed women to talk freely about their lives. The interviews were "collaborative" (Laslet and Rapoport 1975) in that the women actively participated in the process and asked me questions too; we pursued issues they raised and felt were important. My aim was to interview the women at least twice, and I also obtained more information through subsequent telephone calls. After the interviews, when my notes were put away, I encouraged people to discuss how they felt about the process. Most women remarked that they had enjoyed our conversations, although some worried about what I would do with the information. At these times I often received important information, and informants questioned me further about my own life. I later recorded the content of

36. *San Jose Mercury News*, 20 June 1978. San Jose has since been labeled a feminist capital because of the large number of women in public office and because the union for public employees successfully staged a strike on comparable worth for women employees.

these discussions. Ann Oakley (1981) has suggested that in contrast to a positivist view, in which interviews are considered to be value-free data-collection methods, interviewers should invest their own identity in the interview situation.[37] I found this methodological style comfortable when interviewing women. I also did oral histories, usually with male cannery workers and labor organizers.

Some of the interviews were conducted bilingually or completely in Spanish. Although my Spanish is adequate for general understanding, I do not consider myself completely fluent in what is my second language. I explained this to the Spanish speakers who usually laughed in acknowledgment. They were used to translating or speaking bilingually to their children and other *pochos* (limited Spanish speakers) of my generation. They occasionally asked me if I understood what they were saying. If not, they repeated or clarified until I got the point.

Most of my informants worked and were never sure when they would be home; with overtime during the canning season, they put in long days. So I scheduled interviews that were convenient to them, usually in the off-season.

After explaining the nature of my research and assuring them of confidentiality, if I felt it was appropriate I asked to record the interview. Some were clearly nervous initially, and some of the women refused outright to be taped. For those interviews that I could not record, I either taped the content of their responses in my car on the drive home, or I wrote up my field notes immediately afterward. I generally took notes while interviewing, but sometimes I was told, "You don't need to put this down" or "I don't want this to go in the book because I still got to work there." Since those were usually the most interesting parts, I was a devoted listener and recorded them later.

Folklorist Américo Paredes (1977) has raised a challenge that researchers of a Chicano population must take seriously. He suggests that Anglo ethnographers have produced stereotypic studies because they are not familiar with Mexican folklore, particularly joking and the subtle use of verbal art. These ethnographers attribute literal

37. Wayne Cornelius (1982) has claimed that informal interviews increase reliability and validity with undocumented Mexican migrants. A formal interview style raises suspicions that the interviewer represents agencies such as the Immigration and Naturalization Service.

meanings to figurative expressions or to parodies and humorous fiction. The problem arises especially if the cultural expressions arouse the ethnographers' latent biases. Often the outsider is the butt of cultural jokes, and anthropologists can be particularly vulnerable. The context of verbal performance and cultural nuance that is unfamiliar to the uninitiated may be critical in evaluating the nature of the interaction. Particularly when the information is obtained in group context, with many informants contributing to a story, an ethnographer should be wary. Paredes does not consider if this is primarily a male form of artistic expression, although all of his humorous examples of situations in which the social scientist was duped include male performers.[38] In any event, his warnings alerted me to the necessity of viewing interviews as possible performances.

My first interview with Blanca Ramírez was fascinating, a real performance. After hearing about my interests, she shook her head and announced: "I don't know if this is what you want to hear or not, but I speak the truth." She then bitterly launched into her life story (in Spanish), becoming agitated as she went along, yelling obscenities, and chain-smoking. There was no ventilation in the room and only one light shone on Blanca's face. I was mesmerized, as if listening to horror stories. She told me details that Mexican women would not normally reveal to strangers. At one point, based on her son's eyewitness account, Blanca graphically demonstrated how her babysitter once had sex with a boyfriend. She jumped up, lifted up her blouse and bared her stomach, and wildly groped and bumped. She described the argument she had with this woman after she found out and spat out her words with disgust: "Ah, esas cabronas, son of a bitch!" I was shocked.

Verbal art can be expressed for motives other than duping or shocking the naive. My informants, for example, wanted to protect their privacy from public knowledge and either provided vague answers or evaded them altogether until I proved myself. My first interview with Jesse Valenzuela showed him to be skillfully evasive

38. In an analysis of *chingar mentes* behavior (which means to fuck over minds), I concluded that it is a male form of verbal art similar to "playing the dozens" by young Black males. I observed young Chicano males from South Texas spreading false stories or spontaneously duping someone through group verbal performance. According to the performers, the point of these hilarious deceptions was just to *chingar mentes*, but I argue they develop male solidarity and prestige among the participants.

until he questioned me thoroughly regarding my interests and motives. His reason was that he had been involved in the cannery strike of 1931 and had picked up some Communist literature on the ground. Because he had discussed the contents of the flyers with other workers, he was branded as a Communist. During the 1950s an FBI agent came to his home to question him. He was outraged by this and worried that I also could be from the FBI. These were my most frustrating moments, and Jesse allowed me to begin my questions only after I told him about my involvement in the election campaign, and I clarified my political views. In addition, the context of the interviews was tempered by my status as a Chicana.

I agree with Ann Oakley's (1981) suggestion that the micropolitics of interviewing reflect societal relationships, and the usually unequal status of interviewer and informant contributes to those politics. She has claimed that an informal, collaborative interview style is best among women because it is nonhierarchical. However, it is not always possible to keep status differences out of interviews.

I was reared in a very traditional Chicano family in the working-class suburbs of southern California and hoped that I would understand my informants because I was one of them; to a certain extent this was true. My ethnicity and gender provided entrées, and women in particular did not hesitate in allowing me into their homes. This was certainly congruent with other situations in which women researchers have access to women's private lives (Chiñas 1973; Fernea 1969; Wolf 1968). Some women seemed lonely, and they welcomed the chance to talk with me, taking it upon themselves to educate me about canneries or union politics. Other women related family details, such as problems with alcoholism, that were sometimes upsetting.

The question of family may be the most meaningful area of women's lives, and talking with a stranger about domestic adjustment, conflict, or pain is sensitive.[39] My status was problematic at this point, for although women would have few qualms about sharing personal problems with trusted friends or relatives, some of them were reluctant to discuss them with me, even with the guarantee of anonymity. Furthermore, even by raising certain questions, it was implied that

39. Researchers of the National Chicano Survey found that for their one thousand randomly selected Chicano respondents, the topic of family "is clearly the central feature of the respondent's interests, as well as the most critical and problematic focal point for their concern" (Wreford 1981:1). This is probably a universal concern.

I viewed things differently than they did. We were forced to recognize how very different we were.

In part the reticence can be traced to my position as an outsider. Although as a graduate student I had a lower income than many of the informants, who by middle age owned their own homes and had relatively stable life-styles, most perceived me as upper middle class or even "rich." As their questions implied, how else could I afford to go to college and have the luxury of doing esoteric research?

My education was both a barrier and source of prestige. Informants were very conscious of my education and repeatedly advised me to take advantage of the opportunities offered by an education—opportunities they had never had. Some women saw me as a role model for their children or a potential contact for a better job. Yet the "hidden injuries of class" (Sennett and Cobb 1972) and racism were common experiences for these informants. Some took great pains to use big words, to let me know they read books, or to demonstrate other "intellectual" cues. These attempts were fueled by the racist insults they received at work. For example, Daniel Rodriguez overheard a personnel officer respond to a foreman's request for a new worker by asking, "Do you want brains or muscles, a white or a Mexican?" Being questioned by an educated person exposed the perceived limitations and denied aspirations of the informants, so I tried as best I could to acknowledge their efforts to educate themselves, to dispel their illusions of my affluence, and to sympathize with the affronts they endured.

Many informants were old enough to be my parent or grandparent. They had pride in the younger generation's successes, but they also felt nostalgia for the past. The history of their struggles, which included having been subject to official violence and which created the opportunities for the youth today, are buried in memories. They sometimes saw me as a vessel for making that history known, and at these times they tended to gloss over what were considered the banalities of everyday life.

But informants' reticence went beyond the barriers of education and generation and stemmed precisely from my ethnicity and gender. This was brought out in the middle of sessions in which "rapport" was established and personal information was being discussed. A woman would stop and with a meaningful look make a distancing statement such as "Mmm pues, tú sabes, ¿pa' que te digo?" Literally,

[27]

this means "Well, you know, why should I tell you?" but figuratively, it means "What's the point of even discussing it." Others would abruptly end discussions with tantalizing statements, saying, for example: "Things between my husband and me are not as simple as they seem; they are quite complicated, but I can't explain it all." Such statements, which came only from women, occurred when the topic had to do with their husbands' or other men's sexism, arrogance, drunkenness, or marital conflict. They expressed more than offhand disgust, embarrassment, or resignation. They also meant "You should know, I don't want to explain this to you." Even before they spelled out the details, I understood there was pain and vulnerability in their struggles with men, and these moments produced mixed feelings.

I did not want to pressure anyone into pursuing any matters because of the danger of transgressing the cultural principle of *confianza*. This Chicano construction assumes that only certain people outside the immediate family are to be trusted with private information. I felt as if I was committing "symbolic violence" (Rabinow 1977) by intruding into people's privacy; it seemed more insidious because my cultural and female status got me accepted in the first place. By pressing the matter, I would have crossed the boundaries of acceptability and social comfort. To refrain from probing, however, would have been a denial of my research objectives. I was simultaneously an insider and outsider, in a knowledgeable yet difficult position.[40]

On some occasions I changed the line of questioning to less delicate matters. But at other times I was able to maintain the subject by personalizing our exchange. After gesturing sympathetically, I reciprocated and discussed my personal experience or knowledge and invited their opinions. I turned the situation into a mutually intimate one, and in this way we sustained trust. The women felt more at ease and were willing to relate their own experience in greater detail.

40. Yvonne Tixier y Vigil and Nan Elsasser (1976) have found that the status of the interviewer is significant when interviewing Chicanas on the sensitive topics of racial discrimination and sexuality. Their Chicana respondents provided lengthier, more forthright responses to the Anglo interviewer—for example, admitting having abortions while denying them to the Chicana interviewer. The authors have suggested that Chicana respondents may feel more comfortable discussing these issues with an Anglo researcher, who presumably would not pass judgment on them, whereas Chicana researchers are part of the cultural system and could pass judgment. Clearly, the perceptions of the researcher are crucial in how informants respond to sensitive issues.

On the whole, interviews were unusual experiences for informants, since I encouraged them to discuss their feelings in a manner they probably had never known before. Many people initially felt awkward in this new type of situation. At some point during the interview most people noted that those in power paid little attention to them, that "nobody listens to cannery workers." They also inquired, "Why do you want to talk to *me*?" These remarks were indications that they did not ordinarily express themselves on the issues, and in a sense, they were reflecting their devalued sense of self. My reassurances that their views were important and that I was interested even in mundane details were surprising to them. After seeing my response, several informants imagined a book on cannery workers about which they could boast to their friends that they had participated or even that they would receive part of my "profits." Some informants got a sense of perspective on their lives, a summing up, which despite having to recount the pain was a rewarding experience.

In feeling that their lives had broader significance than only to themselves, my informants gained a pleasurable affirmation of self-esteem. For example, despite his seventy-two years, Emilio Soliz was still active in labor organizing and community politics. During the 1950s he was almost deported for being a Communist sympathizer. Yet he trusted me immediately and graciously consented to be interviewed several times. He remarked in Spanish after our initial interview: "I feel obligated to contribute something of my experience. It's as if I am living once again. When one remembers and reflects about the past, the past seems to come to life again. I feel very happy in doing this and satisfied to be able to help out."

I was deeply affected, too, and came away from the interviews fiercely angry about women's painful experiences. I shared in the depression of a woman resigned to her limited options and in the anxiety of an old man's justified fears of police informers. Yet despite their problems, these people's strong sense of dignity and human spirit was truly impressive. I was privileged to have had my informants' confidence and trust, and I am dedicated to guarding it. Throughout this book the names of workers have been changed, and aspects of their lives have been disguised to protect whatever *confianza* was shared with me.

[29]

[2]

Occupational Segregation in the Canning Industry

The canning-production industry differs from other manufacturing industries in that the raw material, fresh produce, is perishable and seasonal. At harvest time, canners must process tons of produce before the crop is lost. Furthermore, the volume of produce varies from year to year, which creates variation in the volume of canned goods that is packed. Because of this agriculturally based production process, canners have tried to minimize their risks and gain some control over production through various means. Nonetheless, canning is like other manufacturing in that each period in the industry's history contains a particular constellation of ownership, market power, technology, employment levels, occupational structure, and resistance by workers (Cardellino 1984).

There are three major phases of development in the canning industry, which are examined here.[1] I argue that as the canning industry industrialized, there developed a bifurcated internal labor market that included occupational segregation by sex and race. The period 1870–1937 included the decline of craft production, the rise of the factory system and general expansion of production, and the various struggles for union representation. At this time, canning developed a "primary" and "secondary" labor force consisting of men and women workers. Between 1937 and 1968 there was first an intense interunion

1. My periodization is a modification of Martin Brown's (1981) framework.

jurisdictional battle, which culminated in unionization by the International Brotherhood of Teamsters in 1946. During this phase bureaucratic union-management relations developed, as well as increased mechanization and mass production. After unionization occurred, Teamster policy and informal practices contributed to the lack of job mobility by women and minorities. From 1968 to 1978 the canning industry matured in terms of production processes, and there was increased labor agitation by dissident Teamsters regarding the lack of job mobility. Along with market pressures and the high wage bill, these forces set the stage for the restructuring and eventual decline of the canning industry in the Santa Clara Valley. This is discussed in Chapter 6. In each of these periods, the contours of occupational segregation changed.

The Canning Industry

Canning and preserving have been major economic activities in California since the late 1850s, when production began in San Francisco. The industry initially consisted of small, individually owned firms. After 1870 the canning industry rapidly expanded production, and new firms opened up. The industry spread throughout the state, with factories being set up in the Santa Clara and San Joaquin valleys, Los Angeles, and Sacramento (Cardellino 1984). James Dawson opened the first cannery in the Santa Clara Valley in 1871 in a small shed. Fruits and vegetables were obtained through door-to-door sales from neighbors in what was considered the countryside as compared to San Francisco. The Santa Clara Valley was an ideal location because it was a center of agricultural production, and there were good transportation facilities by sea and rail. But the industry had occasional bouts of overproduction, so the California Canned Goods Association was formed in 1885 to regulate trade practices. In 1899 the industry's first concentration of ownership occurred. The California Fruit Canners Association joined together eleven companies holding 60 percent of the industry's output. Production continued to expand, and output doubled in each decade (except the 1930s) between 1890 and 1960 (Philips 1980:128–131).

The canning-production process was originally done by hand. From the first, the required skills were divided along gender lines. Boxes

[31]

of produce were delivered by horse-drawn wagons, unloaded by men and boys, and delivered to tables where the produce was initially processed. Preparing the produce for canning (sorting, peeling, cutting, and coring or pitting) required a careful touch and skills usually considered "women's work." These workers also wore "women's" clothes—aprons and hair nets.[2] Skilled operations included can making by tinsmiths, can capping and sealing, and bulk produce cooking, a very complex and delicate operation. (The proper recipes for cooking produce were closely guarded secrets that even canners did not know.) The craft operations, including bulk cooking, were held by men.

Occupational segregation by race has also been part of the canning industry since its inception. In the 1850s women were scarce in postgold-rush California, and there was a general labor shortage. Thus, for preparing the produce, the canners also hired Chinese men, who had been driven out of gold mining and had no choice but to accept the low wages offered by the canners for "women's work." In addition, the canners trained some Chinese men for skilled jobs. As a result, Chinese males represented 60 percent of the San Francisco cannery labor force in 1870. After the 1870s there was intense racial animosity toward the Chinese, and attempts were made by working-class white men to exclude Chinese males from the labor force. Whether or not the California canners subscribed to the racist propaganda of the anti-Chinese agitators, they placed their needs for labor first and resisted pressure to fire the Chinese workers. "Having started with the Chinese and having proven their usefulness as skilled workers as well as floor labor, it was doubly expensive to replace them" (Brown and Philips 1983c:9). With the threat of hiring even more Chinese workers, Chinese employment could also be used as a check on the demands of white male workers for higher wages.

In the 1870s canneries began hiring more women, whose numbers had increased as a portion of California's population. Women were recruited through advertisements that suggested they spend their summer months earning some extra money in tents with other "girls." Chinese men remained in the skilled jobs, but they were usually secluded and worked in sections of the canneries away from the

2. In the twentieth century some canneries have required the women workers to wear uniforms.

[32]

women. The number of women in canning grew rapidly, in the end largely displacing unskilled Chinese workers. In 1900 women represented 70 percent of the canning labor force (Brown and Philips 1983b:39), and Chinese men declined to only 4 percent of cannery workers by 1908 (Brown and Philips 1983c:15).[3]

Except for the few skilled operations, most cannery jobs (for both women and men) were seasonal and "casual"—that is, the work was usually paid by the piece-rate system, with a minimum wage and an additional rate for each box of produce. Women generally earned less than men, primarily because "a higher proportion of women were employed in job categories in which the piece-rate system was employed than were men" (U.S. Immigration Commission, 1911, cited in Brown 1981:141). Workers were often newly arrived immigrants who knew little English and had few job skills. They also frequently moved from field-harvesting to food-processing jobs, creating peak-season labor shortages. In this regard, the work processes of cannery and farm labor before unionization were similar, and canning was viewed as a part of agricultural production. Beginning in 1910, the percentage of women in California canneries began a steady decline, since mechanization gradually eliminated the need for large numbers of hand processers.

Mechanization

Cannery production was mechanized as early as the 1880s and was unevenly introduced into different canneries. Mechanization brought more control to canners over the uncertainties of agriculturally based production, since fluctuating prices of raw produce created unstable profit margins.[4] Mechanization of the skilled jobs also eliminated the power of craftsmen to withhold their labor at critical times and resulted in lowered wages for workers (Brown and Philips 1983a). The introduction of the pressure cooker and capping machine occurred despite the violent resistance by craftsmen.[5] Eventually, all canners

3. Between 1890 and 1910 children made up about 5 percent of the cannery labor force (Philips 1980:85).
4. For a full discussion of the causes and impact of cannery mechanization in the nineteenth century, see Brown and Philips 1983a.
5. One canner was compelled to use a drawn revolver, and later the machines were smashed (Brown and Philips 1983a:14).

succeeded in mechanizing these skilled operations, although mechanization of "women's work" was hampered by the technical difficulty of replicating small-scale hand movements by machine and the low piece-rates paid to women.

Between 1900 and 1930 the canning industry underwent another process of capital concentration and centralization (Philips 1980). Before and during World War I there was a growth in demand for canned products, primarily by the U.S. government. Furthermore, many imports such as tomato paste from Italy were cut off during the war, causing new markets to start up.[6] In 1916 California Packing Corporation (which advertised under the Del Monte label) bought out the large canner association. "Cal Pak" (as it was called) then controlled 50 percent of the canned goods market. By 1920 two firms, Cal Pak and Libby, McNeill and Libby, produced most of the state's output. After the war government orders dropped abruptly, and the industry was forced to develop new markets. At this time the Santa Clara Valley produced 90 percent of the California pack of fruits and vegetables. The search for new markets was successful, and until World War II, the canneries continued their steady expansion; in fact, canning was the most important manufacturing industry in Santa Clara County (Claus 1966; Philips 1980).

To take advantage of economies of scale, canners built large factories that processed several products and established systems of continuous-line production. The new factories were built in urban areas for ready access to labor as needed. These moves greatly increased potential production capacity, but the mechanization of certain skilled jobs also led to production bottlenecks, and other tasks had to be speeded up.

Between 1900 and 1917 the tasks of labeling and filling the cans were mechanized. Conveyor belts were introduced to move the product from the unloading area through processing stages to boxcars for shipment (Brown 1981:42; Philips 1980:216). The "iron slaves" (as the filling and labeling machines were called) greatly increased productivity and cut unit labor costs. Mechanization of these labor-intensive operations allowed canners to have further control over the labor

---

6. Between 1910 and 1920 output from California canneries grew at two to three times the rate of the real gross national product. By 1926 more than 10 percent of California's industrial workers were employed in canneries (Brown and Philips 1983b:8–9).

process since machines displaced unskilled workers on the shop floor. For the female scalding and labeling tasks, "the gender and wage of the workers did not change after mechanization," whereas in packing and wiping jobs, "men took the jobs formerly held by women," presumably because the wages increased (Brown and Philips 1983b:19). In these two mechanized jobs, increases in labor productivity compensated for the higher male wages (Brown 1981:43).

The first two waves of mechanization were introduced to "deskill" (Braverman 1974) the craft labor of men and control the work process of unskilled workers. Although some of women's jobs were converted to men's jobs, most of the women's work remained as hand labor or of a "casual" character (Brown and Philips 1983b:8). Some of the labor-intensive tasks that women typically performed, such as sorting or filling, remained as hand labor as late as 1978 (see Chapter 4). In 1910, 95 percent of the women in California canneries performed unskilled tasks, 4 percent were employed in semiskilled operations, and 1 percent were employed in skilled and supervisorial positions (Brown 1981:123).

With mechanization, men's work increasingly developed a job hierarchy, and through apprenticeships or company policies men were promoted up the job ladder. Women's work, however, had virtually no job ladder. The one exception was promotions to forewoman, but there were few of these positions. Another result of mechanization was that men, unlike women, were usually paid hourly wages. The majority of women's tasks, even those that were mechanized, continued to be paid by the piece-rate system. Thus although mechanization eliminated the informal nature of male cannery work, the cannery labor force was bifurcated into the structured work of men, with hourly wages and promotion prospects, and the casual work of women, with piece-rates and few possibilities for promotions (Brown and Philips 1983b:12–15). Yet the wages of women relative to men had increased significantly. In 1910 women earned about 86 percent of men's wages (Brown 1981:123). Mechanization also contributed to capital concentration, for small firms found it increasingly difficult to purchase the machinery necessary to remain competitive.

Between 1900 and the restrictive immigration legislation of 1924, there was an influx of many European immigrants to northern California, and the ethnic composition of the cannery labor force changed. To supplement open contracting for jobs, in which workers waited to be hired, labor-recruitment practices also came to include the use of ethnic brokers and networks of friends, relatives, and ethnic compatriots. Some of the Italian immigrants had enough capital to start small businesses of their own, and several small canneries were started in the 1910s and 1920s to can tomato paste and products for the rapidly growing Italian market.[7] Later these new canneries expanded and canned other fruits and vegetables. Although they were eventually sold to large corporations, the family firms started by Italians were a source of employment for many Italian relatives and friends (Philips 1980).

In 1908 more than 60 percent of the cannery labor force consisted of first-generation immigrants, with southern European and Asian men and southern European women predominating.[8] By 1920 about 50 percent of the labor force was foreign-born, and southern European immigrants (mostly Italians) still formed the largest groups (Brown 1981:259). Native-born men dominated the semiskilled and highly skilled jobs, whereas immigrant men and women outnumbered the native-born in unskilled jobs (Brown 1981:270).

As early as 1911 there was evidence of new ethnic and racial employment policies that overlapped the sexual division of labor in canneries. The U.S. Immigration Commission found that in cannery employment, "Italians and Portuguese, as well as the English-speaking, are well represented among the forewomen, [f]or with the exception of Asiastics [*sic*] and Mexicans, it is the general policy to employ a number of a given race to supervise the work of the members of that race."[9] Employers usually did not promote Mexican women to higher paid supervisory positions (Ruiz 1982:59). Apparently, besides their race, forewomen were chosen by their ability to enforce discipline. Elizabeth Nicholas, who worked in Santa Clara Valley canneries during the 1920s, recalled: "They [forewomen] were always picked by the companies, and were someone that could have the authority, could be stern, and could tell you off."[10]

7. For example, V.V. Greco packed the first tomato paste in the West in 1916 (Claus 1966).

8. U.S. Immigration Commission, 1908, cited in Brown 1981:257.

9. U.S. Immigration Commission, *Report: Immigrants in Industry*, 1911, cited in Ruiz 1982:38.

10. Oral-history interview with Elizabeth Nicholas conducted by Ann Baxandall Krooth and Jaclyn Greenberg (1978:14).

Women who did hand processing (with piece-rates) had to fulfill production quotas to keep their jobs. Elizabeth Nicholas recalled: "You were checked when you were given this box of uncut fruit, and if you didn't finish it in a certain length of time, equivalent to 29 cents an hour, well then they gracefully sort of eased you out" (Krooth and Greenberg 1978:13). Women stood around tables and faced one another while they worked, and they occasionally helped one another finish a box of fruit:

> It was cooperative. There were women who would like to finish that extra box. They'd help you finish one night; and you'd help them finish another night. . . . There was an understanding, a way of working this out, that you helped each other out. Yet if someone became too hoggish, you just ignored them. There was no discussion. They'd get angry, but nothing was said about it. (Elizabeth Nicholas, quoted in Krooth and Greenberg 1978:14)

Because of this camaraderie, Nicholas recalled: "I liked working in the cannery. I would say that about 30 percent of us did. There was something about the way it was organized, what you were able to do as a group of people, what you were able to put out. . . . There was a certain amount of challenge in this whole thing" (Krooth and Greenberg 1978:14). Nonetheless, women complained when they believed that the checkers did not fully record all of the produce they had processed.

A kind of informal seniority ranking arose since these women who met requirements to be at work on time and on a regular basis were most likely to be retained (Brown and Philips 1983b:14). However, there was no job security: "You were never hired for the season," Elizabeth Nicholas recalled, "but you were hired for a particular crop for as long as it lasted." According to Nicholas, this "was a way of getting rid of people they didn't want" (Krooth and Greenberg 1978:12). Women were paid different rates for each type of produce—apricots were the lowest paid because they matured first, and there were usually plenty of available workers.

Once conveyor belts were introduced into canneries, the piece-rate system pitted women manual workers against one another. To make good wages, these workers had to secure positions on the line near where the produce first entered the department so that they would have plenty of produce to process. One Mexican-American woman, who worked under this system, recalled the competition for produce:

> There were two long tables with sinks that you find in old-fashioned houses and fruit would come down out of the chutes and we would wash them and put them out on a belt. I had the first place so I could work for as long as I wanted. Women in the middle hoarded fruit because the work wouldn't last forever and the women at the end really suffered. Sometimes they would stand there for hours before any fruit would come down for them to wash. They just got the leftovers. Those at the end of the line hardly made nothing.[11]

"Often a disagreement arises between women concerning who shall have the best positions to begin with," one male worker at the time observed (Anthony 1928, cited in Brown 1981:53). Supervisors sometimes favored their friends and members of their own ethnic group (Ruiz 1982:40). When favoritism occurred, "discontent was bound to spread" (Anthony 1928, cited in Ruiz 1982:40).[12] Apparently, forewomen had complete discretion in assigning women to workstations, and if they favored members of their own ethnic group, it created conflict or resentment among the women workers.

Working conditions at this time were bad. Canneries were poorly lit, women stood on their feet all day, and bathroom facilities were poor (Ruiz 1982: chap. 1). Women workers started the shift at five in the morning and worked until all of the day's fruit was processed, occasionally as long as eighteen hours. When they were not actually working, women had to wait around without pay for the raw produce to be delivered.

All of these early twentieth-century conditions were documented by a California Industrial Welfare Commission study, which recommended protective legislation. Beginning in 1913, various protective laws were passed. In 1916 the California Industrial Welfare Commission regulated piece-rates and provided a guaranteed minimum wage of sixteen cents an hour for women and children working a ten-hour

---

11. Interview with Carmen Escobar conducted by Vicki Ruiz on 11 February 1979, cited in Ruiz 1982:39.

12. One of my informants had cored tomatoes at a large cannery in 1956, when this task was still done by hand. Her forewoman, however, allowed the workers to rotate so that each woman had a chance to work at the front of the line.

day in canneries.[13] The commission also regulated conditions in the factories, setting standards for room lighting, rest rooms, and the provision of stools and foot rests for women workers. Since produce is perishable, canneries were exempted from the maximum-hours provisions of the legislation, so workers could work more than ten hours a day or sixty hours a week "in an emergency" situation, which was standard for the industry (Ruiz 1982:47).[14] An audit system was set up by the California Industrial Welfare Commission (in 1919) to check whether women were making an hourly minimum wage. Canners could be forced to raise the piece-rates if two-thirds of the women were not making a minimum wage (Cardellino 1984:48–49).[15]

Compliance with the commission's directives on plant conditions was in effect voluntary. Since there were few provisions for enforcement of these measures, women continually had to struggle with management to gain better working conditions. In one plant women threatened a wildcat strike to get stools on the job (Krooth and Greenberg 1978:24). Various other strikes occurred to gain union recognition and better working conditions.

The Struggle for Unionization

The main issue in a cannery strike in 1917 was low wages. Workers objected when management began adding extra produce to women's boxes without raising the piece-rates, which in effect decreased total wages. The strike was led by the Toilers of the World, an offshoot of the Industrial Workers of the World (Wobblies). The Toilers advocated unionization of farm and cannery workers and wage increases for all unskilled laborers. However, women were not members of the Toilers of the World but participated only as wives and daughters of the male members (Greenberg 1978:9). The strike was unsuccessful for several reasons. The World War I–inspired xenophobia fueled

13. This commission regulated the piece-rate for women until 1937, when piece-rates were regulated by the more stringent Collective Bargaining Agreement (Brown 1981:142).

14. The regulation of the workday was particularly important since some canners would lock workers inside the plants so they would have to work long hours (Smith 1949, cited in Cardellino 1984).

15. The Fair Labor Standards Act (1938) later provided wage rates for overtime work. See Brown 1981.

[39]

fears that the strike was led by alien "conspirators." The Toilers of the World were red-baited, and widespread violence followed mass demonstrations. Since disruption of production was considered an impediment to the war effort, the federal government intervened to negotiate a settlement. Workers were forced to return to work in exchange for wage increases (for male workers only) and with no recognition of the union. Many of the strikers felt betrayed. After another short-lived strike in 1919, the canners gave women a rate increase from twenty-eight to thirty-three cents an hour (Ruiz 1982:81–89; Greenberg 1978). The distinction between "men's" and "women's" jobs remained, and women's wages dropped to about 69 percent of men's wages in 1920 (Brown 1981:123).

Another unionization attempt began in response to a wage cut caused by the Depression. The Cannery and Agricultural Workers Industrial Union (CAWIU) organized a widespread strike in 1931. The strikers demanded the restoration of the 1930 wage scale, an end to favoritism by supervisors, an end to the twelve-hour day, provisions for overtime pay, equal pay for equal work regardless of age or sex, free transportation to work for women, and recognition of CAWIU as the formal bargaining agent (Ruiz 1982:90; Mathews 1975; Krooth and Greenberg 1978:19; Brown 1981:51). The walkout itself was successful. Elizabeth Nicholas recalled, "I think we had every cannery shut down tight. No one came to work that day" (Krooth and Greenberg 1978:19).

However, the American Federation of Labor would not grant a charter to the fledgling union. According to Elizabeth Nicholas, who was an organizer for the CAWIU, it was because the workers were seasonal and could not be depended on for yearly union dues. Additionally, for its broad social aims, the CAWIU was considered "utopian" (Mathews 1975) or even Communist.[16] The CAWIU sought the "unity of all agricultural workers—field workers and fruit and vegetable cannery workers" (CAWIU Union Book, 1938, cited in Brown and Philips 1983b:17). The union also attempted to organize all work-

16. CAWIU had the support of the International Longshoremen's Association (ILA), which was attempting unionization of nonwaterfront warehouses in the Bay Area. ILA leader Harry Bridges was viewed as a Communist and disliked by the American Federation of Labor leadership. See Rose 1972:70–71.

ers without regard to sex or race (Mathews 1975).[17] Furthermore, many of the leaders of the CAWIU belonged to the U.S. Communist party, although most of the workers did not even know this. Elizabeth Nicholas claimed: "I don't think they [the workers] ever thought of it as being Communist," although she noted that many of the European immigrant workers, especially those from Spain, had a "background of radicalism" (Krooth and Greenberg 1978:21,19). The strike was broken by the third day, primarily because of highly repressive law enforcement. A mass demonstration at St. James Park, reportedly held by fifteen hundred people (Jamison, 1945, cited in Mathews 1975), turned into a riot after protestors marched to City Hall and clashed with police and antiunion demonstrators. Emilio Soliz, one of my informants who had been a strike sympathizer, recalled what was then the worst riot in San Jose's history:

> We went to protest there by City Hall. In those times there was an order that the police would not hit the women. They would hit the men all they wanted but not the women. So we decided to put the women and children up front so that the police wouldn't attack us. But then the fire engines came, and they attacked the workers with billy clubs and fire hoses. They put the fire hoses on so strong that they pushed the children behind the women. Well, they gave us a good bath, and we retreated.

Some sixty prounion demonstrators were arrested. The next day about half of the strikers returned to work, and the following day the strike was over. The strike proved unsuccessful because the canners diverted their raw produce to other Bay Area plants, preventing any appreciable strike loss. In the context of the Depression, the canners were in a much better position to hold out than were the workers.[18]

After the failure of the 1931 cannery strike, leaders of the CAWIU shifted to a highly successful campaign to organize field workers throughout California.[19] In response, the Associated Farmers launched

17. CAWIU made overtures to the United Farmers League and other organizations of small and midsized farmers. See the CAWIU Resolutions 1934.

18. Ruiz claims that the lack of organization on the part of CAWIU was a factor in the breakup of the strike (1982:94).

19. For example, 79 percent of the 1933 labor disputes were under CAWIU's leadership. See Ruiz 1982:94.

[41]

a campaign to rid the state of its so-called red menace, various violent incidents followed, and the CAWIU disintegrated when its leaders were jailed for violating the California Criminal Syndicalism Act (1919). After the CAWIU became defunct, the membership was encouraged to join the American Federation of Labor.[20]

The Depression had other consequences for the composition of the cannery labor force. During the Depression, the work force was still composed primarily of white ethnics, with Italians predominating in San Jose and the Portuguese in Santa Clara (Mathews 1975).[21] Mexicans were only 2 percent of the total Santa Clara County labor force in 1928.[22] Furthermore, the white ethnic cannery workers tended to be second generation—the children of immigrants, which meant that they were English speakers—and many resided in cannery worker neighborhoods in the valley (Mathews 1975). One former worker later recalled that the cannery work force was relatively young at this time: "very few [workers] were around after 30 years of age."[23]

The widespread migration to California of people from the dust bowl and other areas during the Depression posed a threat to those with cannery jobs. Because of the high unemployment, cannery jobs were at a premium. In 1933, bowing to political pressure, nearby Monterey and Pacific Grove chambers of commerce instituted a system whereby jobs in local fish canneries would go first to those with six months of residence in the county.[24] Emilio Soliz recalled that these actions were done to protect local people's jobs and to exclude "outside agitators" who were pushing for union recognition. The exclusionist sentiments quickly took hold, and many would-be work-

20. According to the President Donald Henderson, the demise of CAWIU was caused by its isolation from the rest of the trade union movement, in particular the American Federation of Labor's prior hostility, along with the vigilantism against it. Henderson believed that by organizing only cannery workers, CAWIU would have been a more stable organization (1936, cited in Ruiz 1982:97).

21. In Sunnyvale and Mountain View (about fifteen and twenty miles, respectively, to the west of San Jose), there were also large groups of Spanish immigrants, as well as Yugoslavians, in the cannery labor force (Krooth and Greenberg 1978; Robles 1978). According to my informants, Italians and Portuguese dominated Hayward's large plants thirty miles north.

22. Governor Young's Mexican Fact-Finding Committee, *Mexicans in California*, 1930, cited in Ruiz 1982:63.

23. Mike Elorduy, secretary-treasurer of the Teamster California State Council of Cannery and Food Processing Unions, interviewed by Martin Brown, 19 December 1978.

24. *San Jose Mercury Herald*, 9 July 1933.

ers found it difficult to find jobs in Santa Clara Valley canneries. The result was that Mexicans, "Okies," Blacks, and other migrants were restricted from getting jobs in canneries. According to Mexican informant Jesse Valenzuela, during the Depression "the canneries were controlled by the Italians and Portuguese," so he had to lie about his ethnicity and claim kinship with another worker to get hired. A study of seasonal employment in California confirmed my informants' recollections of the difficulties of securing cannery employment at this time. This study found that "between 50 and 60 percent" of the cannery workers interviewed had members of their immediate families working in the same plant. Furthermore, the average duration of state residence of cannery workers was fifteen years, and the percentage of cannery workers from out of state was "practically negligible" (State of California 1939:53–54). According to my informants, and confirmed by Elizabeth Nicholas (Krooth and Greenberg 1978), there were few Mexican-Americans working in Santa Clara Valley canneries before World War II.

Economic factors and increased labor agitation stimulated another phase of cannery mechanization during the Depression. Protective legislation had reduced the advantages of women's casual hand labor, and the union drives threatened to raise further the wages of women's work (Brown and Philips 1983b:9). Therefore, canners began to mechanize the seasonal preparation tasks of women, and various cutting and pitting machines were slowly introduced to different factories (Brown 1981:47–53).[25] With the exception of sorting, women increasingly worked as machine operators.

The consequences of the mechanization of "women's jobs" were contradictory from the workers' point of view. The new machines placed the pace of production in the hands of management, they fragmented the production process further, and productivity increased. Where individual productivity could be measured, the machine operator positions were paid by piece-rates. Women workers at the time indicated that they had preferred the piece-rate system when working by hand, because they could make more money if they worked faster, and it allowed a respite from the fast pace since they

25. It wasn't until the mid-1950s that the automated-line production reached maturity in preparation tasks and was linked up with the automated line in the cookroom. When this happened, most of women's hand labor was eliminated from the production process in canneries. See Brown and Philips 1983b:11.

[43]

could slow down when tired (Brown 1981:60). Women also could converse with one another, as Elizabeth Nicholas recalled, "if you wanted to give the time" (Krooth and Greenberg 1978:13). After introduction of the new machines, there was a sharp rise in the frequency of occupational injuries, indicating that workers were either mentally or physically exhausted and that there were inadequate safety provisions on the new machinery. Under the pressure of piece-rate mechanized jobs, women workers often took risks—for example, attempting to rig the counting device on a peach cutter. Accidents such as severed fingers resulted (Krooth and Greenberg 1978:18). Occupational injury rates increased, reaching their highest point ever in 1942 (Brown 1981:62). Mechanization transformed cannery work from agricultural to industrial labor, however, and this ensured that seasonal cannery workers were included under the provisions of the National Labor Relations Act. Management-controlled production also eliminated supervisory abuse when placing women on the line, which had been a key organizing issue in the 1931 strike.

Many changes had occurred during the Depression. Between 1930 and 1950 the Santa Clara Valley became the most important center of production of canned goods in the United States (Claus 1966). Changes in the production process consolidated a large, urban, and relatively stable work force despite the ethnic diversity, and a persistent militancy developed on the part of cannery workers. Furthermore, in contrast to the agricultural labor market, which remained informally organized, cannery work became industrial labor. These changes facilitated union recognition.

In the fifteen years between the cannery strike of 1931 and unionization in 1946, intense rivalry grew among various unions attempting to organize northern California cannery workers. The International Brotherhood of Teamsters union viewed their jurisdiction as including cannery warehouse workers, so they wanted to organize cannery production workers too. In 1935 the American Federation of Labor began issuing charters for "federal" locals to cannery workers as well.[26] Several of these locals began cannery-organizing drives with the Warehousemen's Union, which was affiliated with the International Longshoremen's Association.

26. Federal locals are individual union locals with charters issued directly from the national office of the American Federation of Labor but administered by the State Federation of Labor. See Brown 1978.

[44]

Mike Elorduy, secretary-treasurer of the Teamster Cannery Workers Council, recalled that their aim was to gain an industrywide union with uniform wage rates, as opposed to craft-union structure, which organized only craft workers.[27] If they could organize this type of union, individual employers would not be able to "whipsaw" the workers—keep wages lower at particular plants by threatening to hire unorganized workers (Brown 1978:6). But the process could work two ways, so without the protection of an association of canners, individual canning firms could be "whipsawed" by pressure to conform to higher union wage rates. California Processors and Growers, a canners association, was formed in 1936 with hopes of forestalling unionization by setting an industrywide uniform wage scale and making provisions to process each other's produce in the event of strikes (Gilb 1957; Ruiz 1982:102–105). A showdown came in 1937, when Stockton cannery workers staged a walkout to gain higher wages and union recognition of one of the AFL "federal locals." The canners resisted by locking out the workers, and picketers were attacked in the worst riot in Stockton's history—later known as "bloody Friday."

Once it became clear that unionization would happen, California Processors and Growers planned to favor a union of their choice. J. Paul St. Sure, the lawyer representing California Processors and Growers at the time, later recalled: "The *quid pro quo* was that in return for assistance in organizing . . . that we might avoid the violence or disturbing problems of organization. . . . We'd come off more cheaply in the long run by having avoided trouble and perhaps by getting an easier deal."[28] The canners also wanted a union that would not organize farm workers, since many of them either owned large tracts of farm acreage (Ruiz 1982:105) or had produce-supplying arrangements with particular farmers (Brown and Philips 1983b:18).

With the help of canning management, the State Federation of Labor engaged in "union substitution" (Thomas and Friedland 1982) by imposing a union that was not the choice of cannery workers. Breaking with the AFL national leadership, State Federation of Labor

27. According to Mike Elorduy, the craft-oriented American Federation of Labor was "not structured to take in industrial unions," and that is why the AFL organized "federal" locals. Oral-history interview conducted by Martin Brown, 19 December 1978, p. 3.

28. Oral-history interview with J. Paul St. Sure conducted by Corrine Gilb (1957:142).

secretary Edward Vandeleur denied the legitimacy of the AFL "federal" union because, he alleged, outsiders were on the picket lines. He recognized instead the Stockton Cannery Workers Union (SCWU); virtually all members of the SCWU held supervisory positions. Members of California Processors and Growers signed an agreement that recognized SCWU as the sole bargaining agent for Stockton cannery workers and stipulated that there would be no connections with the Agricultural Workers Union. This imposition of a "company union" set a precedent. The State Federation of Labor then dissolved the "federal" locals and with the help of management formed new AFL locals throughout northern California.

The first collective-bargaining agreement between California Processors and Growers and the American Federation of Labor was signed in 1937. This brought changes in the organization of production. Management agreed to an eight-hour working day with a forty-eight-hour (six-day) work week. During the processing season, however, the contract allowed a sixty-hour week for men, with a ten-hour work day, before overtime applied, and up to a two-hour recess (without pay) if work was stopped by circumstances beyond the control of the employer. In 1937 there was a simultaneous sharp increase in productivity (as indicated in value-added rates per worker) and in real wages for workers (Brown 1981:40).

Women's working hours, still regulated by the Industrial Welfare Commission, were based on a forty-eight-hour, six-day work week with overtime pay for work beyond twelve hours a day.[29] In fact, the overtime pay for women working less than twelve hours made their hourly wage equal to the regular hourly wages for men. This occurred because of an informal agreement between the union and California Processors and Growers, so that "the women's earnings would not exceed the men's."[30] Furthermore, in 1932 the Industrial Welfare

29. It wasn't until a 1944 ruling by the National War Labor Board that the processing season workday was reduced to eight hours for men and women, and provisions were made for overtime pay after eight hours of work. By 1962 most canners had switched to hourly wages and three eight-hour shifts, which enabled them to run the expensive machinery all day and cut down on fatigue-induced accidents (Brown 1981:63–65).

30. Paul Pinsky, "Economic Material on California Canning Industry" California CIO Council, 1946, cited in Brown (1981:64). This was testimony given before the National War Labor Board, which regulated wages and working conditions in canneries during World War II.

Commission had ruled that women could not lift more than twenty-five pounds. This restricted women from certain men's jobs that required heaving lifting.

Although unionization benefited workers by providing better wages, the contract stabilized a long work day. Canners frequently violated their agreement with the AFL locals by ignoring wage scales or overtime rates (Ruiz 1982:112–113; Rose 1972:68). The collective-bargaining agreement also institutionalized the engendered division of work into "men's" and "women's" jobs and formalized the wage disparities between women and men. Furthermore, in 1939, with the support of the AFL union, unemployment benefits were extended to include seasonal cannery workers. The union lobbied to have cannery workers included in unemployment-compensation legislation—which provided incentives for workers to return to seasonal cannery employment rather than find other jobs—so that the union would have a stable membership (Brown and Philips 1983b:20).

Meanwhile, the United Cannery, Agricultural, Packing and Allied Workers of America (UCAPAWA) had been organizing and recruiting members of the old AFL federal locals as well as independent unions. "The founders of UCAPAWA shared a vision of a national decentralized labor union . . . in which power flowed from below" (Ruiz 1982:131). As stated in its constitution, the UCAPAWA aimed to "unite all workers in our industry on an industrial and democratic basis, regardless of age, sex, nationality, race, creed, color or political and religious beliefs, and pursue at all times a policy of aggressive activity to improve our social and economic conditions" (1938, cited in Ruiz 1982:133). UCAPAWA organizers and officers came from all sectors of the working class, and women and Chicanas in particular held significant numbers of leadership positions (Ruiz 1982:chap. V).[31] The union was left oriented and continually red-baited. But as organizer and international vice-president Louisa Morena noted, it was not a "Communist-controlled" union as was alleged (Ruiz 1982:135).

In 1937 the Santa Clara County local of the UCAPAWA filed a complaint with the National Labor Relations Board (NLRB) alleging that fifteen AFL locals were "company unions" and charging man-

---

31. In the official union pledge members promised "never to discriminate against a fellow worker" and to "defend on all occasions . . . the members of UCAPAWA" (Ruiz 1982:133).

agement with coercing cannery workers.[32] The NLRB ruled in favor of the UCAPAWA in 1940, prohibiting further interference in labor organizing on the part of California Processors and Growers. However, the closed-shop agreement between the American Federation of Labor State Council of the Cannery Unions and California Processors and Growers continued (Ruiz 1982:116).

The union rivalry continued through the duration of World War II. Between 1938 and 1945 AFL cannery union members in Sacramento, Stockton, Modesto, and Sunnyvale managed to take control of their locals. In contrast, San Jose, Oakland, and Hayward continued as "company unions" (Ruiz 1982:206). Informant Emilio Soliz had worked at a Sunnyvale plant and had strong opinions on the contrast between the two unions: "The AFL has always been a 'moneygate' union, nothing more. They never never have been a union which protects the workers." He was a staunch supporter of the UCAPAWA and later an organizer for the Food, Tobacco, Agricultural and Allied Workers Union, which was affiliated with the Congress of Industrial Organizations. "We wanted a union that would be of the workers, that truly responded to the needs of the worker." Despite the fact that the CIO union was continually red-baited, there were more than 124,000 UCAPAWA members in 1939.

World War II brought changes to the cannery work force. There was constant turnover of employees, especially among the men, as workers entered defense-industry jobs or joined the armed forces. Also, the war effort required increased production of canned foods, and canneries were regulated by the National War Labor Board, which cut the length of the workday. The result of these changes was a severe labor shortage. Women and children were recruited from all over the state to work in canneries, schools were used to house and feed workers, and school buses provided transportation (Cardellino 1984:62).

The expansion of the canning industry was part of the war-induced growth in Santa Clara County. From a population of 68,459 in 1940, the county expanded to 95,280 in 1950, 204,196 in 1960, and 445,779 in 1970 (U.S. Census 1982a). During this time, many Mexican-Amer-

---

32. The Wagner Act passed in 1935 had guaranteed industrial workers the right to join the labor union of their choice and instituted the NLRB to supervise and certify fair elections as well as regulate working conditions and employer practices. See Ruiz 1982:115.

icans began settling in San Jose, migrating from south Texas or Mexico. The Mexican-American population in Santa Clara County increased from 35,306 in 1950 to 226,611 in 1970, a growth of more than 600 percent (U.S. Bureau of Census 1950, 1982b).[33] Many of these new residents began working in canneries: "The major economic magnet drawing the Mexican-Americans [to San Jose] was the canning industry which enabled families to have a relatively stable source of employment and to earn enough to stay in one locale throughout the year" (Sánchez and Wagner 1979:9).[34] By 1946 "Spanish-speaking" individuals (which may have included a few Spanish immigrants) made up about one-third of the northern California cannery labor force eligible to vote in union elections (Ruiz 1982:213). These new workers would play an important role in the ongoing union rivalry.

On May 2, 1945, in response to Teamster pressure, AFL President William Green, with the approval of the Executive Board, turned over jurisdiction of California cannery locals to the International Brotherhood of Teamsters. The Teamsters leaders had threatened to destroy the cannery union unless the AFL capitulated.[35] In protest over the Teamster takeover, about which the AFL members had not been informed, workers in Sacramento, Stockton, and Modesto staged strikes or temporary work stoppages but to little avail. The disgruntled AFL members approached the Food, Tobacco, Agricultural and Allied Workers Union (FTA-CIO) for help.[36] In August 1945 the FTA launched a campaign to organize northern California workers for the CIO. For the next four years there was an acrimonious jurisdictional dispute between the CIO cannery unions and the Teamsters.

In 1945 the FTA-CIO won the election for union representation of

33. Data for 1940 are not available, and the data for 1950 are for the "Spanish-surname" population. Hernandez, Estrada, and Alvírez (1973) have discussed problems of census undercounting and changing of definitions of Hispanics.

34. There were some Mexican braceros who worked in the canneries and later became permanent residents.

35. The threat came in a statement made by Dave Beck, leader of the Western Teamsters. See Ruiz 1982:207.

36. At the 1944 national convention, UCAPAWA had changed its name to the Food, Tobacco, Agricultural and Allied Workers Union of America (FTA-CIO) to acknowledge the CIO tobacco workers locals that joined the union. There was no change in leadership, structure, or philosophy (Ruiz 1982:144). The FTA had been successful in organizing southern California cannery workers, in particular the Cal Can Strike of 1939. See Ruiz 1982:chap. 6.

[49]

cannery workers, defeating both the company unions and the Teamsters. However, the Teamsters challenged the election results with the NLRB, claiming that at least a thousand votes were improper. The Teamsters began a major counteroffensive, applying intense political pressure on the NLRB and claiming that the board was dominated by radicals. They also staged an effective national blockage of goods going to and from California canneries. Despite a recommendation by its own staff to certify the election, the NLRB dismissed the election results and ordered a new election.

In the spring of 1946, California Processors and Growers (CPG) and the International Brotherhood of Teamsters, in flagrant violation of the law, defied the NLRB and entered into a closed-shop agreement. J. Paul St. Sure stated that the canners considered the Teamsters to be the more "responsible" union, since it would be the sole bargaining unit for thousands of workers spread over northern California and would represent production and warehouse workers within the same plant. For these reasons the CPG actively encouraged unionization by the Teamsters (Gilb 1957:141). Cannery workers throughout northern California resisted this imposition of a union without a proper election. They staged protests and formed picket lines around canneries. The companies locked out the workers, and the Teamsters retaliated with violence, assaulting even women workers in a "reign of terror" that some likened to "civil war" (Ruiz 1982:221–224; Rose 1972). In addition, California Processors and Growers hired a public relations firm and took out full-page ads in various northern California newspapers, portraying the NLRB as the villain and their own actions as reasonable.

FTA sympathizers were red-baited and subjected to violence and intimidation. On the Sunday before the second election, priests throughout San Jose encouraged the predominantly Catholic Italian and Portuguese cannery workers to vote for the Teamsters. Emilio Soliz recalled the effects of this advice: "Naturally all of the people were Catholic. So how could they vote for the FTA-CIO union if the priests told them they would be voting for a subversive union?" The priests' admonitions were one of many elements exacerbating a tense climate. According to Emilio Soliz, the recent migrants from Texas and Mexico were another problem because they did not want to support any union: "They didn't know anything, and they were afraid to lose their jobs after just arriving." In August 1946 the Teamsters won the second election by 1,400 votes out of a total of 31,800 votes cast.

The FTA challenged the election results, but it wasn't until 1949 that the NLRB found the CPG guilty of unfair labor practices and ordered the reinstatement of workers who had been dismissed for CIO activity. Emilio Soliz recalled that he and his fellow organizers received lump sums of cash, but by the time they received the funds they had already found other jobs. The NLRB also upheld the validity of the Teamster contract, and the FTA locals disbanded.[37]

The Teamsters won the right to represent cannery workers by dubious means. Without a strong base of support and with the Teamsters' reputation for negotiating "sweetheart contracts," the prospects for a strong union did not seem bright. Yet the force of a large, national Teamsters union would help in contract negotiations.

During the period of union rivalry, women's wages relative to men's wages accelerated significantly. In 1947 women received about 83 percent of men's wages (Brown 1981:123). The CIO's aim of equal wages for all workers pressured the AFL to increase women's wages (Brown 1981:124), and the war-induced labor shortage contributed to wage increases.

Maturation of the Canning Industry

After World War II canning greatly expanded in the Santa Clara Valley, and the miles of orchards that supplied fruit to the canneries led one publicist to dub it the "Valley of the Heart's Delight." The canned fruit and vegetable industry was the largest manufacturing employer in California in 1947 (Cardellino 1984). The Santa Clara Valley produced about 90 percent of California's canned fruits and vegetables, which amounted to about 25 percent of the national pack (Claus 1966:48). The war brought enormous increases in profits, especially to the large canners.[38]

At this time another wave of mechanization began, with the major

37. At this time the FTA was undergoing severe internal conflict, and it was expelled from the Congress of Industrial Organizations in 1950 for alleged "Communist domination" (Ruiz 1982:135, chap. 8).

38. For example, Del Monte's profits nearly tripled before 1947 (Cardellino 1984:91).

Table 1. Average annual number of production workers in California canning industry, 1939–72

Year	Production workers
1939	25,093
1947	37,416
1954	37,662
1958	45,146
1963	45,027
1967	44,600
1972	43,400

Source: U.S. Bureau of Census, Census of Manufacturers, 1937–72.

impetus being the severe labor shortage during the war. Many machines and practices that were standard in the industry a generation later were first introduced after the 1940s (State of California 1962). Mechanization spread to various canneries between 1950 and 1960, and in recent years the industry has moved from conveyorized production to full-scale automation.[39] Canners also moved into frozen and dehydrated foods.

The canning industry had spectacular growth in output until 1960; production declined between 1960 and 1970 but then increased again. By 1974 more than 146 million cases were produced in California canneries. Yet employment was declining because mechanization reduced the number of job opportunities in the industry, particularly the unskilled jobs. Throughout the state, annual average wage employment in canneries began dropping after 1958 (see Table 1).[40] In Santa Clara County, the number of cannery-production workers also declined after 1958. From 1950 to 1958 annual average employment fluctuated between 9,300 and 10,300. But from 1958 to 1962 employment was in the range of 8,400 to 9,100 (State of California 1962:35). In the early 1970s, the employment levels were lower than in 1950. Only 8,300 wage and salary workers were employed by canneries in

39. There were other technical improvements, such as storage methods, which extended the canning season.

40. The Census of Manufacturers changed its definition of the California canning industry (SIC code 203) over time: 1939—canned and dried fruits and vegetables (including soups); 1947—canning, preserving, and freezing; 1954, 1958, and 1963—canned and frozen foods; 1967—canned, cured, and frozen food; 1972—canned and preserved fruits and vegetables. See U.S. Bureau of Census 1939–72.

Santa Clara County in 1972. In the following years, the number increased somewhat, so by 1976 canneries employed 9,200 people (State of California 1978).

Canning remained among the top five manufacturing industries in California until 1963 and was among the top ten as late as 1977 (Cardellino 1984:74–76). By the midsixties, however, there was already evidence of maturation in the canning industry as it underwent another process of concentration. From a high of more than 300 California canning firms in 1919, there were only 160 canning firms in 1971 (Philips 1980:181).[41] The industry was dominated by three corporations, Del Monte; Libby, McNeill and Libby; and Hunt-Wesson, which had diversified operations.

Profit margins, which have always been variable, were low between 1968 and 1977, averaging 3 percent and declining in the late 1970s (Thor 1982:Table 4).[42] Canning became increasingly unattractive to investors, and marketing became more competitive. There also has been a decline in the importance of the processors' labels with an increase in the volume packed under labels for retail stores or distributors (the generic brands, which often cost less to consumers).

Furthermore, the market for canned fruits and vegetables (with the exception of tomatoes) has been declining (Brown 1981). The high prices of canned food relative to fresh fruits and vegetables, along with increased awareness of the high salt or sugar levels in canned food, has led to consumer preferences for fresh food (Thor 1982; Goldberg and Wilson 1982).[43] Further concentration of the industry will probably continue as canning firms are bought up by conglomerates with diversified operations or by grower cooperatives.[44] These changes portend a highly competitive and unstable canning industry in years to come.

41. In part this was because of the formation of cannery cooperatives in the 1950s, which were owned by growers to can their own produce and were protected from antitrust concerns.

42. Eric Thor has analyzed national data. More recent data are difficult to obtain, since so many canneries are part of cooperatives (in which profits are calculated differently) or are integrated in multinational firms (Thor 1982:15).

43. In response, canners are producing low-salt and lightly sugared products.

44. Del Monte (which had already diversified into shipping, canning production in Europe, and other enterprises) was purchased by tobacco conglomerate R. J. Reynolds in 1979, and Libby's was acquired by Nestle Co. in 1978.

[53]

The Teamsters Union

Unionization has brought about increased wages and benefits for cannery workers. By 1976 workers enjoyed cost-of-living adjustments, eleven paid holidays, and pension, medical, dental, drug, and vision plans (California Processors, Inc., et al. 1976). However, these union benefits disproportionately favored skilled, year-round workers. At first, the collective-bargaining agreement had classified jobs as male and female. In 1967 under the impetus of the Fair Employment Practices clause (Title VII) of the Civil Rights Act, a system of wage "brackets" (occupational categories with corresponding wage rates) was established, and a distinction between "seasonal" and "regular" (year-round) workers was made. By 1976 *regular status* came to be defined as working fourteen hundred hours a year, and *seasonal status* was achieved when a worker had more than thirty days on the job but less than fourteen hundred hours a year.[45] Regular workers had much better medical benefits and pension plans.[46] As we have seen, the regular workers were predominantly male, whereas the majority of seasonal workers were female.

Teamsters policy, as reflected in the collective bargaining agreements, was not overtly discriminatory toward minority-group and women workers. Rather, informal practices in conjunction with management and the lack of advocacy for the needs of seasonal workers had a discriminatory effect. The union's distinction among workers illustrates the discriminatory informal practice, and its policy on mechanization reflects its inadequate concern with job loss by seasonal members.

Before 1973, and corresponding to this distinction in the labor force, there were two seniority lists, consisting of regular and seasonal seniority workers. Once one was placed on the seasonal seniority list, one was called back to a seasonal job the next season. It was virtually

45. In 1976 there were nine wage brackets, with Bracket V (the lowest) being $4.53 an hour and Bracket IA (the highest) being $7.52 an hour (California Processors, Inc., et al. 1976:49).
46. Howard Winklevoss (1978) found that about half as many seasonal workers as regulars were expected to receive a retirement benefit, and then the amount was far lower than that of retirees who were regular workers.

impossible for seasonal workers to get hired in full-time jobs and achieve regular status.[47]

After 1973 the collective-bargaining agreement was changed so that the seniority lists were merged, with the regular workers placed above the seasonal employees. This merger of the lists came to be known as the "grandfathering" of the lists, in which year-round male workers were given an advantage over the seasonal women workers.

The distinction between seasonal and regular workers created a barrier to job mobility for women and minority-group workers and was maintained by two informal mechanisms. A seasonal employee's rate of pay was based on whether she or he had worked 50 percent of the time at a particular job. For example, label-machine operators would return to this job the following season if they had spent more than half of their time operating this machine, even if they had been assigned to temporary jobs such as sorting. This allowed the workers to "establish the bracket"; that is, the rate of pay would be the higher one regardless of the temporary work assignments.

The second informal mechanism was the "incumbency rule" in the contract. This rule allowed a worker with low seniority to work in a higher-paying seasonal job and to reclaim that high-paying job the following season even if a worker with higher seniority wanted that job. The problem was not in the wording of the contract clause itself, which did not actually specify a previous claim to a job, but in the way it was interpreted. The interpretation by canners was that an incumbent in a high-paying seasonal job had "dibs" on that job the following season. Once workers had spent more than half of their time on the job, they "established their bracket"—could permanently claim the higher-paying position. White male workers were often hired temporarily for higher-paying positions, and then the following season were considered incumbents. Thus, the effect of these practices was to promote white male seasonal workers into full-time jobs. "The incumbency rule may be the single practice which most hinders the movement of

47. Between 1964 and 1973, only 4 percent of the seasonal labor force made regular status (Winklevoss 1978).

women and minority group cannery workers into higher-paying, full-year jobs."[48]

The Teamster policy on cannery mechanization is another example of a union policy that does not intentionally exclude certain workers, but it has discriminatory consequences. The following is the full extent of the Teamster policy on automation-mechanization in canneries: "A joint Committee consisting of an equal number of Employer and Union representatives shall develop procedures for continuation of studies of automation and mechanization in the plants covered by the Agreement" (California Processors, Inc., et al. 1982:77). This provision has remained the same since at least 1976 (through two periods of contract negotiations), despite plant closures, which began in the late seventies. Few of the cannery workers I interviewed had heard of the committee. Apparently, it rarely met and issued one report that claimed that most of the jobs lost because of mechanization were offset by the creation of new jobs with increased production by the cannery (State of California 1962). Yet there were inadequate data to verify this claim. While the canning industry was undergoing massive mechanization, which could decrease the number of cannery jobs, the Teamsters union was studying the problem and pointing out the positive aspects of mechanization. We have seen how mechanization in the past had very serious consequences for women workers.

The union also did not vigorously enforce the retention of wage brackets in the face of mechanization. In the 1976 contract, a clause was inserted that required workers to spend all of their time at a particular job in order to retain the higher wage rates. Since then, when positions have been abolished, workers have been reclassified or "bumped down," and it has been impossible to retain one's wage rate. As a result, workers who have had many years of seniority have dropped to lower wage rates as mechanization has been introduced. Another union provision states: "The company shall notify the local union at least ten days before a job is to be abolished" (California

48. "Trial Brief of Intervenors," Coria, García, et al., María Alaníz et al., Plaintiffs, vs. Tillie Lewis Foods, et al., Defendants, and Related Cases, U.S. District Court, Northern District of California, 9 February 1976, p. 4. This document (in my possession) is a legal brief that contested the Conciliation Agreement and provided the rationale for the objections raised by a group of workers who intervened in the race- and sex-discrimination suit. The clause in question was sec. IX, art. G, of the Collective Bargaining Agreement (California Processors, Inc., et al., 1976).

Processors, Inc., et al. 1982:17). Finally, employees who are permanently laid off as a result of the closure of a processing plant or warehouse unit get thirty days notice and severance pay. In contrast to other unions that take an aggressive stance against displacement of workers by mechanization, the Teamsters union has provided little support for cannery workers who have faced loss of jobs through mechanization or plant closures.[49]

Job Segmentation

There is severe occupational segregation of women, particularly minority women in the cannery labor force. Women represented 47 percent of the Santa Clara County peak season cannery labor force in 1973 (California Processors, Inc., 1974).[50] Yet there were few women in supervisory or skilled positions: In the six highest paying jobs, women represented only 7 percent of the Santa Clara County work force.[51] The concentration of ethnic women in unskilled, low-paying jobs is also clear: 66 percent of the male labor force and 70 percent of the female labor force in northern California canneries were identified as having a Spanish surname in 1973 (California Processors, Inc., 1974, cited in Brown 1981). Yet Chicanas represented only 4 percent of the highest paid workers in Santa Clara County (see Table 2).

When one examines each wage category (or "bracket") separately, the concentration of ethnic women is more striking. All females make up only 3.0 percent of the highest paying jobs (Bracket I), and Chicanas represent only 0.5 percent of that wage group. In Bracket II, the proportion of both women and Chicanas is 2.0 percent each. Women comprise 12.0 percent of the Bracket III jobs; Chicanas alone make up only 7.0 percent of that category.

49. The International Longshore Workers' Union provides retraining and large severance pay when workers are displaced. See Mills and Wellman (forthcoming).

50. These statistics, obtained through a discovery motion by the plaintiffs in Alaniz vs. California Processors, Inc., include information on sixty-seven canneries in northern California. They are at best conservative figures because the question under litigation was the companies' discrimination against women and minorities. The figures include production workers only, and the percentages are based on my calculations.

51. In the whole industry, women made up about 50 percent of the peak labor force in 1970 (Brown 1981:118).

Table 2. Number and percentage of Spanish-surnamed and female cannery workers in top three wage brackets during peak season, Santa Clara County, 1973

Wage bracket	All workers		Workers with Spanish surnames				All female workers	
			Male		Female			
	Number	Percent	Number	Percent of total	Number	Percent of total	Number	Percent of total
IA–I	560	28	225	40	3	0.5	15	3
IIA–II	450	23	303	67	7	2.0	9	2
IIIA–III	959	49	574	60	71	7.0	114	12
All top brackets	1,969	100	1,102	56	81	4.0	138	7

Source: California Processors, Inc., 1974.

Mexican-American men fared slightly better. Chicano men comprised 28 percent of the Santa Clara County peak-season cannery labor force in 1973. Yet they had 40 percent of the Bracket I jobs, 67 percent of the Bracket II jobs, and 60 percent of the Bracket III jobs.

The situation for the off-season labor force—which includes warehouse workers, skilled workers, or high-seniority production workers—is similar. Women, and particularly Chicanas, are disproportionately concentrated in the lower-paying jobs (see Table 3). Only 1.0 percent of the craftspersons were female, and 0.2 percent were Mexican-American women. Women were 6.0 percent of the off-season operatives and 56.0 percent of the laborers. Chicanas were 4.0 percent of the off-season operatives and 38.0 percent of the laborers. Operatives and laborers (Brackets IV and V, respectively) were the two lowest paying categories and together make up 74.0 percent of the off-season jobs. Women had 63.0 percent, and Chicanas had 42.0 percent of these low-paying jobs. The situation for Chicano men was again slightly better. They held 47.0 percent of the off-season craft positions, 66.0 percent of the operative positions, and 36.0 percent of the laborer positions.

This statistical picture is confirmed in interviews with workers, who note that those working on the lines are "puras mexicanas" (nothing but Mexican women). As Emilio Soliz phrased it, "In San Jose, when you're talking about mexicanos, you're talking about cannery workers."

Clearly, there are two labor forces in canneries. Men—especially white men—have the year-round, skilled, or supervisory positions, and women, especially Mexican-American women, fill the lower-level, seasonal positions. Brown correctly argued: "The IBT [International Brotherhood of Teamsters] advocated and effectively carried out a policy of preserving proportionate wage differentials for different level workers . . . and *institutionalized* the predominantly female seasonal labor force into a distinct seniority system which tended to limit their prospects for promotion into the higher level jobs" (Brown 1981:124, emphasis added). The overall effect of various Teamster policies, including the inadequate concern with mechanization, has created differences in job mobility between women and men and has contributed to occupational segregation by gender and race.

In addition, there were marked age differences between regular and seasonal cannery workers. Regular workers were relatively evenly

Table 3. Numbers and percentage of Spanish-surnamed and female cannery workers during off season, Santa Clara County, 1973, by job classification

Job classification	All workers		Workers with Spanish surnames				All female workers	
			Male		Female			
	Number	Percent	Number	Percent of total	Number	Percent of total	Number	Percent of total
Craftpersons	687	26	320	47	2	0.2	10	1
Operatives	567	21	375	66	22	4.0	35	6
Laborers	1,427	53	517	36	537	38.0	806	56
All classifications	2,681	100	1,212	45	561	20.0	851	32

Source: California Processors, Inc., 1974.

distributed in all age categories. However, long-term seasonal workers (those with four or more years of unbroken service) had a greater proportion of older workers (Winklevoss 1978). Increasingly, the seasonal labor force included middle-aged workers, who would be particularly vulnerable once canneries began closing. These differences in age distributions also contributed to the dissatisfaction that many seasonal cannery workers had regarding the lack of job mobility by women and minorities.

The differences in status and benefits among Teamster members are not unique to cannery workers. Teamsters generally tend to negotiate better packages for their "core" members, usually skilled, male workers. This stems from the Teamster philosophy of "business unionism," the notion that union structure is determined by the structure of industry, and workers who are "important" to a firm should be better compensated.[52] Since mechanization increases the proportion of skilled workers, Teamster wage increases favor them. The Teamsters also seek to organize all workers in agriculture vertically, "from field to truck" (sometimes at the expense of other unions). Cannery workers are peripheral since they are a small portion of the Western Conference of Teamsters membership.[53] But there also is a clear pattern of the Teamster's indifference to the interests of women. Between 1971 and 1975, for example, only 12 percent of the grievances that the Teamsters took to the Arbitration Board (the final step of the grievance procedure) were taken on behalf of women. Stated differently, "the Teamsters spent 63 percent of their Arbitration Board time, resources and effort on behalf of Anglo men, who comprised only 30 percent of the cannery workforce."[54]

The cannery workers who intervened in the race- and sex-discrimination suit argued that the canners and Teamsters union officials had not conspired to discriminate against women and minority-group workers but that there was a lack of enforcement of the collective-bargaining agreements, and informal mechanisms that had a discrim-

52. See an interview with the former International president Dave Beck by Donald Garnel, 11 September 1960, cited in Garnel 1972:188.
53. The Teamsters State Council of Cannery and Food Processing Workers is made up of several locals, which negotiate the industrywide contract. It is part of the Western Conference of Teamsters, an affiliation of caucuses representing specific industries, which meet periodically to strategize. See Garnel 1972:169–200.
54. "Trial Brief of Intervenors," 9 February 1976, p. 58.

inatory effect were constructed. "Discrimination has taken place as both canneries [*sic*] and unions ignore the provisions of the collective bargaining contract, and instead, create their own sets of vaguely defined and changeable rules of operation within each cannery and within each department."[55] These informal mechanisms and their discriminatory consequences are evidence of institutionalized racism and sexism (Knowles and Prewitt 1969).

Teamster Discontent

Among my informants, there was widespread dissatisfaction with the Teamsters union. Even relatively apolitical workers had few positive things to say about Teamster leadership or how the union functioned. The major complaints involved the weak grievance procedure, especially regarding the loss of jobs or wage brackets caused by mechanization, and the lack of union democracy.

In 1969 the Mexican American Workers Educational Committee was founded in San Jose. Informant Daniel Rodríguez, one of the founding members, described the concerns that led to the creation of this committee: "Well, I saw many injustices; they would fire workers, almost, as they say, 'for being ugly.' The union didn't do anything for them. . . . *Their* grievances were the only ones that they paid attention to. And as the workers didn't have any consciousness, they would fire them and everything, scold them, humiliate them, and treat them bad, and they would stay quiet." The members began meeting to discuss working conditions and to develop organizing strategies that would serve the interests of Chicano and Mexican cannery workers, as well as seasonal women workers. However, the membership was largely male. The original goals were to educate cannery workers regarding their contractual rights and to agitate from within the union. Rodríguez stated: "We formed the committee to pressure the union to defend the rights of workers, so they [the bosses] would give more weight to the union. We were not against the union, but against the union officials." The Mexican American Workers Educational Committee in San Jose soon changed its name to Comité de Trabajadores de Canería, or Cannery Workers Committee.

55. "Trial Brief of Intervenors," Coria, García, et al., 9 February 1976, p. 13.

At the same time Chicano dissident caucuses were forming in northern California Teamster locals in Sacramento, Hayward, Modesto and Watsonville. The Hayward caucus was founded by women but was originally organized by Chicanas, who had invited the Black and white women to join them. It later joined the regional network of dissident caucuses. Meanwhile, in the Sacramento caucus, women have recently taken over the leadership positions. Most of the San Jose caucus members, on the other hand, whether male or female, were friends, relatives, or *compadres* (fictive kin) with one another, so the caucuses were built on relationships that were already well established (see Chapter 5).

Members of the regional network of cannery-worker caucuses produced a newsletter, conducted informal research on the pension plan, and attended strategy meetings to plan how to take control of locals within the region.[56] The urban caucuses from Sacramento, San Jose, and Hayward were large, and their members were very active in the regional activities.

Disgruntled cannery workers soon found that the Teamster hierarchical structure made change difficult at the local level. The union locals have little power on their own. They elect delegates to attend national conventions where policy is voted upon. Any time a local is considered to be "unstable," it can be placed in "receivership" and administered directly from the national office. In addition to being part of the Teamster formal structure, all cannery locals belonged to the Teamster State Council of Cannery Workers, a council of cannery locals that negotiated contracts and lobbied state legislators (Brown 1978:9). If most member locals voted to approve a contract, a dissenting local was overridden. Yet the locals were responsible for contract enforcement and grievance procedures.

The manner in which the San Jose cannery local functioned did not allow democratic participation by members. For example, before 1978 union elections were held during the winter, when the seasonal workers were laid off and were often not residing in the area or not attending union meetings. To qualify to run for union office, workers had to have paid dues for twenty-four consecutive months before the nomination period and to have attended half the union meetings

56. This strategy has been called creating a "parallel central labor union." See Lynd 1979.

during that period.[57] This provision in effect excluded the participation of seasonal workers.

Members of the regional caucuses decided to mount a series of legal challenges. In 1971 workers from the regional caucuses filed complaints with the State Fair Employment Practices Commission, and after hearings, their complaints were certified as evidence of discrimination.[58] In 1973 workers filed suit alleging race and sex discrimination on the part of California Processors, Inc., and the Teamsters union.

These struggles were given moral and material support by the United Farm Workers Union, led by Cesar Chávez. Many Chicano cannery workers identified with the Chicano nationalist elements of the United Farm Workers movement, since they had either been farm workers themselves or still had relatives and friends who were farm workers.[59] In the early 1970s, when the United Farm Workers and the Teamsters were having a jurisdictional battle over which one would represent food-processing workers, the Cannery Workers Committees attempted to organize several decertification elections to remove the Teamsters. Their aim was "Teamsters for Chávez," to lead cannery workers to the United Farm Workers Union (Brown 1981:246). In 1975 the San Jose caucus ran a slate of caucus members for Teamster union office, a move that was largely symbolic because most of the committee members did not qualify to hold office. After being threatened with an injunction on the election, the Teamster International president agreed to hold peak-season elections in the future.

In 1976 the plaintiffs of the race- and sex-discrimination suit (María Alaníz et al.) won their case against the California Processors, Inc., and the Teamsters California State Council of Cannery and Food Processing Unions. The court ordered the implementation of an affirmative-action program, which would provide access to promotions and better wages by women and minorities. The major changes were

57. See the By-Laws and Rules of Orders, 1973:11.
58. The 1964 Civil Rights Act, a 1971 court ruling that struck down the twenty-five-pound weight limit for women (Rosenberg vs. Southern Pacific, 1971), and the Equal Employment Opportunity Act (1972) provided the legal basis for challenging discrimination.
59. A high proportion of Brown's cannery worker respondents had parents who were permanently employed as farm laborers (1981:19).

the dismantling of the "grandfathered" seniority list and the establishment of plant seniority—based on date of hire regardless of whether it was in a seasonal or regular job—and the elimination of the incumbency rule. The program also established preferential hiring, training programs, and monetary incentives so that women and minorities could qualify for and secure promotions. Affirmative-action "parity"—the goal for hiring victims of discrimination—was defined as women making up 30 percent of the high-paying jobs.[60] "Parity" for minorities would equal their proportion of the county population. For Chicanos, this was 17.5 percent.[61]

The Teamster union was ordered to comply with the changes ordered for the canners, not to intentionally engage in any discriminatory practice, and to provide Spanish translations of all by-laws and collective-bargaining agreements. The Teamsters union and the director of the Affirmative Action Program were ordered to make an annual determination of which minority groups constituted a significant percentage of the union's active membership and to provide translations of by-laws and contracts in the appropriate language if necessary. The union locals were also ordered to record the number of grievances filed by women and minorities and report them to the State Council of Cannery and Food Processing Unions. Furthermore, the Teamsters State Council was ordered to hire minority and female employees in union staff positions in the same proportion as their representation in the work force.[62]

A group of workers intervened in the suit because they found the Conciliation Agreement woefully inadequate for several reasons: The goal of 30 percent of new promotions for women did not equal the proportion of women (approximately 50 percent) in the industrywide cannery labor force. Moreover, by lumping all minority-group men

---

60. The goal for promotions to mechanics was distinguished from other high-paying jobs because it was a skilled position that required special training. The Conciliation Agreement specified that women should receive 20 percent of the mechanics jobs, and minorities should receive a percentage that equaled their proportion of the county population.

61. Actually, this estimate was the "Spanish-origin" population in Santa Clara County—a category that includes greater numbers of people than does the "Mexican-origin" category and was based on 1970 data (U.S. Bureau of Census 1973). So although the cannery labor force was made up of mainly Mexican-American workers, any person of Spanish origin was considered as representing the class of discriminated workers.

62. Conciliation and Settlement Agreement, 19 February 1975.

and women together, they claimed that the true extent of discrimination against Mexican-American women as distinct from Mexican-American men was denied. The intervenors also believed that the Affirmative Action Program did not have adequate compensations for the discrimination suffered by minority men, who had been denied regular status or jobs with higher wages or who had been forced to wait an extraordinary amount of time for promotions. Furthermore, there was a limitation of one-year's back pay, which they found inadequately compensated victims of discrimination, and they proposed that the trust fund should be increased to $12.6 million. Finally, there were no monetary fines placed on the Teamsters union for their insouciance regarding the alleged discriminatory practices. The intervenors argued for a reversal of these shortcomings of the Conciliation Agreement, but their motions were denied.[63]

The Affirmative Action Program that was eventually approved provided promotions for members of minority groups much faster than for women. By defining parity for minorities as their proportion of the county population—which was relatively low—rather than their proportion of the largely minority cannery labor force, the canners could achieve compliance fairly quickly. By 1978, fifty of sixty-four plants participating in the Conciliation Agreement of the suit had achieved their goals for hiring minority males in all of the high-paying jobs (Bracket III and above), and thirty-six had hired enough minorities as mechanics.

The Department of Labor estimated that to gain proportional representation for women, more than half of all promotions would have to be given to females (U.S. Department of Labor 1978). When the María Alaniz suit was filed (in 1973), a pilot-training program had been established, which would provide the necessary training to women and minorities. An evaluation of the pilot-training program showed that only 35 percent of promotions went to women. By 1978 only one plant had achieved the goal for hiring women in high-bracket jobs, and four plants had hired enough women in the mechanics' jobs. There were no separate parity goals set for minority women (Cannery Industry Affirmative Action Trust 1979:2). Since these data are for the northern California canning industry as a whole, it is impossible

---

63. There were a number of other objections with the Conciliation Agreement. See "Trial Brief of Intervenors," 9 February 1976.

to figure out how many women in Santa Clara Valley canneries were affected by the Affirmative Action Program, probably very few. In addition, the overwhelming majority of back-pay claims were eventually denied because of insufficient evidence.

While this litigation was pending, the Teamsters and United Farm Workers renewed their union jurisdictional conflict. After violent incidents in the fields, in which one farm worker was killed, the two unions negotiated a truce in 1977. They agreed that for the next five years cannery workers would remain under the jurisdiction of the Teamsters, whereas farm workers would be organized exclusively by the United Farm Workers. Some cannery workers felt betrayed by this agreement, for it left them in a union that they believed did not meet their needs as workers.

After the truce opened, the dissident Cannery Workers Committee decided to continue its organizing activities and also to infiltrate the Teamsters from within. Despite the changes ordered by the race- and sex-discrimination suit, they believed that the Teamsters were unsatisfactory.

Tony Di Vencenzo believed that the problems of workers were ignored by union officials: "We were very dissatisfied with the present union officials. . . . I was for a time shop steward and for the life of me couldn't get anything done. There's no employee representation—it's all 'big-wig.'" Antonio Ramírez considered the grievance process "a big laugh":

> If you have a minor thing, like they owe you an hour, then you have a very good chance of getting it. But if you have a case where you are going to take records and witnesses, you might as well forget it. Unless you yourself are the witness and produce the records, then you have a good chance. The union does not go out there and investigate; they will not find you the information you need to fight that grievance.

Workers were especially infuriated with the "special assessments" taken from paychecks without their prior knowledge or authorization. Yet the basic problem, as a number of workers perceived it, was the continued lack of representation of cannery workers. Connie García summed up this view:

> Teamsters have never really been responsive to cannery workers.

[67]

Sure they negotiate contracts, and the best they do is get us a little raise. But they never really fight to give us the things that we really need: representation. If we had representation, we wouldn't have to go to all this hassle. Look at me; I'm an unpaid shop stewardess because I am bilingual. People can't relate to them. . . . The biggest problem we've got in the industry is the union just does not stand behind the worker.

The discontent of cannery workers was part of a wider growing militancy by rank-and-file Teamsters. Various dissident caucuses and organizations were formed—such as Teamsters for a Democratic Union (TDU) and The Professional Driver's Council (PROD)—that sought to change the Teamsters from within. Teamsters for a Democratic Union's Bill of Rights included: "Democratic by-laws, direct elections of officers, a fighting grievance procedure, preservation of good working conditions, safety and health, eight-hour day, five-day week, pensions, just salaries for officers, economic equality among Teamsters, and an end to discrimination."[64] Chicano cannery workers were also dissatisfied with the Teamsters because union officials resisted reforms such as translating the contracts into Spanish for the largely Chicano labor force or holding bilingual union meetings. Furthermore, some Chicano dissidents intimated that Teamsters were controlled by "the Mafia," and Teamster officials claimed that members of the Cannery Workers Committee were "radicals."

In 1978 the Cannery Workers Committee ran a multiethnic slate, including one woman, for Teamster union office. The slate had the simple slogan: "Vote for a Change." The incumbent secretary-treasurer (the position with real power) was college educated, and this added to the perception that he could not understand their problems as workers. The Cannery Workers Committee (CWC) sought to replace him with a Chicano worker who would provide leadership regarding the needs of all workers. The CWC also sought translations of the union contract, bilingual meetings, an end to "special assessments," better health and safety at the plants, worker input into contract negotiation, and the education of cannery workers regarding their contractual rights and grievance procedures.[65] The Cannery

64. See *The Fifth Wheel* (newspaper), 4 October 1977.
65. These issues were the subject of leaflets distributed by the Cannery Workers Committee during the local election campaign in summer of 1978, a campaign that I coordinated.

Workers Committee provided basic education on how to vote, since this was the first time that many cannery workers were present for peak-season union elections. This was also the first time the Teamsters had to campaign actively for votes. The Teamsters' candidates sought out the largely Mexican and Chicano labor force by including some highly visible Spanish-speaking candidates on their slate and using the local Spanish radio stations and print media to get out their election message of "Experience and Leadership." The CWC won six out of the ten positions they sought, a victory that symbolized their potential strength to change the Teamsters union.

By September 1978, with funds from the Catholic church's Campaign for Human Development, these efforts at union democracy were given institutional support with the opening of the Cannery Workers Service Center in San Jose. The center offered bilingual classes in shop-steward training, produced a newsletter, and provided legal counseling and referrals to social services. This service center in many ways was modeled on the Farm Workers Service Center established by the United Farm Workers. It won the battle to get the union to provide contracts in Spanish, after a two-year effort. In essence, the Cannery Workers Service Center functioned as a "shadow union" (Brown 1981:247), providing the services and advocacy that the Cannery Workers Committee believed the Teamsters union should have provided.

Conclusion

This overview of the canning industry illustrates the specific mechanisms that contributed to occupational segregation by sex and race. Initially, engendered job skills and employer preferences for male or female workers to perform sex-typed jobs created distinctions among the work force. Jobs that were considered fit for a particular gender became labeled as "women's" or "men's" work. As labor demands grew, immigrants and members of racial groups were incorporated into the labor force. In the case of Chinese men, a labor shortage led to their substitution for women, indicating that there was nothing inherent in processing that made it "women's work." Yet women's work was always paid lower wages than men's work and was clearly for women, not men. Thus the production process included a division

[69]

of labor by sex, in which women, especially immigrant and minority women, were employed in temporary, "casual" jobs. As canning production mechanized, the distinctions between women's and men's work widened. Men had access to full-time jobs and had possibilities for promotions. Women, on the other hand, who were excluded from men's jobs, had virtually no prospects for job mobility. The nature of canning production created two internal labor markets, the mechanized men's jobs and the temporary, manual women's jobs. The higher wages for men's work indicated that men were seen as primary workers—wage earners who supported families — whereas women's lower wages and seasonal work reflected the view that women had primarily responsibility in the home.

The various unionizing attempts aimed to increase women's wages and better their conditions of work. But workers' organizations generally supported the view that women had different needs than male workers and needed special protection. The first Collective Bargaining Agreement institutionalized distinctions between "women's" and "men's" jobs and supported wage differentials.

Mechanization of women's jobs beginning in the 1930s meant that the work processes became similar for men and women. Women began moving into positions as machine operators. With mechanization, the percentage share of women in the cannery labor force also began to decline.

Unionization by the International Brotherhood of Teamsters meant that workers' attempts to resist changes in company policy was largely confined to negotiation between the union and management. Yet the Teamsters union was not an advocate for the largely female, minority cannery labor force. Teamster policies on mechanization, the practices of maintaining wage differentials and distinctions between "regular" and "seasonal" workers, and the lack of concern for the interests of women and Spanish-speaking workers all contributed to the concentration of women, especially Mexican-American women, in low-paying cannery jobs. With further mechanization, only high-seniority workers were able to retain their jobs. The female labor force, mainly long-term seasonal workers, became a largely middle-aged labor force, with few new, young workers entering the canneries.

Chicano workers responded by attempting to change occupational segregation and Teamster policies through litigation. Despite the Affirmative Action Program and victories toward union democracy,

[70]

women's access to full-time cannery jobs was severely restricted by the overall loss of cannery jobs due to mechanization.

The organization of production and actions by employers and union officials were not the only forces contributing to occupational segregation. The women themselves had a hand in limiting their labor-market participation to the cannery labor force.

[3]

"It Was the Best Solution at the Time": Family Constraints on Women's Work

Several contradictory processes occur when women decide to enter the labor market. The nature of the local labor market and the demand for women workers are the major determinants, but women's early labor-market experiences also affect their work expectations and aspirations. The family economy—the need for sources of income and the division of household labor—is another crucial consideration. Women typically earn less wages than their husbands, which provides an economic rationale for a division of labor in which husbands support families while wives perform household duties. Women's socialization often supports this traditional division of labor and plays an important role in occupational choice by women (Marini and Brinton 1984). Yet men's unstable work histories or low wages may push women into the labor force. Working-class wives tend to make a greater financial contribution to family income than middle-class wives. Working-class husbands often perceive that wives gain considerable power when they work (Bahr 1974; Burke and Weir 1976), and they may feel threatened by women entering the labor market. Finally, there is women's desire for employment, for the personal satisfaction of participating in the labor force and contributing to family income.

The decision for women to seek jobs is complex, and we need to understand the context in which the decision is made and how couples balance the various constraints.[1] The discussion here uses interview and life-history material with women cannery workers and illustrates the cumulative process involved when Chicanas decide to enter the labor force.

Profiles

The women I interviewed represent a significant segment of Chicana workers in California. With the exception of one divorced single parent, all of my informants had been married for a number of years (see Table 4). These women had relatively large families, three to four children (except for one childless newlywed), and most resided in nuclear-family households. With the exception of two women in their twenties, most informants were between forty-five and fifty years old. The middle-aged women had been able to retain seasonal cannery jobs because of their high seniority. All of the women had some schooling, with almost half completing high school. The average length of cannery employment for these women was sixteen years. However, since many of the women worked intermittently for several years before becoming permanent workers, they had even longer experience in the canning industry. Two women had worked seasonally in canneries for more than thirty years. The jobs the women performed ranged from entry-level sorter to supervisor, or "floor lady." Only one worked year round and she was the single parent. The rest of the women worked seasonally, between three to six months a year. In the off-season, all were housewives, although one had a part-time job in a packing shed. The seasonal workers earned approximately three thousand to five thousand dollars annually. Together with unemployment benefits, which for some were as much as two thousand dollars, their contributions ranged from a third to more than a half of the total annual household income.

Vicki Gutiérrez, Luz Gálvez, Rosa Zamora, Celia da Silva, and Euleria Torres were in the stage of the domestic cycle when their children were either late adolescent or adults with families of their own. Another group of women—Connie García, María López, Gloria

1. Christine Oppong (1974) has provided a similar contextual discussion of decisions made by African elite couples that leads to a typology of decision making.

Table 4. Characteristics of Chicana informants

Informant	Age	Number of children	Position	Years of seniority	Years in industry
Women with older children					
Luz Gálvez	48	5	"Floorlady"	29	29
Euleria Torres	53	2	Case-off operator	18	21
Vicki Gutiérrez	46	1	"Floorlady"	27	31
Celia da Silva	50	4	Oiler-greaser	28	32
Rosa Zamora	46	3	Sorter	10	10
Women with school-age children					
Lupe Collosi	36	3	Sorter	12	15
Josie Flores	36	3	Sorter	9	9
Connie Garciá	44	3	Shipping checker	16	22
Estela Gómez	47	3	Quality control checker	24	24
Gloria Gonzales	44	4	Line checker	24	24
María López	38	6	Sorter	4	13
Women with preshcool or no children					
Lisa Hernández	24	6	Sorter	2	10
Teresa Maldonado	46	6	Sorter	3	10
Blanca Ramírez	41	4	Sorter	16	18
Cristina Estrada	27	–	Sorter	2	2

Gonzales, Lupe Collosi, Estela Gómez, and Josie Flores—had school-aged children. Blanca Ramírez, Teresa Maldonado, and Lisa Hernández had children under the age of five. Only Cristina Estrada had no children.

For the most part, these women were Mexican-Americans who were born in the United States. Six of them—Lisa, Connie, Vicki, Estela, Lupe, and María—were third-generation Chicanas; that is, both they and their parents were born in the United States. Blanca, Euleria, Teresa, and Cristina were born in Mexico and migrated to the United States as adults. I did not ask them directly, but my impression was that these four Mexican women migrated "with papers," that is, legally. Unlike the others, the four women spoke mainly in Spanish, and our interviews were conducted in Spanish with a few English phrases. In terms of ethnic identification, there was variation. Connie and Lisa preferred the term *Chicana*. The other women used *Mexican* or *Mexican-American* interchangeably, even occasionally using the more euphemistic term *Spanish* (as opposed to *Mexican*), depending on the topic of discussion. Gloria, who was born in Arizona, preferred *Spanish*, whereas the Mexican-born women called themselves *mexicanas* or *Mexicans*.[2]

Five women are very important in this study: Vicki Gutiérrez, Lupe Collosi, Blanca Ramírez, Gloria Gonzales, and Connie García. Each was selected for her position in the domestic cycle, for her type of job, and for her general political views. Since they represent types of female informants encountered in the field, the chapters in this book focus on their experiences more than those of the others. Each deserves an introduction. Following this, all of the women's experiences before entering the cannery labor market are discussed.

Vicki Gutiérrez

Forty-six-year-old Vicki Gutiérrez grew up during the Depression in the agricultural San Joaquin Valley. The oldest of five children, she was born in the United States, her parents having emigrated from Mexico. She considered herself a Mexican-American, although occasionally she used the term *Spanish-American*. Vicki was bilingual,

---

2. The terms *Mexican-American* and *Mexican* are used most frequently by persons of Mexican descent to identify themselves ethnically. See J. García 1981.

but her primary language was English. Her parents were poor farm workers. Her father had also worked on a temporary basis in a packing shed, where she was allowed to accompany him. She attended high school but had no diploma. Vicki was first married at age fifteen to a young man she met at the cannery. She differed from the other women in that she was trained as a dental assistant because her terminally ill first husband had insisted that she gain skills to support herself after his death. She knew that if she were to lose her job, "I'm always going to have that." Yet she continued to do cannery work. Her second husband was a mechanic, who with a partner owned his own shop. Vicki and her second husband had been married for twenty years when I met her, and they lived in a small, tastefully furnished house in East San Jose. They had one son, who lived alone and was a sales clerk at a major retail outlet in San Jose.

Vicki started working in the canning industry in 1947 at the age of fifteen as a sorter and line checker. To get the job, she lied about her age, claiming to be sixteen. Except for one year off, when her son was born, she had worked steadily as a seasonal cannery worker for thirty-one years, twenty-seven of them in the same plant. At one point she was working at three jobs to put her second husband through school. She had worked the past three years as a floorlady, a job she enjoyed, earning $5.80 an hour.

Vicki was a warm, plump, friendly woman, with impeccably coiffed hair. She kept frequent contact with her many friends. (The phone calls kept interrupting our interviews.) She was also close to her three sisters, who lived in San Jose. She seemed lonely during the off-season and enjoyed talking with me. I met her at a party, and she was very helpful in my research. She offered to take me to a union meeting and referred me to other women. Vicki marveled at the idea of a book on cannery workers; as she said, "You *never* see a book about cannery workers." She was obviously pleased to help me, even while being conscious of our educational differences. At one point she told me: "You should work in the cannery so you can see. You won't be stuck working in the cannery for the rest of your life and think, 'God, am I going to be like that?' You'll realize how lucky you are to have an education." I often found myself wondering about her—how could she like her job so much? Yet I liked her and felt comfortable talking with her. I interviewed her twice in person, a total of four and a half hours on tape, and once by telephone.

Vicki represents those women whose children are grown and have moved away. She also represents women who acknowledge that some things need to be changed but are relatively satisfied with their jobs and have few complaints about the union. She preferred seasonal work: "I like some free time; we work six months and stay home six months. I like to draw my unemployment—and it's all tax-free money." She made fifty-eight hundred dollars in wages and twenty-four hundred dollars in unemployment benefits in 1977. "The money's real good." Her husband did not want her to work full time, but he had adapted to her seasonal employment. She therefore had few problems with her husband regarding her job.

Lupe Collosi

The youngest of six children, Lupe Collosi was thirty-six years old and from San Jose. Her father was a construction worker and her mother a homemaker. Lupe's father was born in Mexico, and her mother was born in Los Angeles. Lupe identified herself as "Mexican-American, and although she was bilingual, she preferred English. She graduated from high school, had some clerical training, and met her husband, who was a truck driver, in a local nightclub and married him when she was twenty-three. They had two daughters and a son, all between the ages of six and twelve. Lupe's husband did not like the fact that she worked, and they had separated for a while but were recently reconciled. She lived in a large, wood-frame house in the San Jose foothills, surrounded by orchards.

Lupe had held a number of clerical positions and had worked a total of fifteen seasons in the canning industry. She also had worked in a packing shed during the off-season and had worked for twelve years seasonally at one cannery, where she was a line checker. Like many others (if not Vicki), Lupe was dissatisfied with her job but needed the money to support her school-age children.

Lupe made about four thousand dollars in wages during the 1977 season and then received about one hundred dollars a week in unemployment benefits. Depending on the level of unemployment in the state, unemployment benefits may be extended beyond the usual limit of twenty-six weeks. With full extensions, Lupe sometimes received unemployment compensation until June, when she started working again at the cannery. Her total annual income was more than six thousand dollars.

I met Lupe at a party. She was a warm, likable woman with a wan face but a ready smile. She rarely sat still. The first time I interviewed her, it was more of a running conversation in which she would suddenly sit down to ponder a question, reflect a few moments, and then, after her response, rush off to yet another little chore. She served me coffee in the midst of watching a pot roast and then collected some dishes into the sink, dashed off to find her old pay stub so that I could see how much money she made, planted kisses and gave instructions to her children, and rushed off to work. I thoroughly enjoyed my time with her.

The next visit with Lupe was less hectic. Later it was necessary to call her to clarify certain points, but she always seemed to be busy. She saw her kin regularly but had little time for friends. She saw me as a role model for her children and a source of advice and information. She also was enthusiastic about my research and offered to do whatever she could to help me. For example, she referred me to other informants, one woman in particular whom Lupe hoped would give me a different perspective than the one she had provided. At first Lupe wondered, "Why do you want to talk to *me?*" Later she expressed her pride in my efforts to write a book on cannery workers and stressed that I should feel free to call on her again for anything.

Blanca Ramírez

I was referred to Blanca Ramírez by another cannery worker. Blanca was forty-one years old and was born in Mexico in 1937. She was one of three children and her father was a *campesino* (peasant); her mother, a homemaker, was born in Mexico and still lived there. Blanca identified herself as a *mexicana* and could read and write Spanish well, having graduated from high school in Mexico. She had been a white-collar worker in Mexico before coming to the United States and had met her husband, an American citizen, in Mexico, later moving with him to San Jose; he was a full-time cannery worker at the time of the interview. They had four children, of whom the youngest was four years old and the oldest was a teenager, and Blanca therefore represents women with preschool children. She had worked in canneries beginning in 1960 and had sixteen years of seniority. But she worked primarily for the income and disliked her job. Their modest house in the foothills of San Jose was paid off partially with Blanca's cannery wages, and she was very proud of this, as she pointed out: "Aunque es chiquita, mi casa es bién pagada, y es muy mía" (Even though it's small, my house is paid off, and it's completely mine). She and her husband had been active in labor politics for many years. Although she had few kin in the area, she visited regularly with friends and *comadres* from work. (*Comadres* are bound to each other as mother and godmother of the same child.)

A sharp, articulate woman, Blanca did not mince her words; she was known for voicing her mind during meetings. She was a fair-skinned woman—they called her *la güera* (the fair one)—who also had many health problems. Our interviews were conducted primarily in Spanish, and she was cordial to me and pleased to help out. At the end of our first interview she noted: "Once you get me started I could talk for hours." Her husband nodded. Blanca hoped that by talking with me some change in plant conditions would come about. As we got to know each other during the Cannery Workers Committee union election campaign, she often asked for my advice and called on me to help her with various chores. I originally felt sympathetic toward Blanca and even depressed after our first interview because of her unhappiness and lack of options. Later I could also feel impatient with her, for she could be domineering while working with others.

Gloria Gonzales

Forty-four years old and with school-aged children, Gloria Gonzales was born in Arizona in 1934. Her parents were also born in the United States and were farm workers. For the first ten years of her life, Gloria was a migrant worker's child, following the crops with her family. She worked in the fields along with her nine brothers and sisters. Gloria remembered moving to San Jose when there were still orchards nearby and recalled how beautiful the area had been. Her family settled in one of the Eastside barrios, where she has lived ever since. She spoke bilingually, moving back and forth in Spanish and English, and she referred to herself as "Spanish."

Gloria graduated from San Jose High School, where she met her husband, Frank. He then dropped out of school and went into construction work. They now have four children, three of whom are

[79]

married with families of their own; only their seven-year-old son lives with them.

Gloria started working in canneries in 1954 and had twenty-four years of seniority. In the off-season she also worked as a cafeteria helper at an elementary school. For five years she had been working as a line checker, grading cans for quality and keeping records for the buyer. She told me her job title with some pride. Lab work is preferred over sorting, which Gloria had done during her previous years at a large cannery. Gloria preferred seasonal over full-time work and claimed that she worked only to gain her retirement benefits.

Gloria and Frank had purchased their small frame house on the Eastside and later had another house built at the rear of their property. Frank was able to do much of the work himself. They rented the second house for a third source of income. Because she worked, they could afford a new car every three years; the car belonged to Gloria since her husband did not drive.

The Gonzaleses had few friends—as Gloria explained, "I'm a loner." They socialized with their neighbors, a young Chicano couple who had a preschool daughter. The wife took care of Gloria's son during the canning season. But mainly Gloria and Frank socialized with family—their grown children and grandchildren and other kin in the area. Gloria's oldest son stopped by daily either on his way to or from his job.

Gloria was attractive—slim, lightly made up, usually dressed in a bright pantsuit. She sat quietly with her hands folded during our two interviews and seemed reticent and shy, steering the discussion away from sensitive issues. During the first interview she told me about her job and how much she liked it: it paid well and was not difficult, and if you ran into any problems the union was always there to help. Frank sat with a look of disgust on his face; finally he blurted out, "Ah come on, your job is no good. They work you like a pig. You always used to come home with your back hurting." They were both right. Gloria did not like her job as sorter and was pleased that she had gotten a promotion. She preferred to emphasize her current job and working conditions, rather than dwell on her difficult former position. Thus during the second interview, when I came back to working conditions on the line, she often disclaimed dissatisfaction, with statements such as, "Sure it gets cold in there during the winter, but you can always wear a sweater." Yet much of what she said was interesting and revealing. Gloria originally agreed to "help me out," consenting to an interview as a favor to a friend. She did not show much interest in my research on women workers, and I felt distanced from her, wondering how she could tolerate her husband's apparent verbal abuse.

Connie García

Also born during the Depression, Connie García, forty-four years old, was the oldest of six brothers and sisters. Her parents were both born in the United States, and Connie, who was born in a small town in southern California, considered herself a "Chicana." She spoke primarily in English but was bilingual. Her parents were farm workers, and her mother worked in a cannery. The family had settled in northern California, following the crops. Connie attended high school for a while and worked in the local cannery after school, beginning at the age of fourteen. Like Vicki, Connie also lied about her age, claiming to be sixteen years old. At seventeen she married a friend who was a cannery worker in the Santa Clara Valley. They moved to the northern part of the valley because he worked there, and Connie got a job in another cannery. She had also worked in numerous clerical and sales jobs and worked sporadically in canneries from 1948 on. In all, she had stayed home for only about two years while bringing up her three children. She had sixteen years of seniority at her current cannery job.

When I met Connie, she was the single parent of two sons and a daughter who were twenty, fourteen, and eight years old. They lived in a tract house with beautiful landscaping, and Connie planted and attended the many flowers and trees herself. She was divorced in 1975, worked full time as a shipping checker, had been a political organizer since the early 1970s, was a founding member of a workers' caucus, and participated in a lawsuit against the union and companies. She also ran for a major office in a local union election. Connie was critical not only of the work situation but also of women's traditional role in the family.

Connie had extensive ties with friends but only minimal contact with her kin, who lived several hours away. She was highly intelligent, tense, a chain smoker, and solidly built, with a deep, resonant voice. She was opinionated and articulate, quickly making judgments on

[81]

varied topics. Our recorded interviews were fast paced. Having made many speeches, Connie was used to being interviewed by the local press. She thought some of my questions naive, even silly—"I went to work because I had to!"—and perhaps they were.

I was referred to Connie by a lawyer friend and interviewed her three times, for a total of ten and a half hours. I always came away feeling I had learned a lot. Connie was very helpful with my research and spent numerous hours explaining things, heaping documents and newspaper articles on me. Her experience in the lawsuit against the union and companies and in labor organizing forced her to consider how best to change conditions in the workplace. Connie was cynical concerning the value of a book on cannery workers, but even so, I felt close to her and came away with great respect for her.

Childhood

Most of the women informants had known poverty in childhood, their stories were of struggles to get by, not the least because they typically came from large families. Most resided in nuclear-family households throughout their childhood, with occasional periods in which grandmothers or other relatives resided with them. As children and young adults, they had to contribute to family income by working. They also took care of younger siblings while their parents worked. The American-born women had fathers who worked as farm workers or in unskilled jobs in packing sheds, factories, or construction. Mexican-born women had fathers who were *campesinos,* or petty entrepreneurs. Except for seasonal farm or cannery work, their mothers usually did not work for wages.

Almost all informants had worked in the fields along with their parents. Connie García, who began her work pattern while young, stated: "We all worked out in the fields when we were kids. My parents were not very educated so the only thing they knew how to do was work out in the fields. And of course my mother used to have to drag us along because there was nobody to babysit; the whole family was out in the fields. That was typical of those days. The majority of us *mexicanos* and Chicanos worked out in the fields." Vicki Gutiérrez recalled extreme poverty and instability, but she had positive views regarding her early work experiences: "When I was ten, we got to work in the fields during the war; we got to learn how to pick tomatoes and peas. A truck used to come to pick up all the teenagers and kids because they needed help. I was earning thirty-eight dollars a week. I thought that was real good. So I bought my own bike and school clothes. And we thought it was a lot of fun. I don't say that we went out and got rich, but it didn't kill us."

Moving the whole family in search of work was a common experience. Most women moved to the Santa Clara Valley as teenagers or young adults. The effect of uprooting and traveling hundreds and sometimes thousands of miles rendered childhood a blur of names and places. Many women lost touch with childhood friends. They assumed adult roles early and experienced few if any years of ordinary childhood activities. Rosa Zamora quit school after the fourth grade because of her family's moves; she wistfully recalled: "When I was a little girl, I wanted to go to school so much, Pat! But I couldn't because we were poor." Rosa had to stay home and care for her younger siblings as well as work in the fields. She characterized her life then as "terrible."

Along with having to contribute to their families' income, the women learned female skills that would be applied in later years as wives and mothers. Connie described her training: "My mother is a real lady. She believes you must know how to cook, wash, clean house, crochet, embroider, knit, and do all that good stuff, besides working out in the fields." Vicki's socialization was similar: "My mother taught us to be young ladies, how to cook, clean, be clean with our bodies, speak Spanish, and take care of our money, to be a little thrifty." In describing her childhood, María sighed, "My job was to make tortillas—*every day.*" With a touch of pride, Rosa described the traditional roles of her parents: "My father was very strict, very authoritarian. Whatever he said went. He was very strong, very macho. He came from Mexico and believed in hard work. They don't make men like that any more. My mother was the opposite. She was very warm, loving." Consistent with this, Lisa Hernández described her family's division of labor: "My father didn't do anything around the house; my mom did it all." These backgrounds of conventional divisions of labor in the family conditioned later expectations of married life.

Typically, work histories that began in childhood were carried over into adolescence and adult life. Although sixteen was the legal age for

[83]

full-time work, many of the women lied about their age and began working in the cannery at the age of thirteen or fourteen. Connie explained: "When my mother went to work in the cannery, I worked right along with her. Then I worked at a frozen food place and the cannery nights when I was going to school. And when I got married [at age seventeen] we moved over here. And of course knowing cannery work, I went to work at the cannery here."

Thus lasting economic orientations were formed early in childhood. As Vicki noted: "When you grow up in a small town, you have a chance to do these things [farm work]; you learn what the penny's all about." Other experiences, such as racism in the schools, influenced adult perspectives. Connie bitterly recalled being treated differently from her schoolmates and being punished for speaking Spanish. "The Mexican kids were herded like animals to check their heads for lice. Everyone had it at one time or another, but they never checked the gringos! And they would question the Mexican boys about saying nasty things to the gringo girls, but they never questioned the nasty things that the gringo boys said to the Mexican girls." Her early experiences of discrimination would sharpen Connie's sensitivity to the way Anglos treated Chicano workers in the cannery.

It appears that the girls of the fields and canneries had role models in the adult men and women who struggled to make ends meet. Blanca saw her organizing activities continuing the family tradition, since her father became a respected labor leader in Mexico. For Connie, it was her mother who commanded special respect: "There are some little die-hards like my mother who's going on sixty-two, but she won't retire until she's sixty-five. She's a strong woman. She's very active and enjoys working. And now that we're all grown and married the only thing she knows is how to work."

The recurrent themes in their early lives—large traditional, migrant families accustomed to hard work in the fields, poverty, and experiences of ethnic oppression—created a general attitude that life was difficult. The women carried a legacy of hard work and the need for perseverance into their adult years.

Early Married Life

As they matured, these women often sought relief from the difficult conditions. Young men left home for short periods to work and seek adventure, but women were more constrained, and they often chafed under the restrictions. Rosa's father, for example, wouldn't allow her to date. When she went to the movies with girlfriends, she had to be home early. She recalled hating her father and eloping because "I felt trapped." Other women, however, were allowed some freedom with their friends. Vicki often went "nightclubbing" in San Francisco, for example. Most women met their spouses through mutual friends. Cristina Garza and her husband, both reared in Mexico, met while strolling in the plaza, as is customary. At sixteen they became sweethearts and married; later they moved to San Jose and worked in different canneries. Other couples met at the cannery, and they married young, around age sixteen, and began having children soon thereafter. Along with the usual hopes for happiness and romance, and perhaps escape, most couples sought, in marriage, lives more settled than those of their parents.

The early years of marriage were times of mutual adjustment to the traditional notions of family stressed during their socialization. My informants were sometimes overzealous in their attempts to fulfill the image of a good wife. By the time she was twenty-two, María López, who was reared in South Texas and married at fifteen, had five children.

I was the one! I don't know why I was like that. I had all the kids little, and I used to keep the house spotless—I'd mop in the mornings and in the evenings. I'd start dinner an hour early, so everything would be ready when Víctor came home. He'd just walk in and go straight to the table, and I'd serve him. Everything would still be steaming hot. And we'd all sit down and eat. Then he'd watch TV or whatever, and I'd clean the kids' faces, change their clothes, and put them to bed. Then I'd wash the dishes. I was busy working all day long, and I didn't have to! Victor would tell me, "María don't work so hard. You don't have to do so much." But I felt that I had to.

María would customarily lay out her husband's clothes with the rationale: "He expected to be waited on hand and foot by the woman. He felt that women are there to serve the man. And that's the way I was raised too. My mother did everything for my father." Many women related similar incidents of catering to their spouses or keeping spotless homes with little help from the men. Women expected and even welcomed their child-care responsibilities. María was defensive about this: "I don't think that we should take turns taking care of the kids when they're sick. I feel like that's my responsibility. *I'm*

[85]

responsible for them 24 hours a day. And if they're sick I couldn't let him take care of them. No, do you think he's going to worry about them all day long?" In accordance with this traditional outlook, husbands reciprocated by providing for their families. Women expected marriage to be this way. As Connie remarked, "That's the way it's always been."

María's beliefs about the traditional division of labor are illustrated in a classic argument she had with her brother-in-law, who was also reared in South Texas.

> The other day Ray began talking about how women's work is easier than men's work: "Women just sit around the house and watch TV."
> So I asked, "Ray what time do you get up to go to work?"
> He said, "At 7:30."
> I said, "I see, you go to work at 8:00."
> He nodded.
> "And what time does Linda get up?"
> "6:30."
> "So when you get up she is already working, making tortillas, making breakfast, coffee, and making your lunch. And then after you've gone she has to wash the dishes, and take care of the kids, and wash and iron, and make something to eat for her and the kids. Then you get out at five o'clock, and already by four o'clock you are getting ready to come home. You know that you don't work very hard that last hour.
> "But for the woman, that is when her work has just begun. She has to make dinner and have it ready so that when you get home, she can serve you right away. And then after dinner you go watch TV or whatever. She still has to wash the dishes, get the kids ready for bed, make sure they're clean and covered. And you've already been relaxing for two hours. So the woman puts in more hours than you do."

María has made an effective argument, pointing out the wife's work contribution. She did not want to claim that women's work was more important, however, just equal. So when her brother-in-law responded that men have more responsibilities, she agreed: "A man has the responsibility to bring in the money para hacer los pagos [to make the payments]. And he has to make sure that he has a job. A woman doesn't have that responsibility. If she works, fine; if not, it's all right. So, yes the man has more responsibility, but he doesn't work harder than the woman." María was pleased that she had won the argument.

It was rare to find women like Connie, who felt unhappy with traditional expectations and deference to husbands. After her divorce, Connie recalled:

> I found myself doing things that I didn't agree with. I'd tell the kids: "Be quiet because your father's asleep, and he's tired and he needs his rest." I'd make a meal and leave something for him to warm up. I always had this feeling, "Well he's the daddy; and you respect the daddy, so I'd better make the kids be quiet, and I'd better cook his meals," or whatever. He's a grown man; he could do things for himself. But you're taught to do these things without thinking, because he's the man of the house. It's inbred into you.

Connie's independence, along with a variety of jobs, enabled her later to gain a different perspective on home life. This lack of isolation probably contributed to her frustration with traditional roles.[3]

Few of the conflicts that arose in the early years of marriage were over role expectations. Husbands and wives expected that women would not have to work. Although some women worked during the first few years of marriage, almost all quit after their children were born. These early patterns of behavior would later become a source of adjustment or conflict when the wife went to work and could no longer meet her family members' needs in the manner in which they had grown accustomed.

The first years of married life usually were the hardest economically. Most informants had difficulties establishing a home, bringing up children who were born in quick succession, and handling the husband's unstable work histories. The women's husbands worked in low-paying, unskilled jobs—in construction, packing sheds, farm work, canneries, or other factories. These were the lean years of stretching the paycheck to make ends meet. Rosa's husband also worked in the cannery part time, and his other job was that of a part-time clerk. She described how they managed: "When your husband

3. Mirra Komarovsky (1962) and Lillian Rubin (1976) have pointed out that socially isolated couples maintain closer agreement on marital norms than when they have outside activities or organizational affiliations.

[87]

doesn't have a steady job, you do things. Like we used to have a freezer, and we used to make pretty good money in the summer time. I'd stock my freezer with all the essentials; then in the winter time we'd just skimp by on unemployment." Blanca Ramírez related a similar situation:

> When we got married, we lived in a tiny house; we paid $25 rent. I was pregnant with my first son and was sick because I had a difficult pregnancy. And we didn't have a washing machine, we didn't have a car, and we had to go real far to wash clothes. And since we didn't have money for the dryer, we had to bring the clothes home to dry. And my poor husband didn't have a job. He could only work one or two days out of the week. He was getting unemployment, $39 a week, and we just couldn't make it.

Not being able to "make it" came from the hardship of low wages when work was available and even less when men were laid off. These years created pressures for the wife to help out. Some tried taking in ironing or doing babysitting for others at home, with the children around. But the meager income did not suffice, so the only alternative was to look for a job.

Deciding to Seek Work

Virtually all of the women originally sought work for economic reasons. The actual decision was made after careful deliberation with husbands, although in several instances women had to argue their cases. Some men viewed working wives as a symbol of their own shortcomings as providers. Others worried about the effects on the children or household.[4] In exchange for husbands' support, women agreed to certain restrictions. Lupe succinctly gave the reason for beginning her job search: "I did it for my family. We needed the money. Why else?" Yet as Lupe recalled, her husband "at first never wanted me to work," so she made some concessions. "He put pretty

4. Generally, husbands' attitudes are very influential when married women decide to enter the labor force. See Nieva 1985.

strict conditions for me to get a job. He wouldn't allow me to work nights or take the kids out of the house [for child care]."[5]

For some of my informants, the decision to seek a paid job was also an assertion of their independence.[6] Despite the dire situation of Blanca's family, her husband opposed the suggestion of her working: "He told me that he wanted a woman for his home and not to go to work. But I went anyway to help him, even though he didn't want me to." After long days spent looking for a job, Blanca recalled her husband's advice: "He said, 'Don't go back, you're not going to find a job anyway.' " Blanca shrugged: "Tú sabes que en este mundo, uno tiene que cuidarse a sí mismo" (You know that in this world one has to take care of oneself). Luz Gálvez also went against her husband's wishes: "At first he did mind, when the kids were small. We used to have a lot of arguments. But I went anyway." Rosa was able to persuade her husband to support her entrance into the labor market: "My husband didn't want me to work, period. But I convinced him."

Theoretically, taking a job against the husband's wishes could have jeopardized the marriage. However, several factors mitigated the husbands' opposition. Given the precariousness of their situations, the husbands could not legitimately argue against their wives going to work. Consequently, their protests may have masked their unstated desire to have wives enter the labor force. Indeed Víctor López wanted María to work (while she was pregnant with their sixth child), with the idea that it would be a temporary solution until he found a job. But he said he did not like the idea and grumbled about it.

Married women with children had conflicting demands once they decided to get jobs. Working mothers had to find time to care for their families, yet spend long hours away from home. Recall the independent views expressed by Gloria Gonzales—"Women *should*

5. Recent research on Chicano and Mexican families suggests that working wives have greater influence on decision making than housewives. See Hawkes and Taylor 1975, Zinn 1980, and Ybarra 1982b. Bean, Curtis, and Marcum (1977) have found conjugal decision making to be husband-dominant for almost half (45 percent) of their Chicano sample, which was a slightly higher percentage than in the Anglo sample. They did not ask who made the decision for the wife to work, however, which would probably have altered the findings.

6. Women who decide to enter the labor force tend to be more independent. Myra Ferree's (1976) study of working-class women shows that employed women tend to support the notion of women taking jobs despite the husbands' opposition, whereas housewives tend to defer more to husbands' wishes.

work outside the home, see what they can do for themselves." Yet when asked why she had entered the labor force, she replied, "It was for my kids' benefit that I got a job and not for anything else. My family comes first." Her husband's opposition and her children's needs at home prevented her from seeking a full-time job. By evoking traditional family ideology—"my family comes first"—she could rationalize her seemingly nontraditional actions and minimize her own independence. This would be necessary only for women who believed men should support families.[7]

Lisa and Teresa, both with very young children, had little choice in the matter since they desperately needed jobs. Euleria, Estela, and Cristina's husbands did not object when they went to work since these families needed an additional source of income.

The women did not carry out the job search through formal agencies. They were acutely aware of their limited education, lack of marketable skills or training, and, for a few, limited English. Their past experience as farm workers or as domestics provided no skills for better-paying jobs. They knew, as Chicanas, they faced discrimination in hiring. As a consequence, their job expectations were minimal: "When I started, I was looking for *anything,*" Luz recalled. "I thought, 'there has to be something better than the fields.' "

Local labor needs dictated the jobs they would find. Having to take what they could get, women who entered the Santa Clara Valley labor force after World War II found agriculturally related employment readily available. Vicki recalled: "This was all the type of work there was. Either you would work in the packing house, or you went to work in the canneries. There was no other employment, really, and there was no problem getting a job then [in 1947]." Luz, who entered the cannery in 1949, had an easy time also: "After the war they really didn't care about age." These women's experiences were congruent with the post–World War II expansion in production, which created plenty of cannery jobs. The need for labor was so great that Vicki could stretch the truth and get hired: "They wanted people with experience in apricots, so I raised my hand even though I didn't have any experience. I was scared but I got the hang of it right away."

As we have seen, beginning in the late 1950s the need for cannery

7. Glenn Hawkes and Minna Taylor (1975) have found that among Chicano and Mexican couples, the decision for the wife to work is made jointly 49 percent of the time and by the women only 26 percent of the time.

labor declined. By 1960 when Blanca applied, jobs were scarce.[8] She described her experience: "I waited all day long, from six in the morning until sometimes eight at night. You couldn't even go for a cup of coffee because while you were gone they would take other people. I waited like this for two and a half weeks." María, who was twenty-five and had small children, also had a hard time in 1965 and was ready to give up: "Ya decidí a batallar no más que un día más" (I decided to struggle only one more day). Lisa and Cristina, who had only two years seniority when I interviewed them, had relatives who got them in.

Once the process of seeking cannery work began, one was subject to the industry's informal means of labor recruitment. Gossip networks were the usual way workers found out about job openings. With only word-of-mouth reports that canneries were hiring, crowds appeared outside company gates to wait in the hot sun. Since there are no union hiring halls, getting a job in the cannery was similar to the "shapeups," or casual assemblies of laborers to secure jobs, that farm workers endured before unionization (Galarza 1977). This could be a demeaning experience since there were no standard criteria for how people were chosen for this unskilled work. Once she was selected, Blanca described her "interview": "I didn't even know English. They asked me questions, and I said 'yes' and 'yes' and 'yes'. And with nothing but 'yeses' they gave me work."

By the 1977–78 seasons when I participated in the cannery shapeups, it was almost impossible to get a job. The majority of the job applicants were men, and from the indications of dress, accents, and the use of Spanish slang, most of them were from Mexico. Many of these job hunters were accompanied by kin, neighbors, or friends. I struck up a conversation with a woman from Tijuana after we accompanied one another to the water faucet in the midst of a boisterous group of men. A great deal of laughing and joking went on, but it did not mask the intensity of hoping. Any indication of work possibilities—the offhand word of a secretary going to lunch, a passing friend who heard that "they'll need people on the swing shift in the warehouse"—was quickly circulated and evaluated. Sometimes just a

8. There is also evidence that canners preferred to hire workers who were referred by other workers rather than off the streets, because this method provided a more stable work force. The use of seniority after unionization consolidated the existence of a long-term seasonal labor pool. See Brown 1981:83.

[91]

small handwritten sign, "Hiring at 4:00," created minor traffic jams and much frustration when the "hiring" did not happen. The competition for jobs was stiff; people crowded elbow to elbow on the steps of personnel offices waiting for a chance to be hired. Although a few canneries recruited unskilled labor through the employment office, a referral was no guarantee of an interview, much less a job. I observed applicants with job referrals from the employment office waiting along with the rest of us.

The informal recruitment method allowed a great deal of leeway in hiring, and this sometimes led to abuse as in Jesse Valenzuela's experience. During the Depression he had lied about his ethnicity and had claimed to be the brother-in-law of a worker in order to get hired in the cannery. One Japanese-American informant, who was hired after returning from an internment camp, had to get a job counselor to pressure the cannery to hire her. (For the first month, her job was peeling onions in the basement with other Japanese-American women, isolated from the rest of the workers.) Most of my informants were lucky enough to have friends or relatives working in a cannery and secured jobs with their help. After enduring the shape-up, or having to resort to other means, most women felt lucky to get a job at all. Josie expressed the common feeling of relief after getting her job in the cannery: "It was worth it."

Child Care

Husbands often helped to take care of the children when the women worked. Couples tried to arrange their shifts so that one parent would be home at all times, or they relied on an older child to care for their siblings. Estela claimed that "it's easy to work with young children." Since she started working on the swing shift (3:30 P.M. to 11:30 P.M.) and then switched to graveyard (midnight to 7:00 A.M.), she was home to take care of her children during the day: "It worked out better when the kids were small." Rosa worked nights for four years while her husband took care of the children. She was relatively satisfied with this arrangement: "The kids were real good. Oh they'd tattle, 'Mommy he did this . . . ' but it was more convenient for us. They knew I was there at home [during the day] if they needed me." Josie said: "I have three children aged seven to eleven, and I can't afford

[92]

to pay fifty dollars a week for a babysitter. So I can only work when my husband will be there to take care of them." When Teresa started to work, she had her sixteen-year-old daughter take care of the younger children while she worked days in the summer, until she was able to change her shift: "They could do it [take care of the younger children when they were not in school themselves], but I felt like my boys needed me when the girls weren't there." When she started working nights, her husband took over. Lupe did not have this option: "A lot of fathers cooperate; they are home nights when the mother has to work. My husband was not like that." Estela's husband, however, did not want her to work nights, and she had to change to the day shift so she could be home with her children.

If it was impossible for the family members to trade off work hours, arranging child care could become a major problem. The single San Jose agency that placed children in family day care in private homes had a waiting list of more than three hundred and fifty children in the spring of 1977. Except for a short-lived cannery child-care center in operation during World War II, federal- and state-funded child-care centers were not widely available until the midsixties in the Santa Clara Valley. (This was the case throughout the nation [Baxandall 1975; Wolk-Feinstein 1979].) Given the limited availability of formal day-care agencies, women were forced to make other arrangements. Contrary to findings for Mexican-Americans in other studies, it was unusual for my informants to rely on kin for babysitting.[9] Lisa was one of the few women who had a relative take care of her children. Euleria did not have to worry about child care, since her mother lived with them and took care of her children. By the time her mother died, the children were old enough to care for themselves. Vicki had a sister and then a niece to care for her son until he was eight years old. Then he came home and watched television by himself until Vicki arrived after her shift ended at 3:30 P.M. Most women, however, were not as fortunate. They did not have kin who were in a position to babysit. Even though most informants had some relatives living in the area, extended family members either worked or lived too far away to make it feasible. Therefore, women hired babysitters they

9. Susan Keefe (1979) and Roland Wagner and Dianne Schaffer (1980) have found that compared to Anglos, Chicanos rely more on relatives than friends or neighbors for babysitting, and Chicanos also tend to have more available relatives.

found with references from friends or relatives or through newspaper ads.

Women and their husbands agreed that if they had to pay for child care, the ideal situation was care in a private home with a woman whose reputation was established. A preference for family day care has been noted in other studies of working-class families (Komorovsky 1962; Lamphere, Silva, and Sousa 1980).[10] Women who were Spanish speakers also required that the child-care provider speak Spanish and be familiar with Mexican customs. For this reason, but mainly because they charged less, many working mothers hired undocumented women from Mexico to care for their children.

As for many working women, the availability and quality of child care was a major concern for my informants. Several women had stories about hired babysitters who neglected children or who quit unexpectedly. These were recurring problems with *mexicana* baby-sitters, who often moved from the area giving little notice. Gloria believed that finding and keeping one reliable person to care for her child is so important that, "When you have sitter problems, then you should quit." She could afford to say this since her neighbor of many years cared for her son. Most women, however, made other less dependable arrangements.

Blanca hired a succession of babysitters, "some good ones and some bad ones." She told me of problems with one who stole food, another who would not change her son's diapers, and a third who romanced her boyfriend in front of Blanca's son. Blanca found out about the third babysitter only because she stayed home unexpectedly one day, and the boyfriend walked in unannounced. Blanca confronted her oldest son—"only five years old, fíjate! [mind you]"—and he con-fessed that the sitter had threatened to beat him if he tattled. Blanca recalled: "It was too much. After all the work I did, to find this. I just broke down and began to cry." Lupe hired several women whom she found by putting ads in the newspaper. Unfortunately, several of these women were "weirdies. . . . I had to hire this kind of girl cause I couldn't afford babysitting wages. . . . That's the breaks for me, I had no family." Lupe did have relatives — three sisters in particular. But they also worked in canneries and could not help. Lupe admitted

10. The vast majority of children in the United States, about 75 percent, are cared for by individuals (either relatives or nonrelatives) in private homes. Only 10 to 12 percent are cared for in center-based arrangements (Woolsey 1977, cited in Wolk-Feinstein 1979).

that she kept minor problems with her babysitters from her husband out of fear that he would make her quit work.

Connie was very satisfied with her paid babysitter. When she and her husband could no longer arrange their shifts so that one would always be home, she hired a teenage daughter of a friend from work. Regarding these arrangements, Connie remarked: "I've been very fortunate. She's like family to us now." Luz had a different babysitter every year; some of them were friends who were pregnant and on leave from canneries. She was pleased with the flexibility that cannery work provided: "The cannery was good in that if your babysitter didn't show up or something, you could call in and they would say, 'It's all right, just come in when you can.' " Satisfaction with the quality of child-care arrangements was often crucial to women feeling good about continuing to work.

After entering the cannery labor force, workers did not necessarily remain, since the seasonal nature of the work created a great deal of turnover. Men left seasonal cannery jobs in search of permanent employment. Women worked intermittently during the initial years, a few weeks at one cannery followed by a layoff. They might work off and on for several seasons, perhaps at several canneries. Women took leaves because of family responsibilities and difficulties in arranging child care or to have babies. Connie, for example, worked at nine jobs (including the canneries) in the period between the age of fourteen, when she started in the cannery, and twenty-eight, when she became a permanent worker. Since 1962, she has worked continuously on a seasonal basis for eleven years and for four years as a full time worker. Altogether she had worked for twenty-two years in the canning industry, but she had only sixteen years of plant seniority, since each time she left the cannery, she lost her seniority. Connie's work history is typical of women cannery workers and of female workers in general (Blau 1975). Her typical history embodies the conflicts between a woman's family responsibilities and her need to work for wages.

Work Expectations

Given their previous experience in menial jobs, particularly farm work, most women began their cannery jobs with certain expectations about the work. They knew that it would be physically demanding, but few felt that the relationship of exchanging their labor power for a wage was exploitive. Most women believed that the company was entitled to make profits. Workers expected to be paid a fair wage and to put in a hard day's work for that wage.

Women viewed working in a cannery as a step up from work in the fields. In the hierarchy of agricultural work, fieldwork was at the bottom, packing-house work next, and cannery work best. Although the work was seasonal, the union wages were much higher than those in farm work. (Most of these informants entered canneries long before farm workers were unionized.) As Rosa asked: "Where else can you get a job that pays more than five dollars an hour?" Cannery work was also perceived as being better than farm work because of the working conditions. Workers were not out in the hot sun, and the actual work process was easier than farm work. Rosa characterized her initial feelings about cannery work: "It was so nice; it was a breeze compared to the fields." Cristina recalled: "The fields are the worst; the pay is so cheap, and you work without a contract. It's too much sacrifice to get together a few cents. I heard about the canneries, that they pay more, and the union protects you, so I tried to work there. And I'll never return to the fields!" Women were also pleased that they were hired to work alongside other women they already knew.

Women needed jobs with flexible hours so that they could complete their home duties. One resolution was to work swing (evening) or graveyard shifts. The seasonal nature of the job was an added incentive, since women could resume homemakers' obligations full time during the off-season. The season conveniently occurred during the summer months when the older children were home from school. For these reasons, then, cannery work for women was seen as "the best solution to our problems at the time," as María put it. Lupe agreed: "It made sense."

During the first years on the job, women expected to work temporarily. Luz, with twenty-nine years of work in the industry, recalled: "I was just going to work that one year, but we needed the money." Responses that indicated an expectation of permanency were rare. Vicki, who was childless for many years, said: "I figured that I'd be working there simply because I liked it." Connie stated: "I would have preferred a permanent job [rather] than working the two jobs I had. But at that time women didn't have an opportunity to go into

[96]

something where you could get more hours and become regular." Most women originally hoped their tenures as cannery workers would be brief, something to tide them over until their husbands could find better jobs. They aspired to be full-time homemakers, without the added pressures of a job. Their husbands also expected that their jobs would be temporary. Women's cannery jobs complemented the traditional division of labor, as Connie's remarks illustrate: "I worked in different places, and then I would go back to the cannery because it was seasonal and because it was convenient, and I could work nights because I had small children. It helped out with the responsibilities of the family. It made it lighter for my husband, so that he wouldn't have the full responsibility of all the bills and everything." (Chapter 5 discusses how this shift in responsibility affected other aspects of family life.) After working a few seasons, these women became permanent seasonal cannery workers. The main attraction was the temporary nature of the work. Lupe stated: "I planned to stay seasonal. You work only three months out of the year and can stay home with your kids."

Company practices also facilitated women's retention in cannery jobs. The personnel office would send out cards informing workers of the time to come in and register to work another season, and they registered according to their number on the seniority list. As it got nearer to peak season and the seniority list was exhausted, companies then took applications at the personnel office. The first people allowed to turn in applications were those who had union books, which indicated that they had worked previously in canneries. Once the union members were all hired, canneries took new applications. Women who were considered good workers could expect to be called back the following season.

"Long-term seasonal cannery workers"—those who work seasonally for four years or more—comprised approximately 16 percent of the northern California cannery labor force (Winklevoss 1978). It wasn't until the 1976 Conciliation Agreement established a plant-seniority list that seasonal workers were eligible for full-time work based on the number of seasons they had worked. Thus whether or not they would have preferred full-time work, seasonal work was all that was available for my informants and for a whole sector of the cannery labor force.

[97]

Conclusion

Despite their beliefs that men should bear the major responsibility for supporting families, most women found themselves in economic situations in which their wage contributions were necessary for family maintenance. Despite the need for an added income, however, husbands often protested their wives' decision to seek a job. Women made the decision on their own or got husbands to accept by asserting the maternal right to provide for their children's welfare. Women's beliefs that their jobs would be temporary and would not interfere with family obligations added weight in favor of entering the labor force.

Yet these women faced many constraints in finding jobs. They had high school educations or less, few marketable skills, and, for some, limited English. Cannery jobs were considered relatively good, primarily because they were seasonal.

The evidence suggests that the decision for a woman to seek work was critical and subject to negotiation between husband and wife. Rather than being an example of the couple's usual mode of making decisions, the decision for women to work in the canneries resolved a structural conflict. Given their husbands unstable jobs, women could not afford to maintain their positions as full-time homemakers. As mothers, the primary nurturers of children, neither could they accept full-time jobs. Their home responsibilities gave them leverage with which to assert their will, even if it also prevented them from becoming full-time workers. Uncovering this context of decision making enables us to understand how women can be both powerful and acquiescent. With two sets of constraints—the family and the local labor market—cannery work was considered the best solution to married women's problems. Yet by seeking work that complemented their family obligations, these women ultimately may have contributed to their own segregation at work.

The next chapter follows women to work and examines their experiences within the canneries. In addition to the need for women's wages in families, women's participation in work culture provides another reason to return each season to the canneries.

[4]

"I'm Not Exactly in Love with My Job": Cannery Work Culture

The question of why contemporary workers continue to labor under exploitive conditions is addressed by Michael Burawoy in *Manufacturing Consent* (1979). He contends that the capitalist labor process is defined by the dual structural imperatives of securing surplus value while obscuring its exploitive nature. Under monopoly capitalism with unionization, a hegemonic organization of work emerges in which the coercion of workers is replaced by granting them limited autonomy through collective bargaining. By accepting limited autonomy, workers consent to the restrictions of the labor process. Burawoy has found that workers often engage in the game of "making out"— working at a fast rate to exceed production quotas. By participating in making out, workers consent to their own exploitation, and the hegemony of capitalist production is ensured. [1] The value of Burawoy's formulation here is that it focuses on social interaction among workers. The making out game is not just one played by individuals to beat the rate but one in which they gain prestige with coworkers for "playing" well. Burawoy's analysis can be extended to social relations among workers in other areas as well, to what labor historians have called "work culture."

1. Michael Burawoy has been criticized for ignoring evidence that economic motivations underlie the "consent" that seems socially based and that class struggle on the shop floor shapes the production process (Gartman 1983).

Labor studies document the rich work cultures that flourish in a variety of job contexts. Work culture includes the ideology and practices of workers on the job: the "informal, customary values and rules [that] mediate the formal authority structure of the workplace and distance workers from its impact" (Benson 1983:185). Work culture is created by workers who confront, resist, or adapt to the constraints and possibilities of their jobs. Transmitted by oral tradition, work culture encompasses workers' understandings and definitions of work and their sanctions within work groups. Workers use work culture to guide and interpret social relations on the job.[2]

Both contemporary ethnographic studies and the work of labor historians show how work culture operates on the shop floor. Susan Benson (1978, 1983) has analyzed the "clerking sisterhood," which allowed saleswomen to control the work process and even provided amusement for workers at the expense of customers and management. Novices could neither make sales quotas nor endure their jobs if they were not inculcated with department lore and accepted into work groups. Craftsmen in the nineteenth century enforced a moral code, in which output on the job was regulated so as to respect other workers and protect individuals from speedups, and workers were expected to maintain a "manly," dignified stance toward bosses (Montgomery 1979). Louise Lamphere (1985) has shown how women "bring the family to work" through socializing, joking, sharing information about family members, or celebrating domestic rituals such as weddings. Women's networks are potent organizing vehicles for hospital clerical workers, in which "the potluck is political" (Sacks 1984). Nurses maintain a "culture of apprenticeship" in which professionalism and notions of women as nurturers have provided conflicting views of nurses as the profession has evolved (Melosh 1982).

The significance of work culture is recognized by managers, who attempt to usurp control of work groups in myriad ways: by regulating workers' dress (Benson 1983) and scheduling workplace rituals or busting unionizing attempts (Lamphere 1985). David Gartman (1983) has suggested that Henry Ford attempted to change auto workers' culture and even their personalities to forestall further shop floor

2. See also Melosh 1982, Gutman 1976, Montgomery 1979.

agitation. Wage increases for auto workers depended on their demonstrations of dependability and subservience, and wage policies favored workers in nuclear families who tended to acquire long-term purchases of consumer goods.

Interpretations of work culture reveal the varied consciousness of workers. Kenneth Kusterer (1978) has shown that even unskilled work includes complicated knowledge that workers must master to labor effectively. David Wellman (1984) has suggested that there is great mental labor involved in manual jobs—the "etiquette" of longshoring includes constantly figuring out how to work safely or within the spirit of the union contract. Women jewelry workers use their conceptions of fairness to accept the dictates of the piecerate system or to resist new assignments on the job (Shapiro-Perl 1979). In sum, the workplace is a social world onto itself, one in which workers create and resist within the confines of the conditions and processes of laboring.

Production and Work Processes

In examining the type of jobs and the work processes within the canneries, I describe the production process in a typical large cannery that (in 1978) canned spinach, peaches, fruit cocktail, and tomatoes. The work season for this cannery was nearly continuous from April through September. At the time of my investigation the cannery employed more than one thousand workers and was divided into several departments: receiving, preparation, canning, quality control, maintenance, warehouse, and shipping. The pace was set by the conveyor belt, which began in the preparation section of the cannery. There the produce, in this case peaches, was dumped from large bins pulled by jeeps onto "shakers," which moved the product onto the conveyor belt. The peaches were pitted and halved by machine and then went through a lye solution waterfall. The lye solution was just strong enough to remove the peel without harming the fruit. From there, the peaches moved through steam and cold water sprays and then through a full water wash. The peaches were next inspected and sorted by hand, with only the very bad ones removed. After this, the peaches were cut by machine into slices or pieces to be made into pie. After it was sliced, the product was sorted again. The work processes in the various jobs described so far (except for sorting) were essentially machine tending, with workers overseeing the smooth movement of the product along the conveyor belt or operating the cutting and pitting machines. The jobs of workers stationed along the belt were unskilled and paid Bracket IV and V ($5.88 and $5.58 an hour in 1978). Except for the jeep handling, these jobs were typically performed by women.

Sorting was more like assembly-line work and was done almost exclusively by women. Workers used both hands to sort the produce into various grades—choice, standard, or nectar. They performed the same task all day, had no control over work pace and little control over techniques, and were confined to their stations on the line. They stood in one place, concentrating on doing the job quickly, with between six and ten workers on each sorting line and, depending on the product, between four and six lines. Workers were stationed about two feet from one another, and with the considerable background din, it was difficult to converse. Some of the shorter women stood on wooden boxes in order to reach the belt, and it was not uncommon for them to fall. Workers were allowed short breaks, in between the regularly scheduled ones, to go to the bathroom or get a drink of water, but they had to hurry since no one replaced them.

After the fruit was sorted, it was poured into cans along with the syrup or water. Most canneries have machines to do this, although in some of the older canneries the cans are filled and weighed by hand. The piece rate still existed in some departments with hand labor jobs. For example, Lisa Hernández had worked as a check weigher, placing spinach into cans by hand. She described the work process: "You take a handful of spinach and put it into the can, then tuck in the ones sticking out, and weigh it. Then you put it on the top belt above." Lisa was disgusted at the high quota (two thousand cans a day) required for this task: "I *never* made that limit." Her mother, with years of experience, sometimes made four thousand cans a day.

Piece rates were phased out as mechanization was introduced (Brown and Philips 1983c). The filler and seamer machines were usually attended by women workers. Some were overseers, making sure that the cans moved smoothly or checking for dents and proper seams. Lisa, who also worked as a seam inspector, described this process: "It's hard work. You have to come out of the cookroom, check the code, see if the seams are right, make sure there's no dents. I check five cans and put them back. If they're bad I stop the line."

The supervisor or floorlady usually remained close by, checking the work or even occasionally working alongside the women on the line. Floorladies supervised between thirty five and forty five workers. The rate of pay for supervisors was Bracket III ($6.26 an hour in 1978). This job entailed enforcing work rules (such as no gum chewing) and being constantly on the move, watching the workers, with a lot of pressure to push and instruct workers. There were floorladies for sorting, canning, and seaming lines.

The sealed cans were then loaded into huge cookers. The cookroom was by far the noisiest section of the cannery. The machines were usually operated by men, who were free to move around somewhat and could enjoy brief conversations while doing their jobs. The contrast between the women's quiet absorption in their work and the men's joking and bantering, most of it in Spanish, was highly noticeable. The men displayed boisterous camaraderie. The women, however, gave visitors furtive, resentful glances and communicated with one another nonverbally by rolling their eyes and tossing their heads.

After cooking, the cans were moved by conveyor belt to the warehouse, where they were labeled, cased, stacked on wooden pallets, and then either stored or loaded onto boxcars to be transported to market. One worker, usually a woman, checked for dented cans and moved them aside. Labeling and casing were done by machine, with male or female attendants, and the cases were stacked onto the pallets by hand, usually by a male, or by automatic depalletizers, which were attended by a man or a woman. The pallets were stored or loaded by forklift, usually driven by a male, and some unlabeled cans were stacked and stored to be labeled in the off-season with a skeleton crew.

The atmosphere in the warehouse was much more pleasant. It was cooler and quieter than the preparation or cook areas. The work pace, although still geared to the line, was less hectic. There workers, although generally stationary, could occasionally converse with one another, move around a little, and look around even while attending the label machine or stacking. The forklift drivers seemed to enjoy driving around and bantering with other workers. The maintenance

[103]

workers, who were almost all male, were also relatively free to move around and talk, although at times they were closely supervised in their jobs.

A small department in the cannery is the quality-control section, or the "lab." There samples of cans are checked for sugar content in the syrup, and the grade of the produce pack is inspected. Most of the workers are female, and according to women, these jobs are the best ones for women in the canneries. Quality-control jobs pay Bracket III wages. The machinery for repairing equipment and making parts is located in the machine shop, and the mechanics usually work there. When I was there, all of the mechanics were male. These skilled workers were free to move around and had specific work assignments, which they completed with little supervision.

There were relatively few workers, considering the high number of cans produced per day and the size of the plant. Most of the workers were in the sorting section.

Women's views on the work process reflected their varied positions. Women who worked on the lines as sorters characterized these jobs as the most tedious and boring. Confinement in one place, endlessly repeating a single task, provided little intrinsic reward. Lupe Collosi stated: "I don't like the monotony of the belt. I hate standing all day. It's noisy; it gives me a headache. The line makes me dizzy, and sometimes I get sick." Rosa Zamora revealed the common use of fantasy in alleviating the boredom of sorting: "It's awful! You have to be constantly thinking of something, dreaming of something. I couldn't be thinking about what I was doing! Or else you'll get all down, all depressed. So I'd dream about the kind of job I'd like, or about what clothes I'm going to wear to the dance this weekend. . . . I'm always in a good mood. You can't let it get you down." Estela Gómez defensively made the point that "you do think. You have to figure out which ones to throw out." Line workers also resented that their movements were completely controlled. Blanca Ramírez deplored being confined to the "women's" department: "You can't lift your head or the floorlady comes and asks you, 'What are you looking at, what do you want?' You can't even notice who works where, who walks by, nor how they treat the others, especially the men." Over and over women noted how demanding the work was and how it strained their bodies. Lisa said, "You're just standing there moving your hands, and it hurts your lower back." Women vehemently complained about the dehumanizing aspects of line work, especially the fast pace and speedups. Josie said, "I'm just like a robot, a cog in the machine. It's so unhuman to me."

More than anything, workers resented unfair and disrespectful treatment by supervisors. When floorladies seemed to push them too hard, either to keep up the pace or to conform with work rules, women criticized them severely in private. Connie García bitterly described the demeaning treatment meted out by floorladies: "We were treated just like cattle, just driven constantly. You couldn't even pick up your head a little to look around, or else there would be a floorlady right there wondering why you weren't working hard, and they'd work right alongside of you just to show that you weren't doing your job." Lisa was detached completely from her work: "I hated it! You had to kind of just ignore the fact that you were there, do your work, and try to pass the time as best you could." María López disliked her job, angrily concluding: "Canneries are the *worst* places to work! They work you like a slave. They don't treat you with respect, like a human being."

The women articulated the alienating nature of their work. They believed that supervisors' disrespect was an insult to their dignity. Furthermore, the work itself had little intrinsic value. Most women were not publicly critical, however, for fear of losing the job.

Other women were much less critical of the work process. Vicki worked as a floorlady and supervised predominantly Mexican women sorters. She appreciated the fact that she could speak Spanish in her work and took pride in the responsibility of teaching workers: "I'm happy with my job now. I like working with people. Especially the younger girls that come from Mexico, they don't know how to speak English. So I have to explain everything to them. That's very important." One of the reasons Vicki appreciated her floorlady job so much was because she also worked on the line as a sorter during the beginning of the season. It was only during the peak of the season that she was in charge of six lines of workers. So during her stint as floorlady, Vicki empathized with her subordinates: "I like to feel comfortable; I want my girls to feel relaxed and do their work. You kind of have to pamper them: 'now girls . . .' " She seemed an exemplary supervisor, but she acknowledged that her work was difficult: "There is a lot of pressure; you have to push people." Estela enjoyed the independence of a quality-control job: "I'm my own boss. I walk around outside and all over the place, and check the lines, and train girls if they need to be trained." She also appreciated that she was not often required to work overtime. Cristina, who had worked for three years as a seamer, found it challenging: "You have to keep up with the men to get the job done, but I'm strong enough to do it *porque soy muy macha* [because I'm tough like a man]."[3]

Women who received promotions, either through the pilot training program or the Affirmative Action Program, were generally pleased with the work. They adapted to and accepted the new rigors of their jobs and sometimes even took pleasure in them. Certain aspects of their jobs were highly valued: a measure of independence, freedom of movement, responsibility, and opportunities for interaction with other workers. Workers who had these kinds of jobs were relatively satisfied. Celia had a former "man's" job as an oiler-greaser: "My job is dangerous, but I love it. I work on my own. No one supervises me; no one bothers me. It's not hard. You need to be fast and agile so you can climb up and around the machines. You're on the go all day. I like the independence." A former sorter, she believed that mechanization relieved the difficulty of the work: "Now everything is done by machine. It's easier."

Connie worked in the shipping department as a shipping clerk. She supervised a crew on the railroad dock in the loading and unloading of boxcars, and she worked alongside them. Her job also included stacking cases onto pallets and driving a forklift or tractor. Her job was strenuous and difficult, and she got dirty from climbing around the boxcars. but she believed it was easier than "women's work": "Ever since women have been able to do "men's jobs," we have it easier! It's not standing on a line eight, ten hours a day anymore. I drive a forklift; I sit in an office and write up tally sheets. We're coasting!" These women considered their jobs as challenging and rewarding work.[4]

3. The term *macha* is the feminine form of *macho*, a Spanish word that holds complex meaning in Mexico and in the United States. In the United States, *macho* (male) or *machismo* (maleisms) implies male dominance and, especially in popular feminist parlance, has come to connote expressions of patriarchy. In Mexico, depending on the context, a *macho* is a man who has courage, integrity, strength, or is a good family man; it can refer to a man who holds his liquor well or is a philanderer; or it can refer to a male animal.

4. Women who are highly satisfied with their jobs tend to appreciate both the nature of the work itself, as well as "extrinsic" features such as the quality of interpersonal relations with others (Andrisani 1978).

Working Conditions

Working conditions in canneries seemed bad, especially to the novice. My field notes describe my first plant visit:

> It was incredible. The whole plant was extremely noisy! Our tour guide had to yell the whole time. Even though we were standing right next to him, I still couldn't hear most of what he said until we got to the warehouse. Most of the noise was in the cookroom where the canned fruit is cooked in machinery that is *very* loud. The clatter of the cans crashing against one another as they moved along on conveyor belts above us added to the noise of the machines. The whole cookroom area vibrated. The interior of the plant was dark, hot, and humid, and water was everywhere. The cement floor was essentially wet all over, with puddles of water and piles of garbage (fallen fruit) left lying around. Several times we literally walked through the garbage and puddles as we toured the plant. The metal walkways were narrow and slippery. I almost fell several times. In the peach-washing area the lye solution was so strong it made me nauseous. It was so humid in that department that my glasses fogged up. Afterwards I had a splitting headache and felt dizzy. It made me wonder: If this is how they treat guests, how do they treat the workers?

Some of the newer plants were not as bad as this, but it was fairly representative according to workers' comments and my own observations.

Since most cannery workers are employed seasonally, they experience these harsh conditions in short, intense bursts. Work seasons usually ran from June through September, with the peak of the season in July and August. Some canneries processed spring fruits or vegetables and had a short work season then. During the peak of the season, workers put in as many as ten hours a day and often worked six days a week.

The physical toll of such working conditions was great. Workers came home exhausted, dehydrated, and suffering from swollen feet or varicose veins after long hours of standing. Blanca echoed others in explaining: "On weekends I just lie around and try to recuperate so I can go back to work on Mondays."

The women considered the working conditions to be difficult and physically demanding. Common complaints included work during the summer vacation months, heat and humidity during the summers and cold during the winters, inadequate ventilation, and excessive vibration from the machinery. Women complained that working on the line left them wet and dirty. Along with the tedious but fast-paced work, there was also the unpleasant nature of the food itself. The women who actually handled the produce indicated that the sight and smell of so much food could be sickening. In addition to considerable amounts of rotten produce, sorters working on the line also had to face assorted dead bugs, spiders, snakes, mice, and even rabbits. Lisa made a face: "It's gross!" After a season of intense exposure to these sights and smells, many workers felt a distaste that lasted for weeks. "After the season I don't even want to look at a tomato," Rosa declared.

Canneries are not merely uncomfortable work sites but also one of the most dangerous industries. In the period from 1958 to 1970, canneries averaged nine work-injury rate points higher than all other manufacturing (U.S. Department of Labor 1971:361). In 1976 the food and kindred-products industry had the second highest rate of work-related injuries in California, after the lumber-manufacturing industry. At that time, all California industries (including state and local government) averaged ten occupational injuries and illnesses out of a hundred full-time workers, whereas the canned-fruit and vegetable industry averaged eighteen injuries and illnesses per hundred full-time workers (Department of Industrial Relations 1978:7).

Historical trends show that the number of injuries have declined since 1970 (Brown 1981:62); yet workers perceived them to be on the rise. One informant had four fingers severed, and his was the third such accident in the same factory. Tony DiVencenzo believed that accidents had increased dramatically since the early seventies because there were more Mexican workers who did not understand the safety instructions. He said, "I don't know how they work in Mexico. It isn't a language barrier. You tell these people to be careful, and they just don't pay attention." Yet later he theorized that "ninety percent is supervisory: They get a new person; they just say 'you run that.' They're not trained on the danger."

Chemicals used in processing the produce provided another danger. Women reported that they missed work because the lye solution made them nauseous. Informant Randy Wilson noted that there were no warnings written in Spanish about chemical dangers or listings of

the chemicals in containers stored in his plant. Chemical spills occurred regularly. At one plant a chlorine accident in 1978 hospitalized
seven women working on the line sorting tomatoes. A worker in the
sorting department told me that management turned off the flow of
chemicals, but the water was recycled. "They never closed the line
down and we worked up there, and we finished our shift." She claimed
that no one advised her of the problem or explained why it occurred.

Loss of hearing was an occupational hazard since few workers wore
the company-provided earplugs.[5] Workers were lax about wearing
earplugs because they were uncomfortable. Some workers such as
forklift drivers did not wear earplugs because they needed to have
their hearing unimpaired for safety reasons as they drove in and out
of the plants. In 1978 workers filed a complaint with the California
Occupational Safety and Health Commission to have canners reduce
noise through engineering changes in the plants.[6]

Informants claimed that it was commonplace for workers to slip
and fall, lose fingers, strain their backs, get hit by falling cans, have
hands caught in conveyor belts, or receive chemical burns. One
worker provided me with minutes from the safety committee in her
factory. This plant averaged 1,779 injuries per year in the three-year
period between 1974 and 1977. The safety-committee minutes confirmed my informants' reports about accidents in grisly detail.

Workers were bitter about having to tolerate such conditions, and
they considered the callousness of company officials to safety issues
to be a denial of human dignity. Connie complained: "They don't
relate to cannery workers as people; they try to work us like animals.
There are little things they could do to make working conditions
easier. But it costs money, and they don't want to put out any more
money than they have to." Workers continually fought with management to have these conditions changed. For example, Connie refused
to become certified to load a butane tank because she believed it was
unsafe. She had witnessed an accident in which three persons were

5. OSHA (Occupational Safety and Health Administration) regulations give preference to noise elimination through engineering solutions and consider ear protectors
to be least effective. Engineering solutions to cannery noise were in the pilot-dem-
onstration-project phase as of 1977 (Department of Agricultural Engineering 1977).
6. The ruling was in favor of the workers, but the company appealed because
engineering changes would be too costly. See Petition for Reconsideration, 26 July
1978, a document in my possession.

burned and wanted guarantees that she would not be jeopardized by the carelessness of another worker. Tony DiVencenzo got into numerous arguments with management, finally complaining to OSHA. He said: "Anytime anything breaks down you try to keep the thing going by any means. They're more worried about production than safety."

The union's laxity on health and safety issues was an important organizing issue for cannery workers. One of the leaflets of the 1978 election campaign demanded to know: "What have the union officials done to eliminate dangerous working conditions in the plant?" It provided a reply "*NADA,*" and criticized the fact that the chlorine accident was ignored. Randy was part of the opposition in the election campaign. Concerning health and safety issues, he said: "I've worked in other factories before, and canneries are by far the most dangerous." Other workers agreed with him. In a survey of cannery workers taken in 1978, 33 percent of the workers believed that there were safety hazards; 37 percent complained about excessive noise (Brown 1981:425).

Work-based Networks

The lack of a sizable administrative and clerical staff compared to the production work force indicated that there was a limited emphasis on "industrial relations" and bureaucratic personnel practices in canneries. Most plants, even the larger ones, had a minimum number of administrative employees. Some of the larger companies and multinational corporations had personnel departments and affirmative-action programs, but they were centrally located and covered a number of plants. The directives and procedures are left up to the plant managers, administrators, and supervisors for interpretation and enforcement. In addition, the informal hiring practices allowed considerable discretion to supervisors regarding hiring. Therefore, the informal organizational practices—the work culture—were significant. Cannery work culture involved informal work-based networks, which operated beside the formal division of labor. The composition of these networks generally consisted of friendships or acquaintanceships developed among employees at work.

Two types of coworker networks were particularly important. One set of work-based networks consisted of those with positions of authority—foremen, floorladies, or administrators. Since most of the supervisors were male, these networks were essentially "old-boy" cliques that did not include line workers. The other type of network was worker based. Membership in both types sometimes cut across ethnic or gender lines, but worker networks were usually composed only of members of the same gender and ethnic group, for example, Italian males. Women usually did not participate in men's work-based networks, perhaps because women and men rarely worked together. Some networks also included kin, since a number of workers had relatives working in the same plant. Seasonal workers tended to make friends with other temporary workers, whereas full-time workers had their own networks.

Mexicans and Chicanos often belonged to different networks, since the difference between them diminished ease of interaction. Chicanos often speak a different Spanish dialect than Mexicans or use slang terms, and *mexicanos* deride them for this. Blanca, a *mexicana*, believed that Chicanas were too docile: "They are ignorant of their rights. They go to school here, where they don't teach you anything, and they don't know that they have rights. And I, what little I know, at least I know that I have rights." Blanca believed that Chicanas "se olvidaron de su país, de su sangre" (have forgotten their country, their blood). Chicanas also had their criticisms of Mexicans and may view Mexican men as being of lower status or too old-fashioned. Connie believed that "mexicanos are really hard to work with," whereas Chicanos "aren't quite as 'old country,'" because they show more respect for women. Chicanos often resented the competition for jobs from Mexicans who migrated seasonally to work in canneries. Estela, for example, wished her son could get a cannery job but believed that Mexicans were favored in hiring: "I felt resentful that my son had to wait. Here he was going to school, and we were paying taxes; he has the right."

It became evident that, from the workers' viewpoint, three major groups were competing for entry-level jobs in canneries: native-born Chicanos, Mexican settlers, and Mexican migrants.[7] The status of the supervisor seemed to be crucial in terms of who was hired, with

7. Workers reported that a few Vietnamese had begun entering the canneries in 1978.

Chicano supervisors hiring people referred to them by other Chicanos, and Mexicans hiring members of their own networks.[8] Whether Mexican migrants were in fact displacing U.S. workers is impossible to ascertain.[9]

There were important differences in the way that supervisors' and worker-based networks operated in the plants. Supervisors could assign workstations, provide information on new jobs, or help workers qualify for promotions. In other words, supervisors had a lot of control, and they often favored members of their own ethnic group. The operation of work-based networks created ethnic conflicts not only between Mexican-Americans and other groups but between Chicanos and Mexicans.

Supervisors had discretion in deciding where to place a worker not only with respect to the job but across pay brackets. This created some abuse and irregularities, such as ignoring seniority. Workers reported that there was widespread favoritism and even discrimination in work assignments. Relatives would get jobs that were easier or cleaner or for which there were better working conditions; friends were allowed to work overtime; or sweethearts moved into higher-paying jobs suspiciously fast. Luz fumed: "The foremen place men where they want, because they know each other or are related." Lupe recalled that when she first started work, there was a Spanish floorlady who had so much control that "she had a dictatorship; she had too much power." Blanca explained that "even among sorters there are fast belts and slow belts. All the Italians work the slower belts while the *mexicanas* have to work a belt that is so fast you have to grab four apricots at once to keep up." Blanca described a fight she had with an Italian floorlady who called her a "stupid Mexican" because Blanca

8. There is evidence that Mexican migrants tend to establish "niches" in particular industries (nurseries, for example) or occupations (busboys) in northern California (Cornelius, Chavez, and Castro 1982). Mexican migrants use social networks to find jobs and housing and help other migrants adapt to life in the United States (Cornelius 1982). In the citrus industry in southern California, there was a division between established settlers who were former *braceros* (Mexican contract laborers who came to the United States between 1942 and 1946)—who had better, more stable jobs—and seasonal, migrant Mexican workers. See Mines and Anzaldua 1982, cited in Cornelius 1982

9. The U.S. Select Commission on Immigration and Refugee Policy studied current national evidence on this issue and concluded that there is no strong evidence to support the position that undocumented workers displace U.S. citizens or take jobs that native workers do not want. See Cornelius 1982:30–31.

arrived early and the floorlady thought Blanca had misunderstood her instructions. Blanca responded:

> "Cuando tú naciste, no tenías toda esa ropa de floorlady, tú naciste sin la ropa, sin las papeles, encuerada como yo. ¡No me debes de tratar así, de hablar en esa manera!" Todas me dijeron después: "¡Qué bien dicho! ¡Tú le dijiste bien!" ("When you were born, you didn't have on those floorlady clothes; you were born without the uniform, without papers, naked as I was. You shouldn't treat me like that or talk to me that way!" All the women told me later, "You said it well! You told her off good!")

Lisa discussed her understanding of how supervisors "picked on" the Mexicans: "When my mom started working, it was the Mexicans against the Italians. See, there are professional cannery workers who know how to steal. There's a way in which with the machine, with one can you can mark three cans. The Italians were giving them [their friends] the cans. But right away they pick the Mexicans' cans to check. We all knew, because when you work on the line you know who's working." Lisa herself was able to get off the line for two weeks because one of the "head honchos" put in a good word with another foreman. Luz observed how these abuses were kept quiet: "I filled in for a sick timekeeper, and that's when I learned a lot about the unfairness that goes on. I complained with the personnel man cause I saw Bracket III people doing Bracket V jobs and getting paid for Bracket III. I brought this to his attention, and he told me that I was paid to keep time and not ask questions." Luz said questioning these practices caused her problems: "This is where I had most of the conflict." She was eventually returned to working on the line. Connie observed that instances of ignoring seniority in work assignments had increased. Women believed that there was little use in complaining about favoritism in work assignments.

Undocumented Mexicans were even more vulnerable than other workers, and supervisors took advantage of this through their informal practices. Cristina, who had permanently settled in the U.S. from Mexico, was angry at how foremen used Mexican migrants:

> Los mayordomos, ni Diós no los quiere. Tienen una preferencia a los que vienen de Mexico, que les traen tequila o les dan dinero. Por eso permiten que trabajen sin señoría [*sic*]. Pero nosotros pagamos

taxes, hemos pagado para los derechos de estar aquí. (The foremen, not even God loves them. They prefer those who come from Mexico, who bring them tequila or give them money. That's why they let them work without seniority. But we pay taxes; we have paid for the right to be here.)

Teresa Maldonado, who was born and raised in Mexico but had lived in San Jose for twelve years, disliked the way younger Mexican women were treated: "Those mexicano foremen favor those who come from Mexico over us." Chicanos perceived these practices as favoritism. Foremen could use Mexican workers in these ways because of the threat of deportation.[10]

But race or ethnicity was only one way in which favoritism flowed. Gender was an important basis for providing access to resources or denying it.

Supervisors influenced the decision about who got information regarding promotions. To get a promotion, workers had to sign up or "put in a bid" to the personnel office. Those women with high seniority could "bump" the present jobholder, that is, take his or her job. Women often had an unclear picture of what a higher-paying job actually entailed, however, especially the specific work process. When they inquired about new positions, they were rarely given a written job description. They had to rely on their friends and co-workers to figure out what the job specifications were and, if they were eligible and had enough seniority, whether to apply or to bump the present worker. Women, particularly Spanish speakers who did not have access to this information, were often discouraged from even applying for better jobs. Vicki explained that before the affirmative action program, "just the supervisor and foremen did the placement. You never had a chance to better yourself because you never heard about the jobs."

A Department of Labor study evaluated job training in canneries and found that only 19 percent of trainees knew about the bidding process as a way of advancing. Under these conditions: "one of the biggest barriers to the advancement of women was their lack of knowledge about the jobs, and the rules and processes for advance-

10. Informants reported hearing of instances in which Mexican nationals were allowed to work longer hours in exchange for one hundred dollars to a particular supervisor. The Cannery Workers' Service Center was investigating such allegations.

ment" (U.S. Department of Labor 1978:20). Fifty percent of the Mexican-Americans who received training that provided such information advance one pay bracket the following season (U.S. Department of Labor 1978:26). Martin Brown (1979) argued that this training program did not necessarily cause these workers' advancement, but rather the increase in job advancement was a result of the elimination of dual seniority lists and the incumbency rule in the contract, which allowed a worker to return to his or her job each season.

Supervisors' work-based networks were also critical for women passing job trials. The highly developed internal labor market had no clear lines of progression and had limited entry points. To qualify for better-paying jobs, workers had to pass job trials, which tested their qualifications. Since the collective-bargaining agreement allowed outside contractors to be hired if there were no qualified high-seniority workers, outside skilled workers or people with low seniority were often hired. There was no training program to help unskilled workers gain the skills necessary for promotions. Open entry from the outside routinely permitted men to enter at the higher-paying jobs, and there was little mobility for women. Those few job openings were awarded informally before bidding for jobs started under the collective-bargaining agreement of 1970 (U.S. Department of Labor 1978). Again Vicki explained the former process of gaining promotions: "You didn't apply; they just gave jobs to people."

A pilot training program, conducted between 1972 and 1975, was designed to improve the employment status of women by training them for semiskilled positions. Forty-seven percent of the trainees advanced one or more pay brackets the following season. But only 21 percent of the trainees received the job for which they were trained —the rest of the successful trainees received higher-paying jobs for which they were not trained. Limitations in plant turnover and low seniority of the trainees did not explain this pattern. Rather, the happenstance selection process, particularly the attitude of the supervisor or foreman, was the critical factor. A significantly high proportion (71 percent) of the trainees who passed job trials gave a favorable rating on their foreman's attitude, whereas 51 percent of those who failed gave their foreman the most negative rating. These factors were more prevalent in some plants than in others (U.S. Department of Labor 1978:64–67).

As a supervisor, Vicki observed male supervisors helping their friends qualify for better jobs. She stated: "It's who you know; that's how the girls get into these positions. That's what the big fight is over there at work, because lots of times it's the girls' boyfriends that want them to get in there, and they show them. They want them in there, and they give them the chance." Cristina recalled how tomato sorters had staged a work slowdown in protest when a qualified Mexican woman was not given a supervisory position: "The majority of the floorladies are Italian. This woman wanted the position; she knew everything, she deserved it, and she had struggled with the union to get the position. They didn't want her because she was Mexican, I think." The Mexican woman was eventually appointed as floorlady. Nevertheless, Connie believed, as other Chicanas did, that "they want to keep all the cushy little jobs for their relatives, their girl-friends, and other Anglos." Blanca had no respect for Italians, whom she perceived as clannish: "There are a lot of conflicts between the Italians and the Mexicans. The Italians always stick up for their own race and are very money hungry." To explain this view, Blanca related an incident in which she had observed an Italian-American floorlady, who had supposedly retired, at the unemployment insurance office. This indicated to Blanca that the floorlady was employed at another cannery, since she still qualified for unemployment benefits. Blanca surmised: "She probably quit [the first cannery job] so another Italian could have her place and it not go to a Mexican." Blanca implied that by quitting and working surreptitiously at another job, the floorlady had been able to circumvent the normal process of posting a new job opening, and that management was in collusion by giving the job to another Italian-American. Blanca was convinced that favoritism was rampant.

Whether or not one ethnic group discriminated against another, women perceived ethnic discrimination. The fact that supervisors' work-based networks often were of a different ethnic group from workers made the conflict over jobs and wages seem ethnically biased, and in some instances it may have been. However, these tensions were reflections of the underlying conflict over the scarcity of jobs: there were a few promotions to be had, and all workers with high seniority could apply for them. Connie phrased the conflict this way: "Because of the seniority system, if somebody gets a better job than you, it means more money. If that person doesn't have as much seniority as you, you're going to take that job 'cause, hey, money's the name of the game. And you're always competing for your money. The competition is always there." The operation of supervisors' work-based networks was more than just capricious behavior by supervisors, although this occurred too. More analytically, it was a system of allocation in which access to scarce resources was channeled through informal means. In this regard, cannery work-based networks were a means of "simple control," which allowed supervisors to reward some workers and discipline others and which operated alongside the bureaucratic system sanctioned by the collective-bargaining agreement.[11]

Women were aware of the importance of being in the good graces of supervisors and how the networks operated. Luz, a floorlady, recalled her instructions when she started her job: "She [her supervisor] told me 'if you ever become floorlady, always be nice. You get more work out of people when you're nice.' " María observed: "A lot of times they give a little gift, and they get good little jobs." Blanca derided the "kiss-ups" who "bring the floorlady little gifts, call her sweet names, and tell her how pretty she looks." She refused to do it: "I'm not hypocritical; I'm paid to work, and that's all I do. I'm not paid to kiss up." Women perceived that individual supervisors developed power, particularly through their ability to hand out work assignments. Lisa recalled when a supervisor had refused to allow her to work in the warehouse: "He took my name and yelled at me. They are just trying to enforce respect for authority." Over and over women expressed their intimidation by supervisors and how difficult it was to get around their power. María succinctly summarized women's views: "Es siempre una batalla" (It's always a struggle).

The work-based networks of women workers functioned differently. Coworkers taught new employees how to perform their jobs so that the work was easier. When women first obtained jobs in canneries, they were not formally trained (Brown 1981:81). They were immediately placed on the job and learned by watching coworkers, with on-the-job instruction from the supervisor. New workers were often overwhelmed and felt dizzy or nauseated. Coworkers advised new sorters to adjust to the movement of the conveyor belt by con-

---

11. Richard Edwards (1979) has distinguished between *simple control,* whereby supervision is personal and extreme; *technical control,* which stems from the technology itself (such as an assembly line); and *bureaucratic control,* whereby unions and management negotiate how production is to be organized.

centrating on individual pieces of produce. Training by coworkers was informal, often given during breaks, since talking with coworkers was prohibited, and mandatory earplugs made it difficult to converse anyway. But coworkers found ways to get around this rule. If they talked too much, though, or the floorlady thought they were "playing around," they would be fired. Coworkers also pointed out that keeping up with the fast pace was not possible or even necessary.[12]

Other jobs such as check-weigher allowed more flexibility. Women who were experienced learned to gauge the proper weight with their hands, enabling them to bypass the weighing operations. Since they were paid by the piece-rate, this helped considerably in making more money. Skipping the weighing task also provided a momentary break from the fast pace. Women learned these tricks from experienced workers.

Coworkers also acquainted women with the authority groups. Lisa noted, "It's a big soap opera at the cannery. You know who hangs around the bosses and who makes the cans." Gossip provided important information about who belonged to different cliques. Euleria smiled as she said, "You always know something about everybody."

On the line, women were able to cooperate with one another, and this made the job more pleasant. Connie recalled: "We all got along; you have to when you work that kind of work. We used to sing, make jokes." Furthermore, women could anticipate staying on the line with many coworkers for long hours. Lupe observed: "Usually people in the cannery are good natured; people have no problems. They're all so used to working hard that they don't complain." Workers tried to keep their differences in check because of the constant menace of supervisors and the fear of losing their jobs. Vicki used to work as a sorter and apricot cutter. She noted, "I got along pretty good with everybody. I wanted a job, so I made it a point." Luz said, "If you want to be working, you can't be fighting." These statements contrasted with the antagonisms among women workers when they competed for line positions in the 1920s. The hourly pay, coupled with pressured working conditions, fostered camaraderie among women in the 1970s.

12. There is evidence that the canners encouraged this method of informal training and recognized that it created a relatively skilled work force. See the interview with Mike Elorduy, secretary-treasurer, California State Council of Cannery and Food Processing Unions, cited in Brown 1981:83.

Informal groups socialized women into the work culture. Yet most women claimed, with disgust, that "I trained myself." Although they had help, women did not view their coworkers as constituting a group. The term *work-based networks* better characterizes informal relationships with certain, not all, coworkers. Women's work-based networks usually were social forums too, and women socialized with one another during breaks and lunch.[13]

By contrast, women with relatives in the same plant had ready-made training teams. Lisa, a third-generation cannery worker, described her first season on the job: "It's hard work, but I can't say I didn't enjoy it. Everywhere I looked I knew somebody; I had relatives to talk to. They baby me, give me cans." She went on and described her parents' participation in a work-based network: "My mom and my stepfather live in the same world, the cannery world with all the chismes [gossip]. In the cannery you can see them sitting together talking with all my aunts and their friends. My mom is on a high during the season." Other women initiated friendships with coworkers through the informal training process. Connie observed: "You get to know all these people. You have this intimacy because you work with them at least eight hours a day." Vicki believed that work friendships detracted from the monotony of the job: "You get to know everybody's little problems. It's interesting." Another woman characterized work friendships in a more cynical manner: "You have this *abnormal* intimacy. You make friends with people who are totally different from you, just because you work together." Nevertheless, many women believed they never would have stayed on the job without the help of coworkers.

The ethnic cohesiveness of networks reproduced and perpetuated the ethnic segregation of the work force. Gloria characterized Mexican-Anglo friendships as appearing "weird." One hapless Portuguese-American informant described her social isolation until she made friends with other Portuguese women: "I used to sit with some Mexican women, but they would only speak in Spanish. I felt so left out! I think it's only courteous to speak English." Starting to work on the line, this woman received little help from her coworkers. "I don't know a lot of people; in three months' time you don't get close. This

---

13. Rafaela Castro (1982) has analyzed the sexual jokes of Mexican women who worked in food-processing plants. Women who worked in fish canneries also made sexual jokes, in this case regarding the fish loins (Garson 1972).

Spanish lady who works across from me doesn't speak English. So all we do is say hello or goodbye and smile." After twelve years of work, this woman was promoted to swing-shift floorlady. Her Spanish-speaking cohorts with greater seniority remained behind.

Women tended to distance themselves from those who left line work and no longer socialized with network members. After Connie took on a man's job, she missed the friendship of her former cowork-ers: "It just seems like everytime that someone gets an advancement, there's a lot of things said. Petty things, like 'she thinks she's too good' because she does all this stuff.' A lot of it is just jealousy."

Working on the line, women established friendships with one an-other. Yet because of the working conditions, relationships were difficult to sustain at the cannery. During the peak of the season, workers were on the job six or seven days a week. Breaks were only twelve minutes long, lunches a half-hour. There was not much time to socialize. Besides, women occasionally preferred a silent retreat from the commotion inside the factory: "Sometimes I need to be by myself for that half hour," Vicki observed.

The potential cohesion of work-based networks was undercut fur-ther by conflict over promotions and the chance for better wages. As long as women were in the same positions, it was easier to cooperate. Friendships developed through work-based networks enable women to bear the difficult conditions of their jobs and added solidarity with other workers. Yet working conditions were not conducive to the development of meaningful relationships at work, so women built their work friendships outside of the factories (as discussed in the next chapter). The changes in work organization mandated by the Affirm-ative Action Program would disrupt the informal organization as well.

The Affirmative Action Program

Women had contrasting views about the Affirmative Action Pro-gram, but generally they supported the principle of equal opportunity for women. Cristina noted, "It was about time. We should be equal with men in everything." Lupe believed that "it's really good. Women are going into mechanics, forklift driver, regardless of their race. Everybody in the U.S. should have that right." Vicki agreed with the notion but had questions about whether women could handle men's work: "I'm all for it if you're capable of doing it." Vicki's job injury, incurred while she trained for a man's job, no doubt led to her caution. A woman entering a man's job created a stir. Lupe recalled the first time a woman went to work on the seamer machine: "Everybody was flabbergasted. They said, 'What's the world coming to?' 'This is terrible, a woman doing a man's job!' I was shocked." Workers referred to the program derisively as "women's lib."

There were many reasons why the changes ordered by the Affirmative Action Program would be slow in coming. Most women indicated that they were not adequately informed of the proposed changes and had to rely on rumors. As a floorlady, Luz had not had much direct experience with the program. She shrugged: "things haven't changed that much. I don't think there's too much to it." Gloria, who worked in the lab, also saw few changes. Connie was dissatisfied with the training program because it focused on job bidding: "The affirmative-action training program is a farce." She explained her dissatisfaction:

> The first day we toured canneries. I had them come to my plant and took them all over, even in the basement where the women work and there are all the rats. The head of the training program told me, "you'll do anything to make a point." I told her, "You're right." Then they showed us slides of different jobs, which were right out of the Appendix A book [of the union contract]. [She rolled her eyes.] Next they were going to show us a videotape of how we look when we put in a bid for a job to management. I told them to forget it. I didn't give a shit how I looked when I put in a bid. What really mattered was if I was qualified, if I had the seniority for the job. I refused to participate.

By contrast, Lupe had a positive experience in her plant: "She [the personnel officer] explained it real good, with everything in Spanish and English. She told us about the different positions that would be opened, how you were hired, what wages and health benefits, everything. I was pleased; they had never done it before." Lupe hoped that she would qualify for a promotion in the near future and believed that the Affirmative Action Program was "the greatest thing that ever happened to the cannery." Luz had problems with the training program also: "They don't allow a person to learn the job unless they want that particular person."

[121]

Some women did not support the notion of women taking men's jobs. Estela, for example said: "I don't go for that. Those jobs should be for men; they have a family. I don't like to work hard anyway. I wouldn't take a man's job because they're harder. It's good for widows and divorcees, but if we have our husbands, why bother?" Lupe concurred, believing women are physically weaker: "I myself wouldn't want to work that hard. We can't handle it; our bodies can't handle it." Yet she observed women successfully performing men's jobs: "Women drive semis, work on axles." She had a look of amazement. "Some of them are pretty and are not built that big." Celia felt guilty because she had taken a man's greaser job. "Sometimes I feel bad because I've taken a man's job for the last five years. And I figure we women with hard hats, we took men's jobs." Celia also did not like to see men in women's jobs: "It's unusual for men to work on the line. But when they do, they have to wear a hair net, the women's aprons, gloves, like a woman. It makes me feel kind of funny. To me, they must feel kind of, you know . . ." She couldn't bring herself to conclude her statement, that men in aprons are emasculated. She stammered a bit longer and then pronounced that at least she would not take a warehouse job, "because those are men's jobs."

Vicki believed that conflict among workers was precipitated by the Affirmative Action Program: "Yes, there is competition because of women's lib." Celia did not like the program: "There should be something different." She hoped that "women's lib" would remain confined to the job: "Women should get paid if they work a man's job, but I don't believe in all the other stuff. I like to have my door opened and other things."

Connie, on the other hand, did not support the view that women and men should be confined to certain jobs: "We have families, too, that have to live. And I don't feel like I'm hurting any man by supporting my own family."

The men also apparently believed that women should remain in women's jobs. This can be seen in the harassment women received when they got promoted. Women clearly had difficulties in using plant seniority as a vehicle for moving up the job ladder.

Men were sometimes temporarily assigned to women's jobs, but women had to fight through a series of steps to gain men's jobs. First they had to put in bids, since a man's job almost always meant a promotion. Workers did not wear badges with their seniority numbers on them; the only way women could ascertain another worker's seniority was through gossip networks or a visit to the personnel office. Thus to bump someone took initiative and nerve. Women were discouraged not only by supervisors but through fear of the possible repercussions by their coworkers.

Once they succeeded in getting new jobs, women were often subject to devastating harassment. Supervisors insured that women received inadequate training. Vicki, for example, almost burned her face with acid while working with a cleanup crew because she was not advised of the dangers: "They don't teach you; they're in a hurry, and they don't go for women up there." Women would fail their job trials or receive job-related injuries and get discouraged. Familiar with this scenario, the bold Connie anticipated her treatment when she was promoted to shipping clerk. She told her supervisor and union representative alike: "I want it to go on the record that I have been told already that I'm going to be disqualified. But the only way you are going to disqualify me is to run me over with that boxcar. I am going to make it." She described her training period:

> I learned to stack cases, which weigh up to a hundred pounds, and put up bars to the box cars, which weigh about twenty-five to thirty pounds, and you must lift them over your head. I wasn't taught to drive a forklift until I'd been there about six months. It would have made my job a lot easier, since I have to go up and down the dock, which is about two-and-a-half blocks long. But the boys there weren't allowed to teach me. They were told "definitely not; teach her to hand stack and put up bars." I used to come home so tired I'd just flop out on that bed, and I was out until the next day. I was *completely* exhausted!

Supervisors would add tasks to jobs and even assigned one woman work that formerly had been split between two men's jobs. For example, four-foot-nine-inch Maricela Hernández had to climb a ten-foot ladder to check temperature gauges, a task never assigned to the prior male worker. Lisa observed about her mother's experiences: "They used to hassle her! They turned her meter back; she knew because she wrote the numbers down before she left. It was like a ritual: Every year they'd try and take her job away; she'd call in the union." Lupe observed: "The foremen were really upset because they had to train this one girl. They felt men should have the job because of the prestige; that's mostly what it was."

Patronizing comments by supervisors were commonplace. During her interview for an oiler-greaser job, one woman was told, "We don't want you using your sex appeal to get the men to do your work." Connie observed: "Most company people are male Anglos, and for some asinine reason they don't like working with women. They just don't want to give you the chance to advance."

Women's new male coworkers were also a source of irritation or outright harassment. On a new job, women were alternately ignored and taunted. They were admonished for depriving a man's family of its support, accused of being "man chasers," or called "uppity" or "loud-mouthed bitches." Men made fun of women's awkwardness in a new job with comments such as "leave it to a woman to do that" or teased them with statements such as "you wanted a man's job, now do it." Connie's coworkers were explicit: "They said, 'You're going to learn the hard way. Then its up to you to learn the easy way.'" Luz, who worked temporarily in a higher-bracket job, said, "I know I sound paranoid, but those men who are fair are moved; they were very biased as to who you are. Men assume women can't do it with no testing." Cristina was upset: "They tell us vulgar things; all of this is very bad. It's discrimination, and sometimes even your own race is the worst." Celia had what seems to be a unique experience. She found her coworkers to be "real nice, very helpful. If I needed anything they helped and didn't make me feel like I took a man's job; they made me feel at ease." The fact that her husband, a Portuguese-American, was a foreman in another department in the same plant may have contributed to the cooperation she found from male coworkers.

Even subordinates discouraged the entry of women into better-paying jobs by refusing to respect their authority as supervisors. Connie supervised three crews of workers as part of her job. One of the new male workers refused to follow her directions on how to load the boxcars properly. This was during a rush period and created a lot of tension until she finally confronted him, demanding to know why he refused to work for her. According to Connie, he had responded: "'It's just that I'm not used to a woman telling me what to do, much less yell at me. That made me mad.'" Connie observed: "I get my biggest problems from Chicano men. Any time I get a new worker out there, if he's Mexican or if he's Chicano, he's the one that gives me a hassle." I asked, "Why is that?" "Because Chicano men, Mexican men, have always dominated their women, and they don't want a woman to tell them what to do," she replied. She found it easiest to work with black men: "They have more respect for women." The fact that Chicanas were often placed in men's jobs in which they competed with Chicanos probably made these women more sensitive to slurs from them.

Furthermore, Chicanas may have responded differently to Chicano men because of their prior experiences with them. Connie described her own response to being in a man's role:

> It's just like in your home. Women are much more liberated now; we dare to answer back, but still a lot of times you feel guilty. There's times when I feel guilty, when I have to tell a man "you must do this because I'm telling you to do it." I revert back to when I was a child, and you didn't dare tell Daddy that. And you grew up, and you didn't tell your husband that either. It's just another male you're talking to, but it's the whole mystique of being a man: "you're so big, and you're so strong." Women are supposed to be intimidated by men.

Apparently, male intimidation carried more force when the men were Chicano, because Chicano men conjured up images in Chicanas' minds that were more personal.

Women's complaints did not change things. Vicki noted, "Personnel could care less." Hence besides experiencing the difficulties of learning new jobs, women often felt humiliated and frustrated. Liz said: "I'm surprised I didn't get an ulcer. It was too much: I felt discriminated against as a Chicana and as a woman." Lisa observed, "My mom was a nervous wreck." Connie stated: "Everytime a woman goes into a 'man's' job, she's harassed to the point that some women say 'you can have it.' "

The frequency of such harassment is subject to debate. A U.S. Department of Labor study (1978) claims that only one-quarter of the women they interviewed received such treatment. But every one of the women I interviewed who was working at a "man's" job had received patronizing treatment in one form or another and knew of other women who had also. Almost all of the women I interviewed had heard of such incidents. The consequent "spillover" effect of such intimidation went far beyond the individuals who faced it directly.

Women witnessed management practices that flouted the new system of promotions. Job openings were not posted; a foreman would

[125]

inform friends of coming job openings so that they could apply first and so on. Connie worried because the incumbency rule was being used again. Luz believed that she could get promoted faster if "they ran the whole place fair; if jobs were openly and honestly available." Most women who were Spanish speakers believed that they needed more education and a command of English to move up. Lisa instead recalled the significance of work-based networks: "I'd have to be related to somebody important, to have the right friends and more contacts." Women clearly understood the stakes involved if they tried to move out of the "women's" departments.

The Meaning of Cannery Jobs

Women chose to remain in the cannery for varied reasons. The relatively high hourly wage compared to that for other unskilled jobs was a primary one. Also, seasonal workers are eligible for tax-free unemployment benefits if they cannot find another job. Most women were often unable to find another job during the off-season partially because of their age and lack of skills but also because they were cannery workers. Women believed they were passed over for other jobs because "once they see you have so many years in the cannery, they figure you'll go back," Lupe explained, "so they won't hire you." The probability of receiving unemployment benefits provided an added incentive to remain as cannery workers.[14] Lupe mused: "Sometimes I wish there was no unemployment. A lot of us would have steady jobs. Because you know you are going to have a steady income coming in all winter, you keep going back." Combining wages and unemployment benefits, my informants earned between three thousand and seven thousand dollars in 1978, depending on how many hours they worked. This was always a substantial contribution to family income.

Women preferred seasonal work for another reason: once they

14. In 1976 even the lowest paid cannery worker could qualify for unemployment insurance by working slightly more than one month. About 75 percent of cannery workers were eligible for unemployment benefits (California Employment Development Department 1976, cited in Brown 1981:238). The average level of unemployment benefits received by California cannery workers in 1976 was $1,128. Brown calculates that the lowest paid workers who worked a typical season of four months would receive a subsidy of about two thirds of earned income (1981:240).

adapted to it, it was only a temporary infringement upon their lives. Vicki, with thirty-one years in the industry, shrugged: "You get used to it; it becomes routine. The time goes by fast. Before you know it another season is over." Women learned to *aguantar*, to bear the conditions of their work with patience, strength, and, one hopes, vigor.[15] I asked Cristina about the possibility of seeking a full-time job elsewhere. She shook her head. "I can't, it would be too hard. I don't have enough energy for that." Lisa was stark in her appraisal of seasonal cannery work: "You go through hell for three months. All you think about is your own time, what you're going to do when you're through." These women had only two years of seniority each and had not yet learned to endure, to *aguantar*.

Full-time cannery work had a different meaning for Connie. As a single parent, she had little choice. She struggled to get and keep a man's job because she needed higher wages: "I work because I have to!" she said. "I'm no glutton for punishment. I'm not exactly *in love* with my job." In addition, Connie did not want to seek welfare: "I want to be independent. I don't want to have to accept charity from anybody. And I am willing to work for it." Connie had another reason for persevering despite the obstacles she found on the job: "I wanted to show women that it could be done. And when other women saw that I could do it, I mean I'm not too big, and if I could do it, why couldn't they do it? And I didn't dare not make it!" She laughed as she concluded, "I would have cut my own throat!"

Conclusion

Work-based networks were a central aspect of cannery work culture. Supervisors' networks functioned to channel resources, and women supervisors were in positions to do this also. Participants in male supervisors' networks no doubt also developed camaraderie, but they usually did not include women production workers. Work-based networks, then, expressed the occupational segregation of the canning industry and contributed to the lack of job mobility by women.

Women workers' own networks usually remained fairly exclusive,

15. Ernesto Galarza (1977) has discussed how farm workers take pride in their ability to *aguantar*.

with networks being composed of members of the same ethnic or racial group. This stems in part from the fact that women were segregated on the job, and white ethnic women often worked separately from Mexican and Chicana women. Language barriers also prevented closeness among many of these women and even distanced Chicanas and *mexicanas*. Furthermore, Mexican and Chicana women observed their ethnic female supervisors helping members of their own group secure higher-paying jobs or easier working conditions. For this reason, white ethnic women had an edge in the competition for better jobs, and Chicanas could find little basis for solidarity with them. These ethnic and racial conflicts contrast with the situation of Lamphere's (1985) informants, who included Portuguese and Colombian immigrant women working in textile and apparel factories. Lamphere's informants used women's work culture, particularly short, on-the-job celebrations of domestic rituals such as weddings, to bridge language and cultural differences. Chicanas' cannery work-based networks reflected the structural changes occurring in canneries as women started moving into men's jobs, and Chicanos and Mexicans replaced white ethnic workers. Yet Chicanas and *mexicanas* were also rivals with one another, and this exacerbated the cultural and language differences that already existed between them. Work-based networks served to fragment workers, who focused on antagonisms based on ethnic differences and gender-based discrimination. These antagonisms undermined the potential for collective struggle.

The women I interviewed considered the conditions in which they labored as hazardous, foul, rife with discrimination, and, in a word, oppressive. Women with jobs on the line found the work itself boring, tedious, confining, pressured, but, most of all, difficult. If they were closely supervised, these jobs were considered demeaning. Close supervision and dirty conditions of work violated women's sense of self-respect. Their vulnerable positions as workers often meant that they were unable to challenge or change the affronts to their personal integrity. In the face of these conditions, my informants learned to endure. The relatively high wages, along with the unemployment benefits, were the main reasons women on the line chose to bear through cannery work. When women were able to get off the line and gain some autonomy or responsibility, they found satisfaction in their jobs. These women found the difficulty and independence in their work as challenging.

Although women may not have been thrilled with their jobs, they found many aspects of the cannery "world" to be satisfying. Chicanas' own work-based networks were an important contribution to women's job satisfaction, bringing the camaraderie and sociability women valued highly. Women were also able to support one another in their individual battles to get better jobs. Chicanas' work-based networks functioned in a manner similar to the work groups of sales clerks (Benson 1983, 1979) by inculcating women into job practices and social relations. As Barbara Melosh (1982) has shown for nurses, Chicanas' occupational segregation ironically allowed them to initiate meaningful relationships with other Chicana workers, and work-based networks functioned to "humanize" the workplace. Yet cannery work-based networks could also be a means through which women consented to their own exploitation, for network members made the job seem better and even pressured others to acquiescence.

Cannery jobs held complex meaning for women workers—*aguante* and friendship, difficulty and challenge, struggle and consent—notions that came to be accepted in the role of cannery worker. Apart from the economic incentives, cannery-work culture provided sufficient social reward for women to stay on the job.

[5]

"Everybody's Trying to Survive": The Impact of Women's Employment on Chicano Families

Recent research on the impact of women's employment on families indicates several patterns. Generally, working women gain status and influence in family decision making because of their financial contributions and enhance their families' standard of living (Blood and Wolfe 1960; Safilios-Rothschild 1970; Nieva 1985). Yet despite these positive effects, working wives do not obtain significant help from their husbands with housework. Instead, women tend to add the time spent at work to the time spent on household chores, although working wives decrease the time spent in housework (Vanek 1974). Heidi Hartmann (1981a) has reviewed time-budget research on how much housework married men and women actually perform. She has shown that regardless of the class status of respondents, 70 percent of all housework is usually done by women—husbands and children each contribute about 15 percent—and wives are largely responsible for child care. Wives spend, on the average, forty hours a week maintaining a house and family if they do not work for wages and thirty hours a week if they do. Other research finds that husbands of working wives spend little more time (on the average, two hours a week) on housework than husbands of homemakers. Husbands' proportion of family work does increase when wives work but "only because the wife does less" (Pleck 1979:484; also see Walshok 1979). However,

[130]

the amount of housework increases substantially if there are young children or many children in the household.[1] Clearly, "while husbands of employed wives participated more often than husbands of nonemployed wives in almost all household tasks, their contributions to the time spent on the tasks were small" (Hartmann 1981a:381).

Recent research on Chicano dual-worker families confirms that working women gain power in decision making but also implies that there is considerable sharing of household chores. Leonarda Ybarra (1982b) has found that Chicano husbands and wives have "egalitarian" attitudes on sharing household chores: 94 percent of her respondents agree that a husband should help his wife with housework if she is employed.[2] In terms of actual child-care tasks and housework, Ybarra has found that if a wife works, "the couple is more likely to practice egalitarian values" (1982b:174) and concluded: "If the wife was employed, there is a greater likelihood that household chores and child care would be shared between spouses, and that in general, they would have a more egalitarian role structure than couples where the wife was not employed" (1982b:169).

Zinn has also found that Chicano husbands of working wives are "involved" in domestic activities more than husbands of homemakers and that dual-worker couples have greater equality in conjugal decision making. Since the employed wives made and enforced the decision that husbands help with housework, "their husbands' participation reflects an important alteration in family roles" (1980:53). Zinn has admitted, however, that "the division of household labor was not equal" (1980:52). Since all of her informants subscribed to patriarchal ideology, she has suggested that individuals may adhere to some aspects of traditional family ideology but nevertheless experienced change in household behavior. This is an intriguing phenomenon that will be investigated further.

In family life, many assumptions about how one should behave are considered "natural," and as a result people usually do not spell out what "family" means to them. Our task is to discern the meaning of what are often cryptic or offhand remarks. I agree with Jane Collier

1. Wives spend perhaps eight hours a week in additional chores because of husbands (Hartmann 1981a).
2. Ybarra interviewed one hundred randomly selected Chicano married couples. "Egalitarian" families are "more democratically structured with husband and wife sharing family responsibilities equally" (1982a:34).

and her associates that "the meaning people attach to action, whether they view it as coordinated and therefore shared, or in some other way, is an integral component of that action and cannot be divorced from our analysis" (1982:37). Such a focus helps to clarify the processes of change occurring in Chicano families when wives enter the labor force. Conflict over women's labor is a key to analyzing power relations in the home and to understanding the degree to which men maintain control over women (Hartmann 1981a).

We also need to examine how coworker relationships affect such issues of change in Chicano families, a phenomenon that has been virtually overlooked by researchers. Regarding their participation in support networks, Chicanos are consistently found to rely on kin, maintaining ties through frequent visiting and the exchange of goods and labor. Chicanos are said to regard emotional support from relatives—especially primary kin—as superior to other sources (Gilbert 1978). Contrary to the predictions of classic acculturation theory, the longer Chicanos live in the United States, the more they intensify their kin support networks. The most "familistic" Chicanos, those with extensive kin relations, are the third generation in the United States and, among them, those of highest socioeconomic status. These cohorts of Chicanos tend to have more kin residing nearby and more resources to exchange with them.[3] Chicanos are more "familistic" than Anglos or Blacks because they often have larger kin networks residing in the area and place higher values on closeness among relatives (Wagner and Schaffer 1980; Keefe 1984). Chicanos even tend to migrate to the areas where relatives reside in order to utilize their kin resources (Zinn 1982; Matthiasson 1974).

An implication of this research is that friendship is not considered to play an important part in Chicano support networks. In fact, some go as far as to claim that relatives are the primary source of support "because of the relatively low reliance of Mexican Americans on other informal resources such as fictive kin, friends, neighbors and coworkers" (Keefe, Padilla, and Carlos 1979:148).

My data show several related processes. Women informants and members of their families expressed patriarchal ideology in the way

3. These findings are the result of research on Chicanos' avoidance of mental health agencies, which is explained by institutional discrimination by agencies and Chicano cultural principles, which value seeking support from kin. See Keefe, Padilla, and Carlos 1978, 1979; Keefe 1979.

[132]

they divided housework. Women (and girls) performed most of the household chores, and men did not carry an equal load. In some of the women's families, there was tension or conflict over the household division of labor. Yet the meaning women ascribed to their situation as working mothers included acceptance of their primary responsibility as housekeepers and the need to adapt to the disruption of wage work. Furthermore, in contrast to research on Chicano networks, my informants developed work-related friendship networks, which functioned in a manner similar to kin networks, and these relationships were very meaningful to women.

Women's Perceptions

Consistent with the findings in the literature, the most noticeable change in perceptions that occurred among my informants was in regard to shared responsibility within families. The traditional patriarchal norms that characterized early married life became more flexible after the women began working. To the women, the fact that they were employed embodied a change in role expectations. Women believed that if they worked, they were easing the husbands' responsibilities as providers. They could therefore legitimately request that husbands reciprocate by doing more housework. Connie recalled: "I felt I was helping, taking some of the responsibility off him." María concurred: "I think if I help him out by going to work, then he can help me out around the house, and he can come and serve himself too." I asked when she started to think this way, and she exclaimed: "When I started to work. I had to; it was too much!" Yet she, like the other women, did not expect her husband to share housework equally.

The decision to continue working was faced anew each season (except for Connie who worked year around). In most cases, the woman announced that she got called back, and no objection was raised by her husband. Her family was used to her working and assumed she would continue to do so (even if they may not have liked it to begin with). The women asserted their own desire to continue working, although there were other factors causing them to remain in the labor force.

Most important was the higher standard of living that the women's income supported. Their income was pooled with that of their husbands, and this brought benefits the whole family shared. With the second income, families became more stable economically, and this allowed a respite from the precarious situation the family was in before the wife worked. As a result, women generally had equal say in how money was spent.

The standard of living changed when wives worked; this is revealed in the women's comments on spending patterns.[4] Blanca said, "At first I had to work. But after a few years it was so that we could pay a bill, get a little ahead." Women with children at home provided for their support. Lupe's wages were used primarily to pay for her children's education in Catholic schools. Lisa and Teresa, as well as other women, noted how the need to support their children was primary; yet their wages also enabled them to provide the "extras." As her youngest daughter toddled by, holding a doll that was almost her own size, Teresa remarked: "Por eso trabajo, para mi hijita, así que puedo darle esas cosas" (That's why I work, for my daughter, so I can give her those things). Even Cristina, who had no children, felt the need for two incomes. When her husband suggested that she quit because she was upset with the situation at work, she declined, saying: "If I had quit, then we wouldn't have the extra things. And with prices so high, you need the extra money." Connie observed: "We need to work because our husbands are older than us and maybe not in good health any more, and the doctor bills pile up, and the kids need to go to college. You know, the things of life that go on everyday—it takes money to live." María reiterated: "Both of you have to work to accomplish anything."

As their children grew up, women changed their spending patterns considerably from the days when they first began working. Rather than working to have wages for basic family maintenance, women later worked with specific goals in mind: to buy a color television or new draperies or to save so that their children could attend college. Luz was putting her youngest son through vocational school with her

---

4. In 1977–78, when these women were interviewed, inflation was high. The consumer price index was 7.7 in 1978 and rising (U.S. Bureau of Census 1982b). Unemployment rates were also relatively high in 1977–78 in California, with 7.1 percent for the total population and a 9.7 percent rate for Hispanics (according to U.S. Bureau of Labor Statistics press releases in 1979). Yet unemployment rates had dropped from the highs of the 1974–75 recession (Bednarzik and St. Marie 1977:8).

income, and Rosa partially helped her daughter attend law school. Estela's son was in graduate school, and although she did not help him directly, her supervisor was able to get him a summer cannery job to pay for college expenses. Josie noted: "I used to spend my money on food. But I told my husband, 'You make enough for the food and house payments. I want to *see* what I work for.' " Euleria was proud of the well-furnished home and new patio, which had been paid for with her wages. Vicki also showed off her totally remodeled kitchen, which was paid for with her income. María laughed, "Now we have three cars and my relatives [in Mexico] think we're rich."

The women's families became financially secure with the dual incomes, especially when they were able to buy modest second homes for rental income. Vicki noted how inexpensive it was to purchase her home thirty years ago—it had cost only $7,000.[5] "I'm sorry I didn't grab two of them," she remarked. Vicki and her husband bought another small house after they paid off their first one, and the additional income from rentals made the Gutiérrezes relatively well off. They also owned a small ranch. Vicki explained: "We've been very good about putting our money away and investing our money wisely." They celebrated their tenth anniversary in the Hawaiian Islands and planned a trip to Mexico for their twentieth anniversary.

Celia da Silva worked primarily so that she and her husband could vacation, and they had been to Hawaii three times. After Celia said, "I'm bored with it," the following season they planned an extended cruise with two other couples in which the wives were also cannery workers: "Now I'm looking forward to *that*. It's what we work for, so why not?" Vicki and her husband were planning to join the da Silvas on the cruise, and he announced their upcoming vacation plans at a party with the rationale: "Why not? Vicki deserves it. I owe it all to her."

Vicki's income not only provided financial "rewards" but originally enabled her husband to get the vocational training he used to set up his own business. In addition, Vicki—who managed her income separately from that of her husband—felt free either to save or to spend her money. Some seasons she managed to save up to three thousand

---

5. The median price of homes in the San Jose metropolitan area was $76,000 in 1978 and had risen to $139,000 in 1985, the second highest area in the nation (*San Jose Mercury News*, 9 November 1985).

dollars. Clearly, Vicki's financial contribution was substantial and aided her position in the marriage. Other women were also in this situation, in which their husbands had relatively stable jobs and their own income had become supplemental. In this regard, Celia remarked how "canneries have been good to us." I asked her to explain, and she replied: "Because of canneries we've been able to pay off our duplex, and we've been able to do okay." The more tangible rewards of the women's income were shared by husband and wife. The women's decision to remain in the labor force served both their interests.

Whether women used their earnings for basic support or as supplemental income, they had considerable say in how their money was spent. This gave them leverage within the relationship and brought the women personal satisfaction. Actually carrying out their egalitarian views in the division of labor, however, was harder to accomplish. As the Mexican saying goes, "Entre dicho y hecho hay gran trecho" (Between word and deed there is a great distance) (Ybarra and Arce 1981).

The Division of Housework

Except for Connie, who worked full time, and Lupe, who worked part time at a packing house, the women were housewives during the off-season. This is very important. Their families considered them, and even the women considered themselves, to be primarily homemakers. Yet the women characterized their homemaker duties in an offhand manner: "I just do my thing when I'm not working," Celia remarked. Estela shrugged: "I just clean my house, pay bills, take things easy." Connie laughingly characterized full-time homemaking: "Anyone likes to stay home and be lazy." Housekeeping was not seen in the same way as a job; although it was necessary, housework was not "work."

As the women went back to wage work each season, there was little impact on the division of household duties. My informants characterized two ways in which they shared housework, and these ways related to changes in the domestic cycle. The first pattern was segregated, in which the woman was seen as being primarily responsible for housework and the care of the children, despite the fact that she worked. These women carried the burden of the double day, often because their children were young.[6] Although husbands helped some-what, most of the domestic chores fell directly on the women. About one-third of my informants were in this situation, in which they performed most of the housework. Similar to Leonarda Ybarra and Maxine Baca Zinn's findings, in two-thirds of the families the division of housework altered after the women began working.

Blanca was one of the women who was responsible for most of the housework. She described a typical evening after a grueling day in the cannery: "It's very hard. I have to come home and cook and clean, get my kids to bed, make food for the next day, and set out clean clothes for the kids." With a nervous glance to my notes, she added: "Then when it's after midnight and you finally go to bed, your husband has his things for you to do." I stopped taking notes as she continued: "The husband suffers the most, because he knows you have to take care of the kids first. Sometimes at night I'm too tired to take care of his comforts. Well, what can I do? That's life." Her husband, who happened to walk in during this part of the interview, listened to her comments and then agreed that this situation is difficult. He said, "Poor women, it's hard for them to have to work and then coming home to clean house too." Although I observed him taking care of his youngest daughter on various occasions, it was clear that his wife took care of the house.

Josie is another woman who did most of the housework. She shrugged: "Well, I didn't have any one [to help out] so I had to do it myself." Apparently, she did not rely on her husband when she needed help. Rosa described how she managed: "It's hard, especially when my kids were little, unless you have a husband who can start meals . . . [she shrugged]. Sunday is my only free day, and by the time you do your laundry and prepare for next week, your day is gone." María came home from work "knowing I had to start working right away." Estela said: "There's no effect on the family when I'm working, except for dinner time. All he wants is dinner when he comes home. So I have to come home and cook." Connie described her and Mario's division of labor: "I went in at night until seven in the morning. But it was a convenient shift for us. That way my

---

6. Boyd Rollins and Kenneth Cannon (1974) have found that marital satisfaction is lowest at those periods in the domestic cycle when "role strain" is the highest. For women, the early child-rearing phase is a time of highly demanding and intense social roles.

husband could sleep, be in with the children, and then I'd get home in time for him to go to work." I asked, "And then you'd sleep during the day?" She said, "Yeah, I'd try. Besides I had to clean house, wash clothes, cook dinner by the time the old man got home, make sure that the food was on the table, or else he'd get mad, go shopping, you know." I could not help but interject, "So you had two jobs?" She replied, "Oh, definitely, always." I pursued: "Other than taking care of the children, did your husband help around the house?" She shook her head. "Not much, not much." Since the women were part-time workers, it was easy for family members to ignore the disruption of their jobs and for household routines to proceed as usual. Myra Ferree (1976) has found that part-time women workers are more likely than full-time workers to be responsible for all of the housework. Thirty-six percent of the part-time workers in her sample of working-class women had husbands who did not customarily do any tradition-ally female chore.[7]

Even among the women who indicated that there was a shift in behavior, however, there was no fundamental redefinition of respon-sibility. Women were still seen as being chiefly responsible for house-work, even if they were given more help. Rosa characterized the division of housework in her home during the cannery season: "My husband helps me more when I'm working, but everything runs the same." Estela smiled as she observed: "During the season it's different. The family pitches in. [But] the main change is in the dinner [hour]." So although families altered their schedules, and husbands and children helped more, there was no major change in responsibility.

Part of the difficulty in changing responsibility for home duties is that men limit the tasks they are able to perform. Some men are inept in homemaker skills, such as cooking. Euleria laughed as she re-counted how her husband once tried to cook dinner and burned it terribly: "The kids wouldn't touch it, and that was the end of that." Sometimes Víctor would make dinner, but María explained: "It comes out awful! He made eggs and potatoes once, and the potatoes were all hard. The girls still tease him." Not surprisingly, it was the older children who assisted in household meal preparation.

7. Some recent research suggests that men believe they do more work when their wives are employed (Pleck 1979). Whether men actually contribute more remains to be documented by time-budget research.

Among children, gender often took precedence over age in the division of chores. Girls most often did the housework and cooking, even if they had older brothers. María's oldest sons were responsible for mowing the lawn and taking out the garbage. It was her fourth child, a girl, who was responsible for dishwashing and occasionally making meals. María elaborated: "Now I rely on la negra [nickname given the daughter]. She starts dinner and makes the tortillas." María's boys expected their sisters to iron their clothes, as well as to serve their meals. If María was late from work, her sons would not start dinner for the family but waited for their sisters to cook or for María to come home. Lupe is another example. Her youngest daughter did most of the daily dishwashing and table clearing, whereas her sons' chores included occasionally cleaning the yard or their rooms. Only if no females were available did boys work harder during the cannery season. Estela's oldest children were male: "My boys were real good; they helped a lot."

Even with daughters and sons helping, however, the allocation of duties to children did not insure that tasks were completed. Their "help" might create added frustration for working mothers. María sighed as she explained the difficulties of supervising children's chores:

> Víctor gets mad. He complains when the house is dirty. He says, "María it's your responsibility to see that it gets done. You don't have to do it, but at least get one of the girls to do it; just see that it gets done." I rely on them to help me out, they're old enough. But I don't like to be always telling them, "I want you to do this" or "haz me eso [do that for me]." So I just let it go or I do it myself. And sometimes it doesn't get done.

María was the one who used to mop her kitchen daily, but now "I don't know how long it's been since I mopped, probably weeks. Pues, ni modo [Well, never mind]."

The women who lived alone with their husbands had the most flexible division of labor, probably because there was less work to do. These women's husbands generally helped more and particulary did more housework during the canning season. Vicki admitted that when she is not working, she does most of the housework: "I spoil him; I wait on him hand and foot." But during the season: "He helps me with the chores. On his day off he'll barbecue or make something.

[139]

And he'll pick up around the house. I'll come home and my house is clean. And he'll throw a load of laundry into the washer. He says, 'If I can't throw a load in the washer—all it takes is to push a button.' He helps more when I'm working." Luz used to get up early and make her husband's lunch even though she worked late on the swing shift: "But one day I put on too much mustard, and it dripped on his shirt—he was so embarrassed! So I said, 'Well make it yourself.' So he does, and now he makes his own breakfast in the mornings while he makes his lunch." Cristina noted: "Hay hombres muy buenos para trabajar en la casa; puedan hacerlo. Mi esposo, sí me ayude" (There are men who are very good about doing housework; they can do it. My husband does help me). Celia appreciated her husband pitching in: "He helps me with the housework. When I'm working, he vacuums, puts clothes in the dryer, little things like that."

But even when husbands help out more, roles are not "egalitarian." From these informants' indications, the women are still responsible for completing the majority of household tasks. For example, Vicki's husband still "wouldn't allow" her to work full time, and she agreed to remain a part-time worker and housewife who "waits on him hand and foot." The segregated division of labor should not be surprising since it is a pattern that is found consistently in time-budget research (Hartmann 1981a; Nye 1974; Walshok 1979). I came across no families with an equal division of household labor and virtually no informants who characterized marriage in terms of equally shared responsibility for home duties. Connie came to see marriage as a "50–50 thing," but this was only after her divorce.

Women coped through various means with the difficulties of completing home duties when they worked. The task most disrupted was cooking dinner, since this chore was expected to be done by the "lady of the house." When working, women often resorted to purchasing prepared, fast-food meals, even though they were relatively expensive. Cristina admitted: "When I'm working, it's nothing but Kentucky Fried [Chicken]." Lupe described a second way of insuring that home cooked meals were ready by dinner time: "Everybody uses a crock pot in the cannery." This appliance enabled women to start a slow-cooking dinner before they left for work so that the food would be ready when they got home. María, on the other hand, changed her cooking style in the opposite direction: "I learned to cook dinner real fast, turn up the heat full blast so that everything would cook fast. And if it was cooked right, good, if not: pues, ni modo [well, never mind]."

Finding time to get other housework completed was a more difficult matter. Because of fatigue during the season, many of the women were unable to keep their homes as clean as they would have liked. Women offered a litany of complaints. Josie said: "When I'm working, I just come home, make dinner, and get my clothes ready for the next day. That's all you want to do. I do my housework on Sundays or late at night, but I let things go during season." Gloria admitted that she hated housework because "it's boring." Her husband occasionally helped with housework but "not everyday." She found it more convenient to ignore her tedious home chores during the season since "it's hard to work and clean." Estela complained: "Usually after work, I just come home. I'm tired. I don't like to do nothing. I'm usually in bed by nine o'clock." She said she resented this because during the season "I'm deprived of my TV."

Teresa laughed, recalling changes since newlywed days: "Now I get frustrated with any little thing I have to do, or I make the girls do it. A veces me pone la flojera [Sometimes I just get lazy]. I don't know why, I just say 'Oh well, I don't have to do it today.'" With six children—one was only eighteen months old—her "flojera" when it came to cleaning house was understandable. Cristina (who worked the swing shift) seemed embarrassed to admit: "No atiendo a mi casa. Si no tuviera tanto trabajo, sí lo hubiera. No tengo tiempo de hacer nada." (I don't attend to my house. If I didn't have so much work, sure I'd do it. But I don't have time to do anything.) Connie summarized women's views about the division of labor during the canning season: "By the end of the season, you're glad it's over because it's hard work and because you haven't had time to really clean [house], and your husband is beginning to complain because all the meals are not on time, and the kids are beginning to complain because you can't take them to the movies; you can't take them anywhere."

Women found time to finish the absolutely necessary chores by extending their day, either by going to bed late, getting up early, or doing both. María would iron and clean late at night because "I just didn't have time in the day." After working for as many as ten hours a day during the peak season, women were glad when the season ended. Lisa accurately summed up the meaning of the double day: "Women never stop working. It's like having two jobs."

[141]

Women's views regarding the double day ranged from the practical María's—"I didn't mind; I knew I had to do it"—to the disgruntled Connie's—"never again." Connie realized she was always exhausted after working and then coming home to keep house. She described forcefully how she confronted the unfairness of the double day:

> In those days, I was a fanatic! I never washed the floor. I got down on my hands and knees and scrubbed it. I used to wax the tiles on my bathroom walls with a toothbrush. . . . There's a little bit of a martyr in all of us. I remember one day I was tired. I got off work at seven A.M., after two shifts, and I came home. Before I went to sleep I asked my son and husband to wax the living-room floor. They said "OK," and I went to sleep. About one o'clock I got up and the floor was still unwaxed. I asked them again, and they said "OK," but first they had to watch the ball game. I kept worrying about that floor. So I got up, got down on my hands and knees, and did the floor. And I started crying—I felt so bad! I felt sorry for myself; here I was tired and had worked hard, and still I couldn't get any help. I was just bawling. And I decided that from that day forward I was never going to keep a spotless house again! Now I do what I have to, and my kids help me a lot, but I've got other things to do.

Other women in this situation, however, did not see themselves as martyrs. Blanca expressed the resignation that most women felt when she asked: "What can I do?" Gloria asserted, "It's not that bad." But another woman who accepted the double day was not passive regarding her husband's lack of support. When Víctor López complained that his food was not cooked right, María told me she had snapped: "Pues, si no te gusta, haz lo tú, o vete mejor" (Well, if you don't like it, make it yourself, or better yet leave). She laughed as she recalled, "So he didn't complain after that." Rosa best summed up the women's response to having to complete most of the housework after a day on the job: "Why, after all that, you're too pooped to poop."

Along with the responsibility for arranging child care, the double day places a great deal of strain on a woman. As we shall now see, this can affect her relationship with her husband.

Conflict and Adaptation

Although I did not seek out conflict in dual-worker marriages, the prevalence of underlying tensions and even outright struggle became apparent at the very start of the research. The full significance of that conflict did not become clear to me, however, until after the fieldwork was completed. This was because of the mixed responses received from working women who tried to convey a positive impression regarding the impact of their jobs. Yet the deflection of questions with a defensive response of "it doesn't affect us" was itself an indication of hidden dynamics. It was not until subsequent interviews with a woman that my gentle probing, or her verbal slip, revealed a fuller picture. After I began the data analysis, I realized the extent to which conflict was a part of these women's family lives.

As we saw in the case of Gloria and Frank's argument (described in the preface), a disruption in social interaction also provided important information. During the interviews with Gloria, it became clear that the family depended upon her wages and unemployment benefits to get through the months when Frank was laid off from his construction job. Also, her income enabled them to buy a small second house, which they rented out for added income. From his response to my questions, it was clear that Frank worried about the possibility of Gloria losing her job. Yet he wanted a wife who was a full-time homemaker or who at least kept house the way he wanted it done.

We have seen how most informants desired the life-style of middle-class nuclear families in which wives did not work. The Gonzales were no exception. Because Gloria worked, Frank was continually reminded of his inability to support his family as he wanted. Her income, job satisfaction, and, most important, independence were threatening to him. The expense of paying a babysitter was an added problem. No doubt he did not realize that Gloria considered him "better than nothing" and was economically dependent on him also. Although Gloria claimed that her job "doesn't affect us, I'm home in the evenings," clearly it required an accommodation on Frank's part that he did not want to make. The tension sometimes erupted into open conflict, as when he accused Gloria of being "too lazy to clean."

If there was opposition to the woman's continuing to work, the conflict that resulted involved her domestic labor. Few couples explicitly discussed how they would change patterns of housework and child care when women began cannery work. Thus when expectations were not met, as in the case of Gloria and Frank, tensions surfaced. A woman's position in the domestic cycle created variations in the types of conflict between spouses. For those women whose children were grown, the conflict revolved around the lack of the woman's

[143]

companionship and personal service. Rosa's husband originally did not want her to work because of the need for her at home with the children. Now that their three children were grown, he was more interested in their own relationship. She said: "He doesn't like me to work because I work nights and he works all day. He wants me to be around when he's home at night. He wants me to be pleasant and take care of him." Euleria's husband also preferred that she quit. Yet because he had had a minor heart attack, she began to save money in case he had to quit working. So when he suggested that she quit and spend more time at home, her response was: "How can I?"

Even in homes in which the husband or children did not particularly mind that women worked, tension was inevitable. Vicki remarked: "Sometimes there's squabbles at work, and I come home tired or angry, and I take it out on him. He says, 'Well you know you don't have to work, nobody's forcing you. You can quit anytime.' But I don't want to." Vicki noted that even her son, who had worked one season in the cannery, suggested she quit. He asked, "Mother, how can you stand it?" Vicki had lectured him: "Now you know the opportunities you've had; take advantage of them so you won't have to work in the cannery."

For women who had school-age children, it was difficult to manage the pressures of work and family duties. Lupe described her husband's feelings about her job: "He didn't want me to continue working because he'd say, 'You're so grouchy when you're working. You yell at the kids and just are not a pleasant person to be around.' " With a wary glance at my note pad, she said, "And you don't need to put this down." So I stopped writing and listened as she continued: "And sometimes I'm too tired and our sex life suffers. And that's so important to a man; no matter what anybody says, that's one of the most important things in a marriage. If that's no good, then nothing's good." But she continued working despite her husband's complaints.

Discord also arose from expectations over who would do the housework. Husbands and children resented having to do more around the house. When Lupe asked her daughter (who happened to be nearby during one of our interviews) how she felt about the fact that Lupe worked, Linda exploded: "I hated it! I didn't like you working nights. The man should bring in the money. I didn't like the babysitters; one ran over my cat." Linda's resentment also stemmed from the fact that despite being younger than her two brothers, she had to do more housework while her mother worked. A surprised Lupe had not known her daughter felt that way. When a woman's job is important to family income, such feelings of resentment are not often expressed.

Blanca's husband, who originally did not want her to work, later decided she should continue her seasonal job. But Blanca wanted to quit because a work injury bothered her. She melodramatically announced "I want to die in my own home" and vowed never to return to the cannery. Jaime left the decision up to her. After he left the room, Blanca said: "I can't tell you everything. But sometimes you need your husband more . . . [pause]. I already told him that I can't work and I won't work. And if he doesn't like it, there's the door; he can walk out like a free man. I can't do it anymore." I dropped the issue. Later I found out that Blanca had returned to the cannery for "just one more season."

Connie's husband originally did not seem to mind that she worked. Later he became critical after she decided to let go of her "fanaticism" for cleaning. Also, the fact that she refused to provide personal attention became a major point of contention in their deteriorating relationship. When I asked how Mario felt about her change, she waved her hand in disgust and said, "Mmm, ¿pa' qué te digo?" I pressed her: "He didn't like it?" She described the painful marital discord that even included the children:

> Later Mario used that against me. He'd say: "I don't want to stick around here 'cause it's like a pigsty." I'd look around, and the house was clean. And he'd say things like: "My mother used to work in the cannery, and my shirts were always clean and ironed." So I'd wonder, "Well, maybe he's right, what's wrong with me?" After a while he stopped asking me to do things; he'd ask the kids. He'd get back at me through them. I told them, "Don't do it; he's a grown man; he's healthy; he can do it himself." My daughter would say, "Momma, he's my father. It's all right, I'll do it." Sometimes the kid was so little they'd have to get a chair to get him a glass of water, but they'd do it.

Apparently, Mario expected the household routine to remain the same, and he even hoped for some lavish attention. When Connie not only lowered her standards of housekeeping but refused to defer to him, Mario accused her of being a poor wife. Connie, on the other hand, had different expectations. She felt good about working and

[145]

the fact that she was helping to ease his burden as provider. After she decided not to worry about housework, she had few concerns about neglecting their family. However, when Mario criticized her behavior, she felt guilty and wondered if indeed she was doing the right thing.

If men accept the notion that they are entitled to respect by virtue of the breadwinner role, working wives who contribute a third or more of the family income can seem threatening.[8] When a woman asserts herself, as Connie did, her husband is in a vulnerable position. Not only has he lost personal service and deference, but he cannot adequately care for himself. Women, on the other hand, can be even more vulnerable. With only seasonal jobs to support their families, women need husbands' incomes. It is in both of their interests to resolve the conflict.

There were two main ways that couples managed the tensions generated by the woman's job. One way was for the woman to quit working, either to save the marriage or end at least this particular souce of strain. After much conflict, María and Víctor finally agreed that despite their need for a second income, the best thing would be for her to quit after one more season. It was originally María's decision, since she did not like her job. She announced several times that she would not return to work with no response from Víctor. At last he announced his acquiescence: "Pues, ni modo" (Well, all right). The rationale was that the children needed María at home, and Víctor preferred that she make his meals and take care of family matters. María's reason for "their" decision was: "El me tiene mantener" (He is supposed to support me).

Connie and Mario found an extreme way to cope with their marital conflict. Mario resented Connie's refusal to be the perfect home-maker. His inability to accept her political activism prompted him to demand that she quit organizing. Connie refused, and they remained deadlocked for many months. During this time Mario's drinking increased, and he became estranged from the whole family. Connie recalled: "And I realized that even though I still loved him, I didn't

8. Lillian Rubin has found that in more than a third of her sample of working-class families, husbands complained that working wives were getting too independent (1976:176). A national survey revealed that more than one-third of all workers living in families experienced either moderate or severe work-family conflict, with women and men reporting conflict in equal numbers (Pleck, Staines, and Lang 1980).

like him. We didn't have anything in common. . . . When I was little, I never had a father, and I wanted a family so much, so I tried to keep the marriage together for the kids, so they wouldn't come from a broken home." Connie believed that her political activities, although perhaps exacerbating her marital problems, were not their cause. She said: "It wasn't that my working hastened my divorce, in that it made my marriage worse, like Mario claims to this day. But rather it all allowed me the *freedom* from a bad marriage." Nevertheless, the decision to divorce was difficult and painful.

Connie is an unusual woman. Very few women cannery workers had received full-time jobs since the Conciliation Agreement and were therefore in a position to support families on their own. Female single parents are likely to become impoverished after divorce: Families of women raising children alone are five times more likely to be poor as are families with a man present.[9] Seeking a divorce is an option that few working-class women with children can afford.

Women's employment did not create discord in all marriages. Most families accepted the temporary changes in their lives when wives worked in canneries. Couples with grown children had the easiest time adapting. We have seen how Vicki's spouse did not particularly mind that she worked. After their son left home, her job was even less of a disruption. Luz's husband originally did not want her to work, but he adjusted: "Now he doesn't mind; he expects it." Estela's husband did not want her to work on the swing shift because "then we couldn't go out; we couldn't be together." As long as she worked the day shift, "he likes it. We want to spend money and have a good time, to party." Clearly, these women had great influence with their husbands.

Lupe and her husband finally agreed that she would work until her retirement, since his health was deteriorating, and he needed to retire early. He grudgingly accepted her seasonal grouchiness. When people are forced into a situation they do not want, because of the need for extra income, it's understandable that they are resigned, as was Blanca: "What can I do? That's life."

In sum, the division of labor fluctuated in concert with the work season and evolved as families went through the domestic cycle.

9. National Advisory Council on Economic Opportunity, "Critical Choices for the Eighties," 1980, cited in Power 1984. Also see Pearce 1979, Economic and Social Opportunities 1974.

When the children were young or during the off-season, women performed most of the home work. Men's ineptness or refusals to carry out their share of the load and women's attempts to be model homemakers were contributing factors. Both were reflections of the notion that housework is "women's work." By the time the children were older or grown, or during the cannery season, men helped out more. Even though women received help from husbands and children, it is clear that these women were performing most of the household chores. By participating in long-term cannery employment, they were able to return to homemaking for most of the year, and this facilitated the maintenance of a traditional division of labor.

Work-related Networks

The relationships women established on the job, in what I call "work-related networks," also had an impact on family life. For the most part, work-related friendships started with social motivations, and women visited with one another during the off-season (roughly from October through May). The women visited in each other's homes, telephoned several times during the week, went shopping or to lunch, or went out for drinks. Connie described how work-based networks evolved into work-related networks: "I don't know how many times I remember telling a coworker that I became particularly fond of, 'Hey I'll be sure to come and see you after the season.' I never made it because I have kids to raise, things to do, and I just never got around to it. And then there are others, like Elena, that you become so involved with and become very dear friends." Whereas women initiated these activities with coworkers, once they were established the networks also included husbands. Cannery workers occasionally got together as couples for parties, barbecues, short weekend trips, or even extended vacations. Some of my informants organized large-scale activities in which a number of cannery-worker couples and their kin and friends participated.

The structure of work-related networks varied between two poles. On one end were friendship networks, which were composed entirely of unrelated coworkers, and at the opposite extreme were kin-dominant networks (Graves and Graves 1980). Connie, for example, had a friendship network consisting of about twelve women who started working when she did. "The majority of my friends are people who work at the cannery," she said. Kin-dominant networks were composed almost entirely of cannery workers who were relatives. In many cases married couples had first met one another at the cannery, and it was common for women's children to work at least one season in the cannery before moving on to better jobs. Women in these situations usually had work-related networks in which kin predominated, and networks included members of their own nuclear families. The following description of Vicki's work-related network shows the dense set of kin relationships at its center.

The core members were three sisters, all of whom were permanent seasonal cannery workers. Two of the sisters, Vicki and Estela, worked in the same plant, as did Estela's son for two seasons while he was a college student; Vicki's son also worked one season at the same cannery. A fourth sister, Marylou Johnson, was a seasonal cannery worker too. She was married to an Anglo who was a superintendent at a plant in another county. Because of these circumstances, Marylou was a marginal member of the network. Estela's niece Sally also worked a season in the cannery but quit when her daughter was born. Sally's husband's mother worked seasonally in canneries for fifteen years. (The grandmother's income supported her family for two years while they established a small business. When the business started thriving, the grandmother quit.) Estela's *comadre* Celia da Silva was a friend from work; she and her husband, Manuel (who is Portuguese-American), stood as godparents at the baptism of Estela's daughter, who was named after Celia. Jean Pascual, a Portuguese-American, was the head floorlady where Vicki and Estela worked; her husband was an engineer, and they were also on the fringe of the network. Other women friends and their husbands were part of the network, including informant Luz Gálvez.

The presence of kin in the area who were also cannery workers, however, did not mean that kin and friendship networks necessarily coincided. Lisa considered herself "a third-generation cannery worker." Many of her relatives had been cannery workers, most at the same plant. Besides her mother (who had worked for thirty-five years) and her stepfather (who had twenty-seven years in the same cannery), she had a great uncle who had worked fifty years in the cannery (since the age of fifteen) and had recently retired and three aunts who continued to work there: "The Hernández sisters are famous; everyone knows them." Two other cousins had recently dropped out of high school and "they will be cannery workers; they will carry on that way of life." Lisa, however, did not consider her cannery-worker relatives part of her friendship network. She had different political values and other interests. She considered herself outside of cannery-worker culture.

Regardless of whether they were recent immigrants from Mexico or third-generation Chicanas, women who did not have kin residing in the area developed work networks composed of unrelated friends. Most of Blanca, Teresa, Euleria, and Cristina's kin resided in Mexico, and these women had only friends in their cannery networks. Rosa, Luz, and Gloria had kin residing in the area, but their kin and work-related networks were separate. Gloria socialized mainly with her kin and neighbors; she had three sisters, eight cousins, and a grandmother who lived in San Jose. Gloria did not want to be "bugged" to socialize with coworkers: "We are friends while at work." Besides, she believed: "My time at home is just for my family."

Work-related networks varied in the number of members, and several were "close knit." This was because some of the women's friends were also *comadres* with one another, through Catholic baptismal rites.[10] Usually, a woman chose a friend and her spouse to sponsor a child at baptism with the intention of honoring them and solidifying the friendship (Carlos 1972). The presence of fictive kin among coworkers blurs the distinction between friendship and kin networks but adds to their cohesiveness.[11]

The women themselves organized activities and kept the networks active by communicating with one another. A few women were core members, and they either organized get-togethers or were honored on special occasions. For example, Estela gave a party in honor of Vicki's birthday and Celia and Manuel's twentieth wedding anniversary. Of the fifty or so people who were present, virtually everyone (except myself) was either a cannery worker or related to a cannery

10. Women can also become *comadres* when their children marry one another or when they sponsor children at other Catholic rites such as First Holy Communion or Confirmation.

11. In network terminology, these personal networks are relatively dense and homogeneous since they include mostly working-class Chicanos and are multiplex in content since members participate as workers, friends, and even kin. See Hannerz 1980.

worker. The women had organized the party and had urged everyone to enjoy the festivities while they served the food. The men clustered together near the keg of beer, and the women sat in little groups around tables heaped with Mexican dishes, vegetables, and dips. A handful of *comadres* who had worked together for two decades sat in one corner. They gossiped and laughed over various incidents that had occurred throughout the years. I was introduced as someone writing a book on cannery workers, and several women giggled nervously. One woman was introduced to me as "la veterana" (the veteran), as she had worked in canneries since the age of fourteen. But she did not even want to discuss it. She shook her head and waved her hand as we all laughed in understanding: "¿Pa' que te digo?" (Why should I tell you?) As a small Mexican band retired, the phonograph was turned on, and the women pulled men onto the dance floor. Couples danced to old Glenn Miller and Tommy Dorsey records. Vicki's husband took advantage of a break in the music to toast Vicki and announce their upcoming vacation plans—two other cannery couples, including the da Silvas, were going on a cruise with the Gutiérrezes after "the season" to celebrate their upcoming wedding anniversary.

In many ways work-related networks also operated like kin networks and served as sources of exchange. Network members were good sources of information regarding problems that arose from their work situation. Women found babysitters through their networks or learned how to qualify for unemployment or claim disability pay from coworkers. Work friends were also sources of emotional support, and women discussed work and personal problems, especially those concerning their children. They frequently sought out a work friend when they needed to talk and greatly appreciated such support. Connie observed of her friend from work: "If I needed her, she was there. When I get real down, she is my moral support. Everyone needs someone like that."

Work-related networks also operated in more political ways. The lack of job mobility and unwillingness of the union to meet the special needs of Chicano workers spurred some women into labor organizing. Although only a handful of my informants were politically active, their friends and kin were often also involved in organizing. In some instances, work-related networks became politicized after they were well established as social networks. Connie and her friends

[151]

met frequently, and the conversation inevitably turned to work. They began to devise ways of changing working conditions. After the calloused rebuffs from male union officials, the women decided to organize women workers themselves. They founded a women's caucus (which also included black and Anglo women) and filed a complaint with the Fair Employment Practices Commission. They later became plaintiffs in a lawsuit against California Processors, Inc. In addition, these women wrote articles for a cannery-worker newsletter, and one woman ran for president of the local. Her friends served as campaign manager and volunteers in a bitter election that was narrowly lost. The friendship network evolved into a militant organization.

Political activists' work friends became important in personal ways as well. Many of the women activists had conflicts with their husbands over their political involvement. Husbands complained that organizing took up too much time and that the women were neglecting their families. Indeed, one woman organizer claimed that reluctant husbands were the biggest obstacles to organizing women. Some of these husbands demanded that their wives either stop organizing or restrict their political activities to times that were convenient for their families. Several of the activists eventually divorced their spouses, partially because of their husbands' opposition to their political activism. Most of these women had attained better-paying jobs and were in a position to leave poor marriages. Connie observed: "Once my friends got better jobs so they could support themselves and their families, they didn't have to take that crap!" Work friendships served as a crucial means of support to these women. Connie stated: "I don't know how I would have *survived* without my friends."

A few women intensified their relationships with their husbands through their political activism. These couples got involved with the dissident union caucuses, whose membership was predominantly male. Through the contacts made during political activities, these wives' work networks enlarged. Daniel and Lucinda Rodríguez and Blanca and Jaime Ramírez had each been involved in political organizing for almost a decade. For these couples, politics often involved socializing. They attended fund-raising activities such as dances with other couples in their network and socialized after meetings, leafletting, or tending booths at political events. Friends from work were more than coworkers or *compadres*.[12] They were political allies who

12. The term *compadres* can refer to the father and godfather of a child or to parents and godparents of both sexes.

shared all the frustrations and camaraderie of labor organizing. Even though these activities were often divided by gender, their wider purposes did bring couples together.

Work-related networks also provided pressure for women to accept unfair working conditions. Lisa Hernández avoided visiting her mother during the work season because the job harassment her mother received became increasingly difficult for Lisa to bear. She had advised her mother to talk with a lawyer and explore the possibility of legal action to stop the harassment, but Lisa's mother refused. Lisa believed her mother would not seek legal redress because of the advice of an older sister who was married to a foreman at the plant where Lisa's mother worked. The aunt discouraged her sister from taking any action that might jeopardize her husband's position as foreman. None of the other relatives working at the plant opposed the aunt's advice, so Mrs. Hernández continued working under stressful conditions. Lisa shrugged: "The cannery is a way of life. You live in it and thrive on it."

Whether or not they involved politics, work friendships were important to most cannery women. Especially as their children either left home or no longer required so much attention, women had more time and desire to socialize.[13] Once home responsibilities had decreased and financial obligations for their children were not as pressing, the meaning of the job changed for these women. They felt isolated at home and longed for social contact. Few women saw housework as meaningful in its own right. If the children were grown, not only was there little housework to do, but "housework will always be there"—it could be put off.

Middle-aged women's social needs were different from those they had when they began working and when their children were young. Vicki explained: "I don't have to work anymore; we don't need the money. But if I stay home, all I'll do is watch TV and get fat. I don't have anything to do. There's not really much housework. No way! No way am I going to stay home! I'm going to go work. Plus the extra money is always helpful." Celia said, "You look forward to another season." Josie remarked, "I'm never happier than when I'm surrounded by a bunch of people who know what I'm talking about and

13. Lillian Rubin (1979) has criticized the notion of "the empty-nest syndrome" in which middle-aged women are said to experience crisis after their children leave home. Instead, her informants found new meaning in life after their children left home by taking on careers, seeking education, or participating in social relationships.

we can relate to each other." Connie observed: "Most of the women my age [forty-four] who work in the industry, their kids are all grown. They've got grandkids already. So their life is just cannery. The people they associate with are cannery workers; they can't see beyond anything else that has to do with the cannery." The cannery provided these women with an escape from the isolation of homemaking. Work-related networks became the focus of their social lives.

Women's longevity on the job allowed friendships to endure. Especially if they were *comadres*, women could feel free to develop *confianza* (trust usually reserved for kin) with coworkers. Women whose networks included only friends often characterized the relationships in kinship terms. Connie remarked, "I don't know what I'd do without her; she's been like a sister to me." Vicki described her work-related network: "It's like a little happy family." Clearly, friendship networks were serving needs that kin networks typically provide.

The Meaning of Women's Employment

There is variation in how women felt about being working mothers. The women who had small children generally did not like the fact that they worked. Women whose children were grown tended to focus on the positive relationships they sustained through work and on how a second income allowed them a more relaxed life. In addition, the salience of their identity as workers varied in intensity. Some women were wives and mothers first, and they considered their jobs of secondary importance. Others saw their jobs as central to their sense of themselves.

Luz was among the women who were content with their situations. She summed up her feelings about working: "I'm satisfied. It was good in the winter months, I could take the kids to school. You work hard, but you get used to it. The cannery is not the place to be all the time. You make good money, but they're closing." She offered her rationale for continuing to work: "Why not? The kids are gone, there's nothing for me to do at home, and I like my job. This is all I know." Rosa was also satisfied: "I only work for three months, my husband helps with the housework, and I enjoy the pool and rest." Celia noted: "It's good to get out in the public, to talk with people. I just feel lucky to have a job." Lisa observed that work facilitated marital communication and therefore had a beneficial effect on her parents' marriage: "During the season my parents' relationship becomes super close. It's like a whole new romance, no matter how tired they are. The cannery is all they talk about. When they hassle my mom, they talk it over and it brings them closer. It brings them together because they are in the same situation." She believed these reasons prompted her mother to continue to work, and noted: "They won't say anything [that is critical]; that's their whole life. Because of the cannery they have two houses, three cars; they put their kids through college. According to them, they owe at least loyalty to the cannery." Some of the women who were satisfied did not attach much significance to their status as workers. Estela said: "I just go to work; I just get my check. That's all I want." Euleria conceded: "It's all right if you work until five o'clock. But ya [enough], after five is too much."

Two women had negative assessments of how working affects their families. Blanca resented that she had to continue to work and that because of this she was forced to neglect her children and husband. Her youngest daughter was frail and sickly. She required much patience and attention from Blanca and from the older children who cared for the child after they got out of school. Blanca was bitter: "To me working is a big sacrifice; it costs me a lot to continue to work. It's very difficult. The children suffer a lot, but my husband suffers the most. And I hate to leave my children with a sitter. After all those years of working, I'm worse off." Lisa was in similar circumstances, with three preschool-age children. The difficulties of arranging child care and her worries about leaving them made her decide to quit work. She contrasted her situation with that of her parents: "I would not stay there. It's a lot of money, but it's terrible; it's wet and dirty and awful. To them [relatives] it's a way of life; they've done it for so long. But to me it's horrible." The fact that she hated cannery work made the decision to quit easier. Like Blanca, Lisa considered work too much of a sacrifice.[14]

14. These women's responses are similar to Leonarda Ybarra's (1982b:175) findings. Almost 30 percent of her Chicano dual-worker respondants believe that the "effects of the wife working" are negative, 26 percent believe that the woman's employment has no effect, 24 percent state that the wife's employment has both negative and positive effects, and 20 percent believe that the wife's employment has a positive effect.

Other women were ambivalent about working. They thought that employment brought many benefits to them personally, but they worried about the effects on their families, especially when the children were young. During the first interview, Vicki had a positive view about working: "It was easy to get hired; nobody bothers you, you make good money, you have unemployment and can be with your family in the winter months." But at the end of the interview she commented: "The family really suffers a lot." She did not elaborate and quickly changed the subject. When I raised the issue during our next interview, she denied that working had any negative effect on her family. Later, after I had described my own difficulties in finding a job, she offered advice and then opened up. She reversed her earlier position and expanded on the negative effects of work on family life. When her son was a teenager, he ran away from home several times and had problems with drugs. Vicki and her husband were very confused and hurt by this since they had tried to provide the best for him. She lamented, "They want more; they want to grow up too fast. They're spoiled." Besides, "all these kids don't have anything to do," and so they spend their free time "looking for trouble." Vicki noted how different this was from when she was a teenager. She recalled her own hard work in the fields—"It was beautiful."

Vicki believed that the fact that she worked had not been detrimental because she did not work full time. Yet she felt guilty that somehow she had failed her son since she was not home in the afternoon when he arrived from school. After we discussed her son's problems, Vicki provided a more sober perspective about working: "I really don't mind, as long as I have my health and all my friends are there. It's really ideal. It's good for a woman to get out. I'm comfortable there." Then she echoed the refrain of several other women: "This is all I know." To Vicki, the relationships she sustained through work allowed some release from the pain at home. Yet she did not want a full-time job: "I like some free time and to draw my unemployment. I get about twenty-four hundred dollars, and that's tax free. You can't beat that for not working." Like other women, she did not consider her home duties as "work."

Lupe is another woman who had mixed feelings about working. She liked the fact that she worked part time and could spend the school-year months with her children. Yet she worried about them being alone and her family's inability to spend time together during the summer: "The part I hate the most is sometimes you have to work ten hours, six to seven days a week. We like to go camping. All these summers I've missed that part." Lupe and her husband had recently separated. Since she now had sole responsibility for supporting her children, she wished she had a different job: "You should set a better example for your kids; they're going to follow your tracks. I wish I had stuck to other kinds of jobs [she has had various clerical jobs]. I'd like to start a business." Lupe hoped to send her children to college so that they would have more opportunities than she had found. She summed up her views on working in the following manner: "It's not so bad. Everybody's trying to survive. You work so your kids will have it better. I don't want them to be cannery workers. I want them to be somebody. That's life, huh? You want your kids to have better. They're my whole world." Many other women echoed her sentiments and pinned their hopes on a better future for their children.

Gloria's contradictory views were more pronounced. The first time I asked her "how do you feel about your job?" she shrugged, "It's all right." She elaborated: "It pays better; you have more time at home. It makes sense." Recall her independent views about women working: "Women *should* work outside the home, see what they can do for themselves. If they don't like it, they can quit, but they can do for themselves. It brings you satisfaction to earn your own money when you're old and your husband is gone." When I asked how having a job affected her family, Gloria denied there was any effect at all: "There's none." Yet as she continued, a defensive edge came into her voice: "I feel I'm a good mother—although too soft, too lenient. But I try." With a toss of her head she emphasized: "My family comes first." I sensed that she felt that even asking this question was a presumption on my part, for of course she could be a good mother despite the fact that she worked. My question implied that she might be neglecting her family. Her husband's presence and criticisms no doubt added to her unease in discussing this issue. During the second interview when we were alone, she admitted: "It's not really good. I miss staying home with the children in the summer. They understand that if I don't work they don't get the extras. But it's hard for a person to work all the time. You have no time when you can relax once in awhile." Gloria's strategy was to continue working for another season despite her husband's objections. With the rental income, her small pension, and her husband's wages (who, after all, was "better than

[157]

nothing"), Gloria would be allowed the rest she desired after retirement.

Connie was the most reflective woman I interviewed. She observed various changes in her life as a result of her working status. The most noticeable impact was on her children. Connie took pride in her children's self-reliance and flexibility regarding gender roles: "My children mean the world to me. I love them very much. But I raised them to be independent. They love me but they don't need me. They can get along by themselves if they have to. Even my son, they keep this place spotless." Because she worked, there even had been a beneficial effect on her relationship with Mario: "My ex-husband works at a cannery. And I could sit down with him and his friends when they were talking and playing cards, and I understood what they were talking about—you know, they fixed this machinery or the fork lift did that. And I wasn't bored; I mean I could relate to what they were saying." As we have seen, Connie was very critical of working conditions and how the union handled complaints. I asked her about the possibility of leaving the cannery. She laughed and dismissed the idea:

> Sure I could get a different job. I was the head of inventory; I've worked as a sales clerk. But I've worked in the cannery for so many years. Eighteen years is a long time. It would be very hard to adjust. I know everybody at the cannery. I've been there for so long that I know everything, how the whole place runs. And besides, I could never live off a salary of a secretary. I couldn't support my family. I *need* a man's wages.

During a later interview she was more agitated: "Where would I go? Cannery work is all I know! And at my age [forty-four] what can I do? For us women, this is all we know." At the end of our last interview, Connie was philosophical after reflecting on the pain of divorce and the insults she endured in her struggles to organize workers. She recalled that a coworker had observed that she was bitter. Connie had replied: "I'm not bitter, I'm resentful. Being bitter is when you expect the world to hand you a living; being resentful is when the world expects certain things from you because of who you are, because you're Mexican or a woman. There's a big difference! Nobody understands the anger that I feel." Angry and resentful, resigned to remain in the cannery, Connie summed up her goals in life: "All I want is a good home for my kids, what I can afford to give them, and love. I wish I had raised my kids to be more loving."

Conclusion

There were several changes occurring within the families of these women. Probably the most radical change was a shift in the family budget from working members pooling their income for family maintenance to the women reserving portions of their wages for luxury items and leisure activities. The data also reveal the economic vulnerability of women workers. Women did not make enough to support themselves and the children remaining in the household. Women's seasonal jobs significantly increased the standard of living and increased their autonomy, but it was still necessary to pool cannery income with a husband's earnings to maintain their families. By continuing in seasonal cannery jobs, women preserved their economic dependence on their husbands.

Christine Oppong (1974) has argued convincingly that the competing interests of wives and their husbands' matrikin (female relatives on his mother's side) are the basis of much conjugal conflict among urban elites in Ghana. My data also show that conjugal conflict stems from competing interests; however, for my informants, the conflict was over the use of women's time and labor. Husbands' interests were in women continuing to provide personal service to them, whereas women favored more autonomy. Because women were considered primarily as homemakers who happened to work, husbands (and even children) expected the women to continue deferring to them and maintaining the needs of family members. When women contested these assumptions, conflict emerged.

Regarding family ideology, women came to see the need for providing material support for their families as a joint responsibility. In some instances, especially when they started on the job, there was little choice. But after a time, many of the women no longer had to work for the sake of their children. Now, they indicated, they worked to provide a higher standard of living. Tied to these shifts in perceptions about family responsibility was the notion that the domestic division of labor should change as well. Women decided that husbands and children should help at home while the women worked.

[159]

Yet most women continued viewing primary responsibility for houshold work as theirs. Their expectations of help at home varied during the year—they expected more when they were at work in the canneries and less when they were "unemployed" during the rest of the year. But even when they received the help they desired, women admitted to putting in long days. These families could not be considered egalitarian. Some couples were involved in marital confict, as husbands attempted to enforce their standards of housekeeping or preferences regarding whether women should work and women resisted. There was also a shift on the women's part from nurturing children to providing services to husbands, as children matured and left home and husbands aged. Women's values concerning children were consistent. They believed the children's needs should receive priority, and mothers should sacrifice their own needs for their children. Women saw their wage work as a way of providing more educational opportunities for their children, who they hoped would enjoy some upward social mobility in the next generation.

The data on women's networks indicate several processes. The networks appear "women centered" (Yanagisako 1977); that is, women were the organizers and nurturers and members of network activities. Friendships established at work were clearly important to my informants. Women's work friends were in similar situations, and therefore they could understand each other's problems. My data do not contradict the familistic behavior previously reported for Chicanos. Rather, women enlarged support networks to include friends from work. Those Chicanas who had nearby relatives relied on kin and friends; those who did not relied on friends. I suggest that friendship networks are more important than previously noted and that we examine the conditions under which Chicanos expand kinship networks to include friends, work mates, and neighbors.[15]

Women who had kin-dominant networks tended to integrate friends into kinship activities and to regard friends as surrogate kin. In some cases, after as much as two-and-a-half decades of working in the same factory, women's coworkers indeed became "like family." Whether women had kin- or friend-dominated work networks, the

15. Interviews with young, married Chicana electronics and apparel factory workers (Zavella 1983) show that women not only valued work friendships highly but at times preferred discussing sensitive matters with friends rather than kin because friends were socially distant and would not get involved in the problems.

conditions in which networks were established and maintained account for the fact that networks endured. The conditions on the job allowed limited social interaction with coworker friends, and so women engaged in social activities with work friends outside the factories. Furthermore, women's extended kin did not seem to place an economic drain on the women. Therefore, these women focused on socializing with kin, and this facilitated the inclusion of kin and friends in networks.

The women's statements revealed a construction of the meaning of family that contrasted with the meaning of work. Contrary to the Japanese-Americans of Yanagisako's study (1985), who define their families as Japanese or Japanese-American in contrast with their views of American families, my Chicana informants were less conscious of ethnicity. They did not compare their families to Anglo families. Rather their ideas about family reflected their place in the public world of work and the broader forces of the labor market's expansions and contractions. It was these institutions that affected their views of their families. Women with younger children placed family obligations first, before work. Women with older children used family ideology to justify their personal desires to continue working. These women valued highly their relationships with coworkers and the personal autonomy of leisure activities and socializing that did not interfere with family responsibilities. For the Chicana cannery workers, the perceptions of family and of work were intimately entwined. The meanings of work and family they constructed varied, but one could not be understood, or even discussed, separate from the other.

[6]

Six Years Later

After the 1978 union elections, cannery labor organizers soon realized that they would have a short-lived victory. By the late seventies, the canning industry had begun relocating outside the Santa Clara Valley, a development that would ultimately undermine the organizing efforts of workers in the dissident caucuses. Cannery-worker activists faced a dilemma: on the one hand, they gained significant victories in turning back occupational segregation by race and sex in the industry and in making the union more democratic. On the other hand, the union was seemingly powerless in the face of plant closures. Furthermore, the employers claimed that worker agitation was itself a factor in the plant closures. With low profit margins, they said, production costs had to be cut in order for canners to remain competitive. Instead, canners faced increased production costs brought on in part by union wage less increases. By 1984 the lowest wage category had risen to $7.92, and the highest wage category was $12.97 (California Processors, Inc., et al. 1982:53).

The industry pointed to other problems, including increased truck-and rail-transportation rates and inflated energy costs (Goldberg and Wilson 1982).[1] Also, cannery waste disposal placed a

1. Upon analyzing national data for all food-processing industries, Roy Goldberg and Len Wilson claimed that labor costs had lower growth rates than any other production cost (1982: Exhibit 18).

burden on the local sewage-treatment facilities.[2] By relocating out of the Santa Clara Valley, canners could save on transportation and energy costs and avoid the sewage problems. As a consequence of competitive pressures and labor militancy, canners either packed up the factory machinery and moved out of the Santa Clara Valley or built new, large, technologically advanced canneries in rural areas of California.

Cannery-plant closures and relocations are part of a national trend toward "deindustrialization"—the decline of basic manufacturing in the United States (Bluestone and Harrison 1982). Following growth in total manufacturing employment in California in the 1970s (especially in high-technology industries), basic industrial employment began to decline around 1979.[3] Between January 1980 and June 1984, 744 manufacturing plants closed in California, and nearly 118,000 workers lost their jobs. Several hundred thousand other workers also lost their jobs during the same period as a result of layoffs and reductions in operations.[4] Most of these closures and layoffs occurred during the 1981–82 recession. California's unemployment rate reached 11.1 percent during the depth of the recession in 1982.

The food-processing industry in particular experienced a sharp decline, with the second highest number of recorded plant closures after "transportation equipment"—the auto and aerospace industries. Eighty food-processing plants closed in California between January 1980 and June 1984, putting 18,396 workers out of jobs.[5]

Santa Clara County recorded the fourth highest number of plant

2. The limitations of the municipal sewage systems had been a problem as early as 1968, with one canner calling it a "virtual invitation to vacate existing plants." See *San Jose Sun*, 21 February 1968.

3. Data on plant closures is difficult to obtain since the California Economic Development Department began generating data only in 1980. The department calculates that usually two-thirds of the work force has been laid off before actual plant closures, and data is gathered only for plant closures of one hundred or more workers, which include only 40 percent of the affected workers.

4. Large establishments (with more than two hundred fifty employees) accounted for 52 percent of the jobs lost in California between January 1980 and June 1984. See Shapira 1984.

5. Employment Development Department, "Closed Business in California," cited in Shapira 1984:14. Because of the difficulties of identifying and recording plant closures, these data significantly underestimate the number of closures and associated job loss.

Table 5. Estimated number of workers affected by eight cannery closures, Santa Clara County, 1980–84, by company

Company	Year closed	Workers affected
Glorietta, San Jose	1980	960
Stokeley Van Kamp	1981	285
Tri/Valley Growers	1981	1,500
California Canners and Growers (three plants)	1982–83	5,000
Del Monte (two plants)	1982–83	900

Source: State of California, Department of Commerce, Economic Adjustment Unit, 1985.

closures among counties in the state.[6] There were 13,236 recorded jobs lost in Santa Clara County, with 118 plant closures (Shapira 1984:16).[7] Of them, just eight closed canneries accounted for 8,645 cannery workers who lost their jobs (see Table 5).

Clearly, in Santa Clara County the majority of jobs lost because of plant closures were in the canning industry. The number of canneries in the Santa Clara Valley dropped from the high of fifty-eight in 1930 to eleven in 1982.[8]

The Valley of the Heart's Delight has been transformed into the Silicon Valley, as electronics production has become the new major industrial base. Closed canneries are being converted into "high-tech" production facilities or office complexes, and the expanding real estate market makes these conversions lucrative for developers. A recent conversion of the Glorietta cannery into an industrial park for electronics production has been one of the most profitable redevelopment ventures in recent history.[9]

Plant closures have had a negative impact on union membership. Between 1973 and 1983 the proportion of union members in California, where union activities are traditionally well organized, dropped

6. Large urban counties containing much of California's industrial base have lost the greatest number of jobs through shutdowns. Los Angeles, Alameda, and Orange counties suffered the heaviest losses.

7. These figures include all workers, not just those in manufacturing, although manufacturing accounts for most of recorded plant closures in most counties.

8. *San Jose Mercury News,* 22 August 1982.

9. *San Jose Mercury News,* 25 October 1984.

from 36.1 percent of the manufacturing work force to 23.4 percent.[10] During these years, the number of union members in the food and kindred-products industry declined 14.6 percent (Shapira 1984:19).[11]

Plant closures in the valley also provided an opportunity for canners to impose wage cuts. In the 1983 collective-bargaining agreement in the Modesto local, a new category called "beginners" was instituted. Beginners are those workers who have less than ninety days seniority in one season and who perform Bracket IV or V jobs. Beginners, however, receive two dollars less than Bracket IV and V wages (California Processors, Inc., et al. 1982:54).[12] The ninety day cut-off point is significant, since it raises the length of time before a cannery worker can be considered a seasonal worker. Thus beginning seasonal cannery workers receive significantly lower wages, and by working for only ninety days, beginners do not receive the same benefits as other seasonal cannery workers. By introducing the category of beginner, the cannery labor force has once again become internally bifurcated.

What happens to cannery workers who are laid off? A study of the Hunt-Wesson B Street plant, which closed in 1978 and left 1,580 workers out of jobs, is illustrative.[13] Two hundred of the unemployed had been full-time workers and were transferred to other Hunt-Wesson operations. Sixty percent of the rest of the laid-off workers, of which the majority were Hispanic females, were enrolled in a publicly funded Comprehensive Training and Employment Act (CETA) program designed to provide retraining. Eighty percent of the participants in this program eventually obtained permanent employment in other industries, but their hourly wages were generally significantly lower than those provided by cannery jobs.

Plant closures have had a devastating effect on my cannery informants. Only five of the twenty-four (three women and two men) are still employed in canneries, and four of them transferred to the

10. Not all of the decline in union membership can be blamed on plant closures. Some of this is accounted for by the growth of high-technology and other industries, which do not have unionized labor forces.

11. The principal unions were the International Brotherhood of Teamsters and Bakers and Confectionary Workers.

12. There have also been problems of cannery workers retaining their seniority but losing their wage brackets when they transfer to another cannery. California Rural Legal Assistance, personal communication, 23 July 1985.

13. This discussion is from a report by the Associated Community Action Program (1980).

Central Valley when their factory closed. Given the relatively advanced age of the women, I would predict that most of them were forced into "early retirement," that is, full-time homemaking. At the times of our interviews, many women had indicated that they felt too old to enter fast-paced electronics production.

The decline of canning in the Santa Clara Valley, however, did not end the organizing efforts of northern California cannery workers. In 1982 the California Senate Industrial Relations Committee held hearings on a proposed bill requiring employers to give one-year notice before plant closures. Although the bill did not pass, the hearings and subsequent media coverage provided increased public awareness of the problems of plant closures. Furthermore, San Jose cannery activists received renewed funding from the Catholic Campaign for Human Development to continue the activities of the Cannery Workers Service Center.[14] The struggle between cannery workers and management undoubtedly will continue for some time to come.[15]

14. *San Jose Mercury News*, 5 November 1985.
15. In the fall of 1985 the mainly Chicano food-processing workers in Watsonville, California (in nearby Santa Cruz County), led by Teamsters for a Democratic Union, staged a strike in protest of wage cuts.

[7]

Conclusion

This book has used both historical and ethnograpic evidence to uncover the interplay between women's position in families and in the labor market. It has examined the complex set of forces operating to keep Chicanas in seasonal cannery jobs in the Santa Clara Valley. These women's experiences are not necessarily unique. The structural position of Chicana seasonal cannery workers is no doubt similar to that of women in other seasonal work situations. In even broader terms, the experiences of Chicana and Chicano workers in canning are similar to those of Mexican-American workers throughout the Southwest, who are concentrated in declining industries and occupations (Kane 1973).

Originally a small industry, canning grew into one of the top ten California industries after World War II. The Santa Clara Valley emerged as the center of canning production in the United States. As canning output increased in the early part of the twentieth century, a larger labor force was needed. Immigrant and ethnic minority populations formed large portions of the expanding cannery labor force until World War II. After the war—with a huge increase in demand for canned goods and with great labor turnover—there was a labor shortage. Mexican-Americans began moving to the Santa Clara Valley, in part attracted by cannery employment, and they soon dominated the cannery labor force.

Beginning in the 1950s the canning industry experienced several important changes. Cannery cooperatives began forming to protect growers, and production costs steadily increased. Mechanization led to skilled labor forming larger portions of the labor force, and Teamster policy that favored skilled workers threatened further increases in wages. The contractual agreement between the Teamsters and management favored white male workers over women and minorities.

As the market for canned goods became increasingly competitive, profits declined. Increased capital concentration marked the industry as canners were acquired by conglomerates with diversified, global operations. In the face of declining profits and high production costs, the Santa Clara Valley lost its attraction as a production site. The threat of further labor agitation no doubt was a factor in the process of plant relocations. Dissident Teamsters were pushing for more participation in contract negotiations, which threatened to raise wages, especially for seasonal workers. All of these pressures resulted in a wave of plant closures in the Santa Clara Valley, beginning in the late 1970s, and massive unemployment for cannery workers. The restructuring of the canning industry ultimately had a devastating effect on Santa Clara Valley cannery workers. Chicano workers became entrenched in an industry that underwent fundamental transformation, and their attempts to change the working conditions and the union ultimately contributed to the demise of cannery jobs.

The decline of canning in the Santa Clara Valley is but one example of the global restructuring of capital that has occurred in other industries in the post–World War II period. Barry Bluestone and Bennett Harrison (1982) showed how manufacturing industries have found competitive pressures and rising production costs, including the high price of union labor, to be incentives for alternative business strategies. Plant closures have become widespread throughout the country, leaving cities and regions devastated by "deindustrialization." Clearly, broad societal changes are critical considerations when organizing workers on the local level.

Yet broad structural changes were not the major concern when these women entered the labor market. Particularly when their children were young, and with few child-care resources, women needed jobs, yet had limited options in securing employment. Women's family obligations and their commitments to a traditional family ideology made them prime participants in occupational segregation within the canning industry. Struggles with husbands also pressured women to seek temporary jobs. The unemployment benefits, with which women saw themselves as being paid for "not working," were an important additional incentive to remain in canneries. For all of these reasons, cannery jobs were the "best solution" to "women's problems." Seasonal jobs—in which they anticipated remaining only temporarily—complemented women's home obligations.

Once they entered the cannery labor force, Chicano women found limited and contracting job opportunities. Their access to better-paying, full-time jobs was restricted by many factors. These factors included job labeling, in which certain jobs were considered "men's" or "women's" work; mechanization; distinctions in the collective bargaining agreements between "seasonal" and "regular" workers; the need for "men's" job skills to qualify for high-paying jobs; the operation of work-based networks; and sexual harassment by male workers. Furthermore, the evidence suggests that there were also important structural differences between Chicanas and other women. In particular, the operation of work-based networks at times excluded Chicanas from knowledge about better job opportunities, and the favoritism by some supervisors kept Chicanas in the worst jobs.

Despite the limited opportunities in the workplace, however, women did gain leverage in the home when they became employed. Their influence over decision making and family-income expenditures increased. Although Chicana workers have more power in families than women who do not work for wages, it appears that Leonarda Ybarra (1977, 1982b) and Maxine Baca Zinn (1980) have overstated the case when they argue that women's employment leads to "more egalitarian" family structure in dual-worker Chicano families. Chicano families are clearly not as rigid as suggested by the "machismo" model; nonetheless, they contain family conflict and patriarchal notions that stem from traditional family ideology. My informants were in situations in which they continually moved from being homemakers to being workers. The household division of labor did change when they were working, and women did receive more help, but there was no fundamental transformation of family roles. To the contrary, husbands, children, and the women themselves viewed household work as women's responsibility. Even when women came to expect more help from family members, none of my informants pushed for an equal division of labor. This stems from several things, but primary was their position as temporary workers. Although they returned to canneries year after year, these seasonal cannery workers were not employed for significant periods. Assuming the direction of household work during the off-season seemed "natural" to them. Some of them may even have felt guilty because they were receiving substantial unemployment benefits when not working.

The resistance to family-role redefinition by their husbands (and children) was another crucial factor. Women were in vulnerable positions if they contested men's expectations, for there was the ultimate threat that the husband would leave the marriage. Women retained their economic dependence on husbands, in part because of the lack of job mobility in the canning industry, where women were segregated in seasonal jobs with low annual wages. But women also were pressured not to seek full-time jobs elsewhere or they chose seasonal jobs, further limiting their economic independence within their marriages. So although women may have gained more control over family matters, their subordinate position in the labor market ultimately preserved their vulnerable economic positions relative to their husbands. These families did not undergo a fundamental transformation. The ethnographic data suggest that when women had access to "men's" wages, they were in better positions to enforce change in their families, including leaving conflict-ridden relationships. But the data also show that it is almost impossible for seasonal cannery workers to move into full-time jobs.

I suggest that close attention to women's position in the labor market and the conditions of women's work is necessary for analyzing the impact of women's employment on family structure. Chicana working mothers face occupational segregation by race and sex on the job and the double day at home. While perhaps providing temporary shifts in behavior, seasonal jobs have kept women economically dependent on husbands. Little egalitarian practice has been evident. As workers in a declining industry, in which there were nonetheless powerful incentives to keep working, seasonal cannery workers remained in marginal structural positions. The rigidity of the cannery labor market, then, supported and reinforced traditional family roles. Yet the meaning women ascribed to their jobs and their status as working mothers was complex, varied, and changeable over time. Cannery work has both set in motion and suspended changes in Chicana concepts of family life and gender possibilities.

The case study presented in this book illustrates the usefulness of a socialist feminist framework and how such a perspective must be modified. Although socialist feminism guides our analysis to structural features that create and maintain women's subordination and examines conflict between women and men, it has been inadequate in explaining the differences and similarities between groups of women based on racial status and historically specific experiences in American institutions. I suggest that such a conceptual focus will serve us well in future inquiry into women's experiences that aims to build cooperative endeavors to change the conditions of all women.

References

Acuña, Rodolfo. 1981. *Occupied America: A History of Chicanos*, 2d ed. New York: Harper & Row.

Aguilar, John L. 1981. Insider Research: An Ethnography of a Debate. In *Anthropologists at Home in North America*, ed. D. A. Messerschmidt, pp. 15–26. Cambridge: Cambridge University Press.

Allen, Ruth. 1931a. *The Labor of Women in the Production of Cotton*. Study no. 3. Austin: University of Texas, Bureau of Research in the Social Sciences.

——.1931b. Mexican Peon Women in Texas. *Sociology and Social Research* 16(1):131–142.

Almaguer, Tomás. 1975. Class, Race, and Chicano Oppression. *Socialist Revolution* 25:71–99.

——.1981. Interpreting Chicano History: The World-System Approach to Nineteenth-Century California. *Review* 4(3):459–508.

——.1984. Racial Domination and Class Conflict in Capitalist Agriculture: The Oxnard Sugar Beet Workers' Strike of 1903. *Labor History* 25(3):325–350.

Almaguer, Tomás, and Carlos Arce. 1984. Chicanos and the U.S. Class Structure. Manuscript.

Almaguer, Tomás, and Albert Camarillo. 1983. Urban Chicano Workers in Historical Perspective: A Review of the Literature. In *The State of Chicano Research on Family, Labor, and Migration Studies*, ed. Armando Valdez, Albert Camarillo, and Tomás Almaguer, pp. 3–32. Stanford, Calif.: Stanford Center for Chicano Research.

Blau, Francine D. 1975. Women in the Labor Force: An Overview. In *Women: A Feminist Perspective*, ed. Jo Freeman, pp. 211–226. Palo Alto, Calif.: Mayfield.

Alvírez, David, and Frank D. Bean. 1976. The Mexican American Family. In *Ethnic Families in America: Patterns and Variations*, ed. Charles H. Mindel and Robert W. Habenstein, pp. 271–292. New York: Elsevier–North Holland.

Andrisani, Paul J. 1978. Job Satisfaction among Working Women. *Signs* 3(3):588–607.

Año Nuevo de Kerr, Louise. 1975. Chicano Settlement in Chicago: A Brief History. *Journal of Ethnic Studies* 2(4):22–32.

Arroyo, Laura E. 1973. Industrial and Occupational Distribution of Chicana Workers. *Aztlán* 4(2):343–382.

Arroyo, Luis Leobardo. 1975. Chicano Participation in Organized Labor: The CIO in Los Angeles, 1938–1950, An Extended Research Note. *Aztlán* 6(2):277–304.

Associated Community Action Program. 1980. Retraining and Job Placement: Community Response to the Hunt-Wesson Cannery Closure Layoff. Report to the Alameda County Training and Employment Board, Hayward, Calif. Presented to the California Senate Industrial Relations Committee Hearings on Plant Closures, 1982.

Bahr, Stephen J. 1974. Effects on Power and Division of Labor in the Family. In *Working Mothers*, ed. Lois Wladis Hoffman and F. Ivan Nye, pp. 167–185. San Francisco: Jossey-Bass.

Barrera, Mario. 1979. *Race and Class in the Southwest: A Theory of Racial Inequality.* Notre Dame, Ind.: University of Notre Dame Press.

Baxandall, Rosalyn F. 1975. Who Shall Care for Our Children? The History and Development of Day Care in the United States. In *Women: A Feminist Perspective*, ed. Jo Freeman, pp. 88–104. Palo Alto, Calif.: Mayfield.

Bean, Frank D., Russell L. Curtis Jr., and John P. Marcum. 1977. Familism and Marital Satisfaction among Mexican Americans: The Effects of Family Size, Wife's Labor Force Participation, and Conjugal Power. *Journal of Marriage and the Family* 39(4):759–767.

Bednarzik, Robert W., and Stephen M. St. Marie. 1977. Employment and Unemployment in 1976. *Monthly Labor Review* 100(2):3–13.

Beller, Andrea H. 1984. Trends in Occupational Segregation by Sex and Race, 1960–1981. In *Sex Segregation in the Workplace: Trends, Explanations, Remedies*, ed. Barbara F. Reskin, pp. 11–26. Washington, D.C.: National Academy Press.

Benson, Susan Porter. 1978. "The Clerking Sisterhood": Rationalization and the Work Culture of Saleswomen in American Department Stores, 1890–1960. *Radical America* 12(2):41–55.

——. 1983. "The Customers Ain't God": The Work Culture of Department Store Saleswomen, 1890–1940. In *Working Class America: Essays on Labor, Community, and American Society*, ed. Michael H. Frisch and Daniel J. Walkowitz, pp. 185–211. Urbana: University of Illinois Press.

Benston, Margaret. 1969. The Political Economy of Women's Liberation. *Monthly Review* 21(4):13–27.

Blau, Francine D. 1975. Women in the Labor Force: An Overview. In *Women: A Feminist Perspective*, ed. Jo Freeman, pp. 211–226. Palo Alto, Calif.: Mayfield.

——. 1984. Occupational Segregation and Labor Market Discrimination. In *Sex Segregation in the Workplace: Trends, Explanations, Remedies*, ed. Barbara F. Reskin, pp. 117–143. Washington, D.C.: National Academy Press.

Blauner, Robert, and David Wellman. 1973. Toward the Decolonization of Social

[173]

Research. In *The Death of White Sociology,* ed. Joyce A. Ladner, pp. 310–330. New York: Random House.

Blaxall, Martha, and Barbara Reagan, eds. 1976. *Women and the Workplace: The Implications of Occupational Segregation.* Chicago: University of Chicago Press.

Blood, Robert O., and Donald M. Wolfe. 1960. *Husbands and Wives.* New York: Free Press.

Bluestone, Barry, and Bennett Harrison. 1982. *The Deindustrialization of America.* New York: Basic Books.

Borrego, John. 1983. Chicanos in the World System. Manuscript.

Braverman, Harry. 1974. *Labor and Monopoly Capital: The Degradation of Work in the Twentieth Century.* New York: Monthly Review Press.

Briggs, Vernon M., Jr., Walter Fogel, and Fred H. Schmidt. 1977. *The Chicano Worker.* Austin: University of Texas Press.

Brown, Lorin W., Charles L. Briggs, and Marta Weigle. 1978. *Hispano Folklife of New Mexico.* Albuquerque: University of New Mexico Press.

Brown, Martin L. 1978. Oral History with Mike Elorduy, Secretary-Treasurer, Teamsters California State Council of Cannery and Food Processing Unions, 19 December 1978.

———. 1979. Comments on Cannery Industry Affirmative Action Trust. Paper.

———. 1981. A Historical Economic Analysis of the Wage Structure of the California Fruit and Vegetable Canning Industry. Ph.D. dissertation, University of California, Berkeley.

Brown, Martin, and Peter Philips. 1983a. Focusing on the Binding Constraint: Craft Labor and Mechanization in Nineteenth Century American Canning. Discussion Paper no. 83-14. School of Behavioral and Social Sciences, California State University, Chico.

———. 1983b. Industrialization, Unionization, and Labor Market Structure. Working paper. Institute for Human Resource Management, University of Utah, Salt Lake City.

———. 1983c. Usurping the Places of Women: Competition, Racism, and Hiring Practices among Early California Manufacturers. Discussion Paper no. 83-11. School of Behavioral and Social Sciences, California State University, Chico.

Burawoy, Michael. 1979. *Manufacturing Consent.* Chicago: University of Chicago Press.

Burke, Ronald J. and Tamara Weir. 1976. Relationship of Wives' Employment Status to Husband, Wife, and Pair Satisfaction and Performance. *Journal of Marriage and the Family* 38 (May):279–287.

California Processors, Inc. 1974. Breakdowns of Employees on Seniority Lists. Document obtained through discovery motion.

California Processors, Inc., and Teamsters California State Council of Cannery and Food Processing Unions, International Brotherhood of Teamsters, Chauffeurs, Warehousemen and Helpers. 1976. Collective Bargaining Agreement, 31 July 1976.

———. 1982. Collective Bargaining Agreement, 16 June 1982.

Camarillo, Albert. 1979. *Chicanos in a Changing Society.* Cambridge: Harvard University Press.

[174]

Campa, Arthur L. 1979. *Hispanic Culture in the Southwest*. Norman: University of Oklahoma Press.

Cannery Industry Affirmative Action Trust. 1979. Status Report, 21 September.

Cannery Warehousemen, Food Processors, Drivers and Helpers, Local 679, Santa Clara County, Calif. 1973. By-Laws and Rules of Order, 13 November.

Cantarow, Ellen, Susan Gushee O'Malley, and Sharon Hartman Strom. 1980. *Moving the Mountain: Women Working for Social Change*. Old Westbury, N.Y.: Feminist Press.

Cardellino, Joan. 1984. A Case Study of the California Fruit and Vegetable Canning Industry, 1860–1984. Master's thesis, University of California, Berkeley.

Cárdenas, Gilberto. 1975. United States Immigration Policy toward Mexico: An Historical Perspective. *Chicano Law Review* 2 (Summer):66–89.

——, ed. 1976. Chicanos in the Midwest. *Aztlán* 7(2). Special issue.

Carlos, Manuel L. 1972. Traditional and Modern Forms of *Compadrazgo* among Mexicans and Mexican-Americans: A Survey of Continuities and Changes. Atti Del XL Congresso Internazionale degli Americanis, 3–10 September. Rome and Genoa: Tilgher.

Castro, Rafaela. 1982. Mexican Women's Sexual Jokes. *Aztlán* 13(1–2):275–294.

Cesara, Manda. 1982. *Reflections of a Woman Anthropologist*. New York: Academic Press.

Chapa, Jorge. 1981. Wage Labor in the Periphery: Silver Mining in Colonial Mexico. *Review* 4(3):509–534.

Chiñas, Beverly L. 1973. *The Isthmus Zapotecs: Women's Roles in Cultural Context*. New York: Holt, Rinehart & Winston.

Cicourel, Arron V. 1964. *Method and Measurement in Sociology*. Glencoe, Ill.: Free Press.

City of San Jose. 1974. Housing Element. The General Plan. May.

Claus, Robert James. 1966. The Fruit and Vegetable Canning Industry in the Santa Clara Valley. Master's thesis, San Jose State University.

Coles, Robert, and Jane Hallowell Coles. 1978. *Women of Crisis: Lives of Struggle and Hope*. New York: Delta/Seymour Lawrence.

Collier, Jane, Michelle Z. Rosaldo, and Sylvia Yanagisako. 1982. Is There a Family? New Anthropological Views. In *Rethinking the Family: Some Feminist Questions*, ed. Barrie Thorne and Marilyn Yalom, pp. 25–39. New York: Longman.

Cooney, Rosemary Santana. 1975. Changing Labor Force Participation of Mexican American Wives: A Comparison with Anglos and Blacks. *Social Science Quarterly* 56(2):252–261.

Cornelius, Wayne A. 1982. Interviewing Undocumented Immigrants: Methodological Reflections Based on Fieldwork in Mexico and the U.S. Working papers in U.S.-Mexican Studies, 2. University of California, San Diego.

——. 1983. Competing Paradigms for the Study of Mexican Immigration. In *The State of Chicano Research on Family, Labor, and Migration Studies*, ed. Armando Valdez, Albert Camarillo, and Tomás Almaguer, pp. 187–200. Stanford, Calif.: Stanford Center for Chicano Research.

Cornelius, Wayne A., Richard Mines, Leo R. Chávez, and Jorge G. Castro. 1982. *Mexican Immigrants in the San Francisco Bay Area: A Summary of*

References

Current Knowledge. Research Report Series, 40. San Diego: University of California, Center for U.S.-Mexican Studies.

Coyle, Laurie, Gail Hershatter, and Emily Honig. 1980. Women at Farah: An Unfinished Story. In *Mexican Women in the United States,* ed. Magdalena Mora and Adelaida R. del Castillo, pp. 117–144. Los Angeles: University of California, Chicano Research Center Publications.

Cromwell, R. E., and R. A. Ruiz. 1979. The Myth of Macho Dominance in Decision-Making within Mexican and Chicano Families. *Hispanic Journal of Behavioral Sciences* 1(4):355–373.

Cromwell, Vicky L., and Ronald E. Cromwell. 1978. Perceived Dominance in Decision-Making and Conflict Resolution among Anglo, Black, and Chicano Couples. *Journal of Marriage and the Family* 40(4):749–759.

Dalla Costa, Mariarosa, and Selma James. 1972. *The Power of Women and the Subversion of the Community.* Bristol, England: Falling Wall Press.

Davis, Angela. 1981. *Women, Race, and Class.* New York: Random House.

Department of Agricultural Engineering. 1977. *Research in Cannery Noise Control.* Davis: University of California.

Department of Industrial Relations. 1978. *Occupational Injuries and Illnesses Survey, California, 1976.* Sacramento: State of California, Division of Labor Statistics and Research.

di Leonardo, Micaela. 1984. *The Varieties of Ethnic Experience: Kinship, Class, and Gender among California Italian-Americans.* Ithaca, N.Y.: Cornell University Press.

Durón, Clementina. 1984. Mexican Women and Labor Conflict in Los Angeles: The ILGWU Dressmakers' Strike of 1933. *Aztlán* 15(1):145–161.

Economic and Social Opportunities. 1974. Female Heads of Household and Poverty in Santa Clara County. Report. San Jose, Calif.

Edwards, Richard. 1979. *Contested Terrain: The Transformation of the Workplace in the Twentieth Century.* New York: Basic Books.

Ehrenreich, Barbara, and Deirdre English. 1975. The Manufacture of Housework. *Socialist Revolution* 26 (Oct.-Dec.). Reprinted in *Capitalism and the Family,* ed. Mina Caulfield et al., pp. 7–42. San Francisco: Agenda.

Eisenstein, Zillah. 1979. Developing a Theory of Capitalist Patriarchy and Socialist Feminism. In *Capitalist Patriarchy and the Case for Socialist Feminism,* ed. Zillah R. Eisenstein, pp. 5–40. New York: Monthly Review Press.

Elsasser, Nan, Kyle MacKenzie, and Yvonne Tixier y Vigil. 1980. *Las Mujeres: Conversations from a Hispanic Community.* Old Westbury, N.Y.: Feminist Press.

Fernández-Kelly, María Patricia. 1983. *For We Are Sold: I and My People, Women and Industry on Mexico's Frontier.* Albany: State University of New York Press.

Fernea, Elizabeth Warnock. 1969. *Guests of the Sheik: An Ethnography of an Iraqi Village.* New York: Anchor Books.

Ferree, Myra Marx. 1976. Working-Class Jobs: Housework and Paid Work as Sources of Satisfaction. *Social Problems* 23(4):431–441.

Fogel, Walter. 1967. Mexican Americans in Southwest Labor Markets. Mexican-American Study Project, Advance Report no. 10. Los Angeles: University of California.

[176]

Friedland, William H., and Robert J. Thomas. 1974. Paradoxes of Agricultural Unionism in California. *Society* 11(4):54–62.

Galarza, Ernesto. 1964. *Merchants of Labor.* Santa Barbara, Calif.: McNally & Loftin.

———. 1972. Mexicans in the Southwest: A Culture in Process. In *Plural Society in the Southwest,* ed. Edward H. Spicer and Raymond H. Thompson, pp. 261–298. New York: Interbook.

———. 1977. *Farm Workers and Agri-business in California, 1947–1960.* Notre Dame, Ind.: University of Notre Dame Press.

Gamio, Manuel. 1930. *Mexican Immigration to the United States.* Chicago: University of Chicago Press.

García, John A. 1981. Yo Soy Mexicano . . . : Self-Identity and Sociodemographic Correlates. *Social Science Quarterly* 62(1):88–98.

García, Mario T. 1980. The Chicana in American History: The Mexican Women of El Paso, 1880–1920—A Case Study. *Pacific Historical Review* 49(2):315–337.

———. 1981. *Desert Immigrants: The Mexicans of El Paso, 1880–1920.* New Haven: Yale University Press.

Garnel, Donald. 1972. *The Rise of Teamster Power in the West.* Berkeley: University of California Press.

Garson, Barbara. 1972. *All the Livelong Day: The Meaning and Demeaning of Routine Work.* New York: Penguin.

Gartman, David. 1983. Structuralist Marxism and the Labor Process: Where Have the Dialectics Gone? *Theory and Society* 12:659–669.

Geertz, Clifford. 1973. *The Interpretation of Cultures.* New York: Basic Books.

Gilb, Corrine. 1957. J. Paul St. Sure: Some Comments on Employer Organizations and Collective Bargaining in Northern California since 1934. Oral History Project, Institute of Industrial Relations, University of California, Berkeley.

Gilbert, M. Jean. 1978. Extended Family Integration among Second-Generation Mexican-Americans. In *Family and Mental Health in the Mexican American Community,* ed. J. Manuel Carlos and Susan E. Keefe, pp. 25–48. Monograph no. 7. Los Angeles: Spanish Speaking Mental Health Research Center.

Goldberg, Ray, and Len Wilson. 1982. Processed Fruits and Vegetables, California Canning Industry. Paper presented at California Senate Industrial Relations Committee Hearings on Plant Closures, Sacramento.

Gómez-Quiñones, Juan. 1981. Mexican Immigration to the United States and the Internationalization of Labor, 1848–1980: An Overview. In *Mexican Immigrant Workers in the U.S.,* ed. Antonio Ríos-Bustamante, pp. 13–34. Los Angeles: University of California, Chicano Studies Research Center Publications.

Gonzales, Phillip B. 1985. A Perfect Furor of Indignation: The Racial Attitude Controversy of 1933. Ph.D. dissertation, University of California, Berkeley.

González, Rosalinda M. 1983. Chicanas and Mexican Immigrant Families, 1920–1940: Women's Subordination and Family Exploitation. In *Decades of Discontent: The Women's Movement, 1920–1940,* ed. Lois Scharf and Joan M. Jensen, pp. 59–84. Westport, Conn.: Greenwood Press.

Graves, Theodore D., and Nancy B. Graves. 1980. Kinship Ties and the Preferred Adaptive Strategies of Urban Migrants. In *The Versatility of Kinship,*

References

ed. Linda S. Cordell and Stephen Beckerman, pp. 195–217. New York: Academic Press.

Grebler, Leo, Joan W. Moore, and Ralph C. Guzman. 1970. *The Mexican-American People*. Glencoe, Ill.: Free Press.

Greenberg, Jaclyn. 1978. Organizing the Great Cannery Strike of 1917. *Harvest Quarterly* 3–4:6–11.

Gross, Edward. 1968. Plus ça change . . . ? The Sexual Structure of Occupations over Time. *Social Problems* 16 (Fall):198–208.

Gutman, Herbert G. 1976. *Work, Culture, and Society in Industrializing America*. New York: Vintage Books.

Hannerz, Ulf. 1980. *Exploring the City*. New York: Columbia University Press.

Hartmann, Heidi I. 1979. Capitalism, Patriarchy, and Job Segregation by Sex. In *Capitalist Patriarchy and the Case for Socialist Feminism*, ed. Zillah R. Eisenstein, pp. 206–247. New York: Monthly Review Press.

——. 1981a. The Family as the Locus of Gender, Class, and Political Struggle: The Example of Housework. *Signs* 6(31):366–394.

——. 1981b. The Unhappy Marriage of Marxism and Feminism: Towards a More Progressive Union. In *Women and Revolution*, ed. Lydia Sargent, pp. 2–41. Boston: South End Press.

Hawkes, Glenn R., and Minna Taylor. 1975. Power Structure in Mexican and Mexican-American Farm Labor Families. *Journal of Marriage and the Family* 37 (November):807–811.

Heller, Celia S. 1966. *Mexican American Youth: Forgotten Youth at the Crossroads*. New York: Random House.

Hernández, José, Leo Estrada, and David Alvírez. 1973. Census Data and the Problem of Conceptually Defining the Mexican American Population. *Social Science Quarterly* 53(4):671–687.

Hernández-Alvarez, José. 1966. A Demographic Profile of the Mexican Immigration to the United States, 1910–1950. *Journal of Inter-American Studies* 8(3):472–496. Reprinted by Institute of International Studies, University of California, Berkeley.

Hoffman, Abraham. 1974. *Unwanted Mexican Americans in the Great Depression: Repatriation Pressures, 1929–1939*. Tucson: University of Arizona Press.

Hooks, Bell. 1984. *Feminist Theory from Margin to Center*. Boston: South End Press.

Humphrey, N. D. 1944. The Changing Structure of the Detroit Mexican Family: An Index of Acculturation. *American Sociological Review* 9:622–626.

Jaggar, Alison M., and Paula S. Rothenberg. 1984. *Feminist Frameworks: Alternative Theoretical Accounts of the Relations between Women and Men*, 2d ed. New York: McGraw-Hill.

Jiménez, Andres E. 1981. The Political Formation of a Mexican Working Class in the Arizona Copper Industry, 1870–1917. *Review* 4(3):535–570.

Joseph, Gloria. 1981. The Incompatible Ménage à Trois: Marxism, Feminism, and Racism. In *Women and Revolution*, ed. Lydia Sargent, pp. 91–108. Boston: South End Press.

Joseph, Suad. 1983. Working-Class Women's Networks in a Sectarian State: A Political Paradox. *American Ethnologist* 10(1):1–22.

References

Kamerman, Sheila. 1979. Work and Family in Industrialized Societies. *Signs* 4(4):632–650.

Kane, Tim D. 1973. Structural Change and Chicano Employment in the Southwest, 1950–1970: Some Preliminary Observations. *Aztlán* 4(2):383–398.

Kanter, Rosabeth Moss. 1977. *Men and Women of the Corporation*. New York: Basic Books.

Keefe, Susan Emley. 1979. Urbanization, Acculturation, and Extended Family Ties: Mexican Americans in Cities. *American Ethnologist* (Spring):349–365.

——. 1984. Real and Ideal Extended Familism among Mexican Americans and Anglo Americans: On the Meaning of "Close" Family Ties. *Human Organization* 43(1):65–70.

Keefe, Susan E., Amado M. Padilla, and Manuel L. Carlos. 1978. The Mexican American Extended Family as an Emotional Support System. In *Family and Mental Health in the Mexican-American Community*, ed. J. Manuel Casas and Susan E. Keefe, pp. 49–68. Los Angeles: University of California, Spanish Speaking Mental Health Research Center.

——. 1979. The Mexican American Family as an Emotional Support System. *Human Organization* 38(2):144–152.

Kessler-Harris, Alice. 1982. *Out to Work: A History of Wage-Earning Women in the United States*. Vol. 1. Oxford: Oxford University Press.

Komarovsky, Mirra. 1962. *Blue-Collar Marriage*. New York: Vintage Books.

Knowles, Louis L., and Kenneth Prewitt. 1969. *Institutional Racism in America*. Englewood Cliffs, N.J.: Prentice-Hall.

Krooth, Ann Baxandall, and Jaclyn Greenberg. 1978. Elizabeth Nicholas: Working in the California Canneries. *Harvest Quarterly* 3–4:12–25.

Kuhn, Annette, and AnnMarie Wolpe, eds. 1978. *Feminism and Materialism: Women and Modes of Production*. London: Routledge & Kegan Paul.

Kusterer, Kenneth 1978. *Know How on the Job*. Boulder, Colo.: Westview Press.

Lamphere, Louise. 1985. Bringing the Family to Work: Women's Culture on the Shop Floor. *Feminist Studies* 11(3):519–540.

——. 1987. *From Working Daughters to Working Mothers: Immigrant Women in a New England Industrial Community*. Ithaca, N.Y.: Cornell University Press.

Lamphere, Louise, Filomena M. Silva, and John P. Sousa. 1980. Kin Networks and Family Strategies: Working Class Portugese Families in New England. In *The Versatility of Kinship*, ed. Linda S. Cordell and Stephen Beckerman, pp. 219–249. New York.: Academic Press.

Laslet, Barbara, and Rhona Rapoport. 1975. Collaborative Interviewing and Interactive Research. *Journal of Marriage and the Family* 37(4):968–977.

Leonard, O. E., and Hannon, J. H. 1977. Those Left Behind: Recent Social Changes in a Heavy Emigration Area of North Central New Mexico. *Human Organization* 36:384–394.

Limón, Jose E. 1981. The Folk Performance of *Chicano* and the Cultural Limits

[179]

of Political Ideology. In *"And Other Neighborly Names": Social Process and Cultural Image in Texas Folklore*, ed. Roger D. Abrahams and Richard Bauman, pp. 197–225. Austin: University of Texas Press.

Lynd, Staughton. 1979. Where Is the Teamster Rebellion Going? *Radical America* 13(2):67–74.

McKay, Roberta V. 1974. Employment and Unemployment among Americans of Spanish Origin. *Monthly Labor Review* (April):12–16.

Madsen, William. 1964. *The Mexican Americans of South Texas*. New York: Holt, Rinehart & Winston.

Marini, Margaret Mooney, and Mary C. Brinton. 1984. Sex Typing in Occupational Socialization. In *Sex Segregation in the Workplace: Trends, Explanations, Remedies*, ed. Barbara F. Reskin, pp. 192–232. Washington, D.C.: National Academy Press.

Mathews, Glenna. 1975. A California Middletown: The Social History of San Jose in the Depression. Ph.D. dissertation, Stanford University.

Matthiasson, Carolyn J. 1974. Coping in a New Environment: Mexican Americans in Milwaukee, Wisconsin. *Urban Anthropology* 3:262–277.

Melosh, Barbara. 1982. *"The Physician's Hand": Work Culture and Conflict in American Nursing*. Philadelphia: Temple University Press.

Melville, Margarita B. 1978. Mexican Women Adapt to Migration. *International Migration Review* 12(2):225–235.

——, ed. 1980. *Twice a Minority: Mexican-American Women*. St. Louis: C. V. Mosby.

Metzgar, Joseph V. 1974. The Ethnic Sensitivity of Spanish New Mexicans: A Survey and Analysis. *New Mexico Historical Review* 49(1):49–73.

Milkman, Ruth. 1976. Women's Work and the Economic Crisis: Some Lessons Learned from the Great Depression. *Review of Radical Political Economics* 8(1):73–97.

——. 1982. Redefining "Women's Work": The Sexual Division of Labor in the Auto Industry during World War II. *Feminist Studies* 8(2):337–372.

Miller, Michael V. 1975. Variations in Mexican-American Family Life: A Review Synthesis. *Aztlán* 9:209–231.

——. 1976. Mexican Americans, Chicanos, and Others: Ethnic Self-Identification and Selected Social Attributes of Rural Texas Youth. *Rural Sociology* 41(2):234–247.

Miller, S. M., and Frank Riessman. 1961. The Working Class Subculture: A New View. *Social Problems* 9(1–4):86–97.

Mills, Herb, and David Wellman. Forthcoming. Contractually Sanctioned Action and Workers' Control: The Case of San Francisco's Longshoremen. *Labor History*.

Mindiola, Tatcho. 1981. The Cost of Being a Mexican Female Worker in the 1970 Houston Labor Market. *Aztlán* 11(2):231–249.

Mirandé, Alfredo. 1977. The Chicano Family: A Reanalysis of Conflicting Views. *Journal of Marriage and the Family* 39(4):747–756.

Mirandé, Alfredo, and Evangelina Enríquez. 1979. *La Chicana*. Chicago: University of Chicago Press.

Montejano, David. 1981. Is Texas Bigger Than the World System? A Critique from a Provincial Point of View. *Review* 4(3):597–628.

References

Montgomery, David. 1979. *Workers' Control in America: Studies in the History of Work, Technology, and Labor Struggles*. Cambridge: Cambridge University Press.

Montiel, Miguel. 1970. The Social Science Myth of the Mexican-American Family. *El Grito* 3(4):56–63.

———. 1973. The Chicano Family: A Review of Research. *Social Work* 18(2):22–31.

Moore, Joan. 1970. *Mexican-Americans*. Englewood Cliffs, N.J.: Prentice-Hall.

Mora, Magdalena. 1981. The Tolteca Strike: Mexican Women and the Struggle for Union Representation. In *Mexican Immigrant Workers in the U.S.*, ed. Antonio Ríos-Bustamante, pp. 111–118. Los Angeles: University of California, Chicano Studies Research Center Publications.

Mora, Magdalena, and Adelaida R. Del Castillo, eds. 1980. *Mexican Women in the United States*. Los Angeles: University of California, Chicano Research Center Publications.

Nakano Glenn, Evelyn. 1980. The Dialectics of Wage Work: Japanese-American Women and Domestic Service, 1905–1940. *Feminist Studies* 6(3):432–471.

Nieva, Veronica F. 1985. Work and Family Linkages. *Women and Work: An Annual Review* 1:162–190.

Nye, F. Ivan. 1974. Emerging and Declining Family Roles. *Journal of Marriage and the Family* 36(2):238–245.

Oakley, Ann. 1981. Interviewing Women: A Contradiction in Terms. In *Doing Feminist Research*, ed. Helen Roberts, pp. 30–61. London: Routledge & Kegan Paul.

Onís, Jose de, ed. 1976. *The Hispanic Contribution to the State of Colorado*. Boulder, Colo.: Westview Press.

Oppenheim Mason, Valerie. 1984. Commentary: Strober's Theory of Occupational Sex Segregation. In *Sex Segregation in the Workplace: Trends, Explanations, Remedies*, ed. Barbara F. Reskin, pp. 157–170. Washington, D.C.: National Academy Press.

Oppenheimer, Valerie Kincade. 1970. *The Female Labor Force in the United States*. Population Monograph Series, no. 5. Berkeley: University of California.

Oppong, Christine. 1974. *Marriage among a Matrilineal Elite*. Cambridge: Cambridge University Press.

Paredes, Américo. 1971. The United States, Mexico, and Machismo. *Journal of the Folklore Institute* 8(1):17–37.

———. 1977. On Ethnographic Work among Minority Groups: A Folklorist's Perspective. *New Scholar* 6(1/2):1–32.

———. 1982. Folklore, *lo Mexicano* and Proverbs. *Aztlán* 13(1–2):1–11.

Pearce, Diana. 1979. Women, Work, and Welfare: The Feminization of Poverty. In *Working Women and Families*, ed. Karen Wolk Feinstein, pp. 103–124. Beverly Hills, Calif.: Sage.

Peñalosa, Fernando. 1968. Mexican Family Roles. *Journal of Marriage and the Family* 30(4):680–689.

———. 1970. Toward an Operational Definition of the Mexican-American. *Aztlán* 1(1):1–12.

Philips, Peter. 1980. Towards a Historical Theory of Wage Structures: The

References

Evolution of Wages in the California Canneries—1870 to the Present. Ph.D. dissertation, Stanford University.

Pitt, Leonard. 1970. *The Decline of the Californios: A Social History of the Spanish-Speaking Californians, 1846–1890*. Berkeley: University of California Press.

Pleck, Elizabeth H. 1976. Two Worlds in One. *Journal of Social History* 10(2):178–195.

Pleck, Joseph H. 1979. Men's Family Work: Three Perspectives and Some New Data. *Family Coordinator* 28(4):481–488.

Pleck, Joseph H., Graham L. Staines, and Linda Lang. 1980. Conflicts between Work and Family Life. *Monthly Labor Review* 103(3):29–32.

Portes, Alejandro. 1979. Illegal Immigration and the International System: Lessons from Recent Legal Mexican Immigrants to the United States. *Social Problems* 26(4):425–438.

Power, Marilyn. 1984. Falling through the "Safety Net": Women, Economic Crisis, and Reaganomics. *Feminist Studies* 10(1):29–58.

Rabinow, Paul. 1977. *Reflections on Fieldwork in Morocco*. Berkeley: University of California Press.

Ramírez, Manuel, III. 1967. Identification with Mexican Family Values and Authoritarianism in Mexican-Americans. *Journal of Social Psychology* 73:3–11.

Ramírez, Oscar, and Carlos H. Arce. 1981. The Contemporary Chicano Family: An Empirically Based Review. In *Explorations in Chicano Psychology*, ed. Augustine Baron, Jr., pp. 3–28. New York: Praeger.

Ramos, Reyes. 1973. A Case in Point: An Ethnomethodological Study of a Poor Mexican-American Family. *Social Science Quarterly* 53:901–919.

Rapp, Rayna. 1978. Family and Class in Contemporary America: Notes toward an Understanding of Ideology. *Science and Society* 42(3):278–300.

Reskin, Barbara F., ed. 1984. *Sex Segregation in the Workplace: Trends, Explanations, Remedies*. Washington, D.C.: National Academy Press.

Ríos-Bustamante, Antonio, ed. 1981. *Mexican Immigrant Workers in the U.S.* Los Angeles: University of California, Chicano Studies Research Center Publications.

Robles, Elena, ed. 1978. Oral History Project. Unpublished document, Mountain View Public Library.

Rollins, Boyd C., and Kenneth L. Cannon. 1974. Marital Satisfaction over the Family Life Cycle. *Journal of Marriage and the Family* 36(2):271–282.

Romano-V., Octavio I. 1968. The Anthropology and Sociology of the Mexican-Americans. *El Grito* 2(1):13–26.

———. 1970. Social Science, Objectivity, and the Chicanos. *El Grito* 4(1): 4–16.

Roos, Patricia A., and Barbara F. Reskin. 1984. Institutional Factors Contributing to Sex Segregation in the Workplace. In *Sex Segregation in the Workplace: Trends, Explanations, Remedies*, ed. Barbara F. Reskin, pp. 235–260. Washington, D.C.: National Academy Press.

Rosaldo, Renato. 1984. Antropological Perspectives on Chicanos, 1970–1980. In *Chicanos and the Social Sciences: A Decade of Research and Development (1970–1980)*, ed. Isidro D. Ortiz, pp. 59–84. Working Paper. Santa Barbara: Center for Chicano Studies.

[182]

Rosales, Francisco A., and Daniel T. Simon. 1975. Chicano Steel Workers and Unionism in the Midwest, 1919–1945. *Aztlán* 6(2):267–276.

Rose, Gerald A. 1972. The March Inland: The Stockton Cannery Strike of 1937. *Historical Society of Southern California*. (Spring, Summer, Fall):67–82;155–176;255–275.

Rubel, Arthur J. 1966. *Across the Tracks: Mexican Americans in a Texas City*. Austin: University of Texas Press.

Rubin, Gayle. 1975. The Traffic in Women: Notes on the "Political Economy" of Sex. In *Toward an Anthropology of Women*, ed. Rayna R. Reiter, pp. 157–210. New York: Monthly Review Press.

Rubin, Lillian Breslow. 1976. *Worlds of Pain: Life in the Working-Class Family*. New York: Basic Books.

———. 1979. *Women of a Certain Age: The Midlife Search for Self*. New York: Harper & Row.

Ruddick, Sara. 1982. Maternal Thinking. In *Rethinking the Family: Some Feminist Questions*, ed. Barrie Thorne and Marilyn Yalom, pp. 76–94. New York: Longman.

Ruiz, Vicki L. 1982. UCAPAWA, Chicanas, and the California Food Processing Industry. Ph.D. dissertation, Stanford University.

———. 1984. Working for Wages: Mexican Women in the Southwest, 1930–1980. Working Paper no. 19. Tucson: University of Arizona, Southwest Institute for Research on Women.

Sacks, Karen. 1984. Computers, Ward Secretaries, and a Walkout in a Southern Hospital. In *My Troubles Are Going to Have Trouble with Me: Everyday Trials and Triumphs of Women Workers*, ed. Karen Sacks, pp. 173–190. New Brunswick, N.J.: Rutgers University Press.

Safilios-Rothschild, Constantina. 1970. The Study of Family Power Structure: A Review, 1960–1969. *Journal of Marriage and the Family* 32:539–552.

———. 1976. Dual Linkages between the Occupational and Family Systems: A Macrosociological Analysis. In *Women and the Workplace: The Implications of Occupations Segregation*, ed. Martha Blaxall and Barbara Reagan, pp. 51–60. Chicago: University of Chicago Press.

Samora, Julian, and Richard F. Larson. 1961. Rural Families in an Urban Setting: A Study in Persistence and Change. *Journal of Human Relations* 9(4):494–503.

Sánchez, Armand J., and Roland M. Wagner. 1979. Continuity and Change in the Mayfair Barrios of East San Jose. *San Jose Studies* 5:7–9.

Sánchez, Rosaura. 1977. The Chicana Labor Force. In *Essays on La Mujer*, ed. Rosaura Sánchez and Rosa Martínez Cruz, pp. 3–15. Los Angeles: University of California, Chicano Studies Center Publications.

Saxenian, Annalee. 1980. Silicon Chips and Spatial Structure: The Industrial Basis of Urbanization in Santa Clara County, California. Master's thesis, University of California, Berkeley.

———. 1984. The Urban Contradictions of Silicon Valley: Regional Growth and the Restructuring of the Semiconductor Industry. In *Sunbelt/Snowbelt: Urban Development and Regional Restructuring*, ed. Larry Sawers and William K. Tabb, pp. 163–200. New York: Oxford University Press.

Segura, Denise. 1984. Labor Market Stratification: The Chicana Experience. *Berkeley Journal of Sociology* 29:57–91.

References

Seifer, Nancy. 1976. Practical Politics, Rosalinda Rodriguez. In *Nobody Speaks for Me!* New York: Simon & Schuster.

Sennett, Richard, and Jonathan Cobb. 1972. *The Hidden Injuries of Class.* New York: Vintage Books.

Shapira, Philip. 1984. The Crumbling of Smokestack California: A Case Study in Industrial Restructuring and the Reorganization of Work. Working Paper no. 437. Institute of Urban and Regional Development, University of California, Berkeley.

Shapiro-Perl, Nina. 1979. The Piece Rate: Class Struggle on the Shop Floor. Evidence from the Costume Jewelry Industry in Providence, Rhode Island. In *Case Studies in the Labor Process,* ed. Andrew Zimbalist, pp. 277–298. New York: Monthly Review Press.

Simons, Margaret A. 1979. Racism and Feminism: A Schism in the Sisterhood. *Feminist Studies* 5(2):384–401.

Slatta, Richard W. 1975. Chicanos in the Pacific Northwest: An Historical Overview of Oregon's Chicanos. *Aztlán* 6(3):327–340.

Smith, Joan. 1982. The Way We Were: Women and Work. *Feminist Studies* 8(2):437–456.

Smith, Ralph E., ed. 1979. *The Subtle Revolution: Women at Work.* Washington, D.C.: Urban Institute.

Sotomayor, Marta. 1971. Mexican-American Interaction with Social Systems. *Social Casework* 52(5):316–322.

Staples, Robert. 1971. The Mexican-American Family: Its Modification over Time and Space. *Phylon* 32:179–192.

State of California. 1939. A Study of Seasonal Employment in California. Report submitted to the 53d Session of the California Legislature by the Unemployment Reserves Commission.

———. 1962. Employment Trends in California's Canning and Preserving Industry, 1950–1961. Division of Public Employment Offices and Benefits Payment.

———. 1978. Wage and Salary Employment by Industry, San Jose Metropolitan Area, 1972–1976. Sacramento: Employment Development Department.

———. 1985. Cannery Closures in Santa Clara County, 1980–84. U.S. Department of Commerce, Economic Adjustment Unit. Memorandum.

Strober, Myra H. 1984. Toward a General Theory of Occupational Sex Segregation: The Case of Public School Teaching. In *Sex Segregation in the Workplace: Trends, Explanations, Remedies,* ed. Barbara F. Reskin, pp. 144–156. Washington, D.C.: National Academy Press.

Stromberg, Ann H., and Shirley Harkess. 1978. *Women Working: Theories and Facts in Perspective.* Palo Alto, Calif.: Mayfield.

Taylor, Paul S. 1980. Mexican Women in Los Angeles Industry in 1928. *Aztlán* 11(1):99–131.

Tharp, Roland G., Arnold Meadow, Susan G. Lennhoff, and Donna Satterfield. 1968. Changes in Marriage Roles Accompanying the Acculturation of the Mexican-American Wife. *Journal of Marriage and the Family* 30(3):404–412.

Thomas, Robert J., and William J. Friedland. 1982. The United Farm Workers Union: From Mobilization to Mechanization? Working Paper no. 269. Center for Research on Social Organization, University of Michigan, Ann Arbor.

Thor, Eric. 1982. The Fruit and Vegetable Canning Industry. Paper presented to the California Senate Industrial Relations Committee Hearings on Plant Closures.

Thorne, Barrie. 1982. Feminist Rethinking of the Family: An Overview. In *Rethinking the Family: Some Feminist Questions*, ed. Barrie Thorne and Marilyn Yalom, pp. 1–24. New York: Longman.

Thornton Dill, Bonnie. 1983. Race, Class, and Gender: Prospects for an All-Inclusive Sisterhood. *Feminist Studies* 9(1):131–150.

Tienda, Marta. 1983. Residential Distribution and Internal Migration Patterns of Chicanos: A Critical Assessment. In *The State of Chicano Research on Family, Labor, and Migration Studies*, ed. Armando Valdez, Albert Camarillo, and Tomás Almaguer, pp. 149–186. Stanford, Calif.: Stanford Center for Chicano Research.

Tilly, Louise A., and Joan W. Scott. 1978. *Women, Work, and Family.* New York: Holt, Rinehart & Winston.

Tixier y Vigil, Yvonne, and Nan Elsasser. 1976. The Effects of the Ethnicity of the Interviewer on Conversation: A Study of Chicana Women. In *Sociology of the Language of American Women*, ed. Betty L. DuBois and Isabel Crouch, pp. 161–169. San Antonio: Trinity University Press.

Trujillo, Larry. 1981. Race, Class, Labor, and Community: A Local History of Capitalist Development. *Review* 4(3):571–596.

U.S. Bureau of Census. 1937–72. *Census of Manufacturers*, State of California. Washington, D.C.: U.S. Government Printing Office.

——. 1950. Persons of Spanish Surname. *1950 Census of Population*, Special Reports, pt. 3, chap. C. Washington, D.C.: U.S. Government Printing Office.

——. 1973. *Census of Population: 1970.* Characteristics of the Population, vol. 1, pt. 6, California, sec. 1. Washington, D.C.: U.S. Government Printing Office.

——. 1977. Persons of Spanish Origin in the United States: March 1976. *Current Population Reports*, Series P-10, no. 310. Washington, D.C.: U.S. Government Printing Office.

——. 1982. *Provisional Estimates of Social, Economic, and Housing Characteristics*, PHC80-S1-1. Washington, D.C.: U.S. Government Printing Office.

——. 1983. *Condition of Hispanics in America Today.* Presented at the Hearings of the Subcommittee on Census and Population, House Committee on Post Office and Civil Service. Washington, D.C.: U.S. Government Printing Office.

——. 1984. *Statistical Abstract of the United States: 1985,* 105th ed. Washington, D.C.: U.S. Government Printing Office.

U.S. Department of Labor. 1971. *Work Injuries in the Canning and Preserving Industry.* Report no. 101. Washington, D.C.: U.S. Government Printing Office.

——. 1978. *Layoff Time Training: A Key to Upgrading Workforce Utilization and EEOC Affirmative Action: A Case Study in the Northern California Canning Industry.* R & D Monograph no. 61. Washington, D.C.: U.S. Government Printing Office.

Vaca, Nick C. 1970. The Mexican-American in the Social Sciences, 1912–1970. Pt. 2: 1936–1970. *El Grito* 4(2):17–51.

Valdez, Facundo. 1979. "Vergüenza." In *The Survival of Spanish American*

References

Villages, ed. Paul Kutsche, pp. 99–106. Research Committee Report no. 15. Colorado Springs: Colorado College.

Valdez, Luis, and Stan Steiner, eds., 1972. *Aztlán: An Anthology of Mexican-American Literature*. New York: Vintage Books.

Vanek, Joan. 1974. Time Spent in Housework. *Scientific American* (November):116–121.

Vázquez, Mario F. 1980. The Election Day Immigration Raid at Lilli Diamond Originals and the Response of the ILGWU. In *Mexican Women in the United States*, ed. Magdalena Mora and Adelaida R. Del Castillo, pp. 145–150. Los Angeles: University of California, Chicano Studies Research Center Publications.

Wagner, Roland M., and Diane M. Schaffer. 1980. Social Networks and Survival Strategies: An Exploratory Study of Mexican American, Black, and Anglo Female Family Heads in San Jose, California. In *Twice a Minority: Mexican American Women*, ed. Margarita B. Mellville, pp. 173–190. St. Louis: C. V. Mosby.

Walshok, Mary Lindenstein. 1979. Occupational Values and Family Roles: Women in Blue-Collar and Service Occupations. In *Working Women and Families*, ed. Karen Wolk-Feinstein, pp. 63–84. Beverly Hills, Calif.: Sage.

Wellman, David. 1986. Learning at Work: The Etiquette of Longshoring. In *Becoming a Worker*, ed. K. Borman and J. Reisman. Norwood, N.J.: Ablex.

Wells, Miriam J. 1981. The Rural Mexican American Family. In *The Family in Rural Society*, ed. R. Coward and W. Smith, pp. 96–105. Boulder, Colo.: Westview Press.

Welter, Barbara. 1973. The Cult of True Womanhood: 1820–1860. In *The American Family in Social-Historical Perspective*, ed. Michael Gordon, pp. 224–250. New York: St. Martin's Press.

Westwood, Sallie. 1984. *All Day, Every Day: Factory and Family in the Making of Women's Lives*. Urbana, Ill.: University of Chicago Press.

Wilson, Michael, and Deborah Silverton Rosenfelt. 1978. *Salt of the Earth: Screenplay and Commentary*. Old Westbury, N.Y.: Feminist Press.

Winklevoss, Howard. 1978. Report on Seasonal and Non-Seasonal Workers Covered by the Western Conference of Teamsters Pension Plan. Manuscript.

Wolf, Margery. 1968. *The House of Lim*. New York: Appleton-Century-Crofts.

Wolk-Feinstein, Karen. 1979. Directions for Day Care. In *Working Women and Families*, ed. Karen Wolk-Feinstein, pp. 177–194. Beverly Hills, Calif.: Sage.

Wreford, Mary. 1981. Reactions from the Chicano Survey Respondents: No Más Silencio. *La Red/The Net, Newsletter of the National Chicano Research Network* 33 (August):1.

Yanagisako, Sylvia Junko. 1977. Women-Centered Kin Networks in Urban, Bilateral Kinship. *American Ethnologist* 4(2):207–226.

———. 1985. *Transforming the Past: Tradition and Kinship among Japanese Americans*. Stanford, Calif.: Stanford University Press.

Ybarra, Lea, and Carlos H. Arce. 1981. Entre Dicho y Hecho Hay Gran Trecho: The Division of Household Chores in the Chicano Family. Paper presented at Meetings of National Association for Chicano Studies, April 1981, Riverside, California.

Ybarra, Leonarda. 1977. Conjugal Role Relationships in the Chicano Family. Ph.D. dissertation, University of California, Berkeley.

———. 1982a. Marital Decision-Making and the Role of Machismo in the Chicano Family. *De Colores, Journal of Chicano Expression and Thought* (1 and 2):32–47.

———. 1982b. When Wives Work: The Impact on the Chicano Family. *Journal of Marriage and the Family* 44(1):169–178.

———. 1983. Empirical and Theoretical Developments in Studies of the Chicano Family. In *The State of Chicano Research on Family, Labor, and Migration Studies*, ed. Armando Valdez, Albert Camarillo, and Tomás Almaguer, pp. 91–110. Stanford, Calif.: Stanford Center for Chicano Research.

Zaretsky, Eli. 1976. Socialist Politics and the Family. In *Capitalism and the Family*, ed. Mina Caulfield et al., pp. 43–58. San Francisco: Agenda.

Zavella, Patricia. 1976. Towards a Sociological Perspective on Chicanas and the Chicano Family: A Critical Assessment of the Literature. Paper presented at meetings of National Association of Chicano Social Scientists, El Paso.

———. 1983. Support Networks of Young Chicana Workers. Paper presented at meetings of Western Social Science Association, Albuquerque, April.

———. 1984. The Impact of "Sun Belt Industrialization" on Chicanas. *Frontiers* 8(1):21–27.

Zinn, Maxine Baca. 1975. Chicanas: Power and Control in the Domestic Sphere. *De Colores* 2(3):19–31.

———. 1979a. Chicano Family Research: Conceptual Distortions and Alternative Directions. *Journal of Ethnic Studies* 7(3):59–71.

———. 1979b. Field Research in Minority Communities: Ethical, Methodological, and Political Observations by an Insider. *Social Problems* 27(2):209–219.

———. 1980. Employment and Education of Mexican-American Women: The Interplay of Modernity and Ethnicity in Eight Families. *Harvard Educational Review* 50(1):47–62.

———. 1982. Urban Kinship and Midwest Chicano Families: Evidence in Support of Revision. *De Colores* 6(1–2):85–98. Special issue.

Index

[189]

Index

Anthropology of Contemporary Issues

A SERIES EDITED BY

ROGER SANJEK

Library of Congress Cataloging-in-Publication Data

Zavella, Patricia, 1949–
    Women's work and Chicano families.

    (Anthropology of contemporary issues; 8)
    Bibliography: p. 172
    Includes index.
    1. Women cannery workers—California—Santa Clara
Valley—Family relationships. 2. Mexican
American women—Employment—California—Santa Clara
Valley. 3. Family and work—California—Santa
Clara Valley. 4. Working mothers—California—
Santa Clara Valley. I. Title. II. Series.
HD6073.C272U596 1987   305.4'3664   87-5245
ISBN 0-8014-1730-9 (alk. paper)